ROME

UNABELLAVISTA • How to tour italy

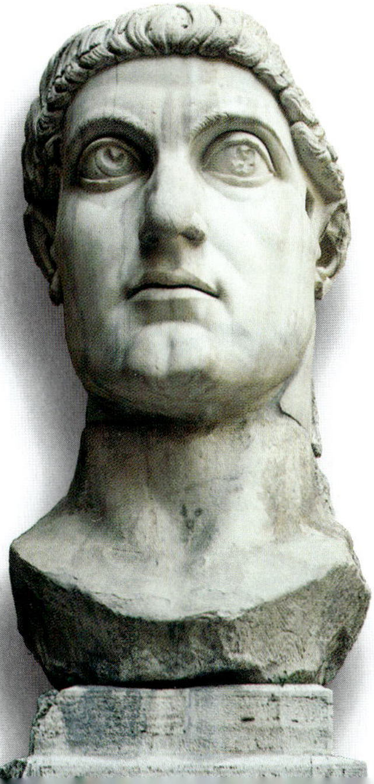

Published by Bella Industries Publishing
ISBN 0-9794552-0-9

Bella Industries Publishing
1300 Iroquois Avenue
Suite 125
Naperville, Il 60563

In loving memory
of Nonna, Nonno, Papa, Denise,
and my Father Orlando.

A very special thank you to Bella, Brian Mazza, Brian Kennefick, Dan Hersom, Bret Schafbuch, Judy Potrzeba, Kevin Potrzeba, Mom, and Nana...who loves you Nana?

I could not have completed Unabellavista: Rome without the dedicated effort of the experts from:

PUBLISHING DYNAMICS: Tim Reeder, David Albert, Jeff Lock, Eric Rosson, Michael Leis, and Christine Wandt.

EUROGRAF DESIGN: Kasia Biela and Robert Nowak

Walks inside Rome: Marilena, Tosca, and Sal.
Thank you for your beautiful contribution to Unabellavista on the Roman Forum and Palantine Hill

How Unabellavista will help you plan your trip to Italy

Unabellavista.com

- Planning guide
- Top Ten Lists of sights and artists
- Giornata – plan your days in Rome with our "Rome In a Day" series
- Links to great tours
- Links to important sights
- Find and book your hotel
- Buy your train passes
- Gourmet Italian food and wine at home
- Italian language schools in Italy
- Travel forum

Podcast & Newsletter

- Focuses on the Italian Lifestyle, Art, Artists, Culture, Food & Wine, and Travel Advice for Italy

Unabellavista:Rome Audio Guide

- Buy the audio guide to enrich your visit to Rome
- On CD from Amazon.com or Unabellavista.com
- Digital download from iTunes, Yahoo Music, and HMV.com

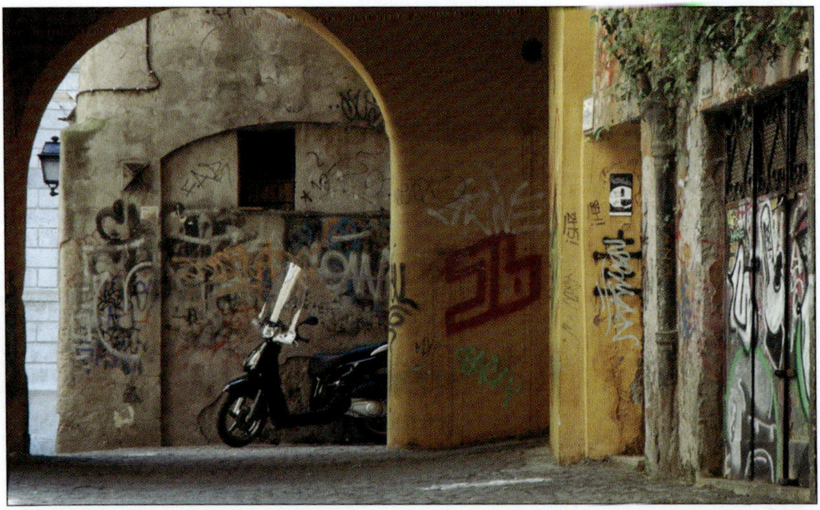

Audio Track Guide

	CD One		CD Two
1	Capitoline Museum & Campidoglio	37	Pauline Bonaparte as Venus Victrix
2	Marcus Aurelius	38	David
3	Capitoline Doves	39	Apollo and Daphne
4	Dying Gaul	40	Pluto and Proserpina
5	Colossus of Constantine	41	Goat Amalthea Nursing Zeus
6	Spinario	42	Aeneas, Anchises, and Ascanius
7	Capitoline Wolf	43	Saint John the Baptist
8	Medusa	44	Sick Bacchus
9	Commodus as Hercules	45	Saint Jerome Writing
10	Arch of Titus and Constantine	46	Madonna dei Palafrenieri
11	Colosseo	47	Boy with a Basket of Fruit
12	Trajan's Market	48	David with the Head of Goliath
13	Trajan's Column	49	Deposition
14	Belvedere Torso	50	Sacred and Profane Love
15	Laocoon	51	Fontana della Barcaccia
16	Entombment	52	Trevi Fountain
17	Transfiguration	53	Giordano Bruno
18	Raphael Rooms Overview	54	Piazza Navona
19	Expulsion of Heliodorus	55	Fontana dei Quattro Fiumi
20	Liberation of Saint Peter	56	Calling of Saint Matthew
21	Mass at Bolsena	57	Martydom of Saint Matthew
22	School of Athens	58	Pantheon
23	Parnassus	59	Risen Christ
24	Disputa	60	Glorification of Saint Ignatius
25	Fire in the Borgo	61	Triumph in the Name of Jesus
26	Sistine Chapel Ceiling	62	Triumph of the Barberini
27	last Judgement	63	La Fornarina
28	Constantine the Great	64	Narcissus
29	Pieta	65	Judith Slaying Holofernes
30	Saint Longinus	66	Ecstasy of Saint Theresa
31	Baldacchino	67	Moses
32	Saint Peter's Exterior	68	Domus Aurea
33	Castel Saint Angelo	69	Baths of Caracalla
34	Ponte Saint Angelo	70	Blessed Lodovica
35	Crucifixion of Saint Peter	71	Galatea & Polyphemus
36	Conversion of Saint Paul		

Rome in Color

Overview Map showing colored regional itineraries

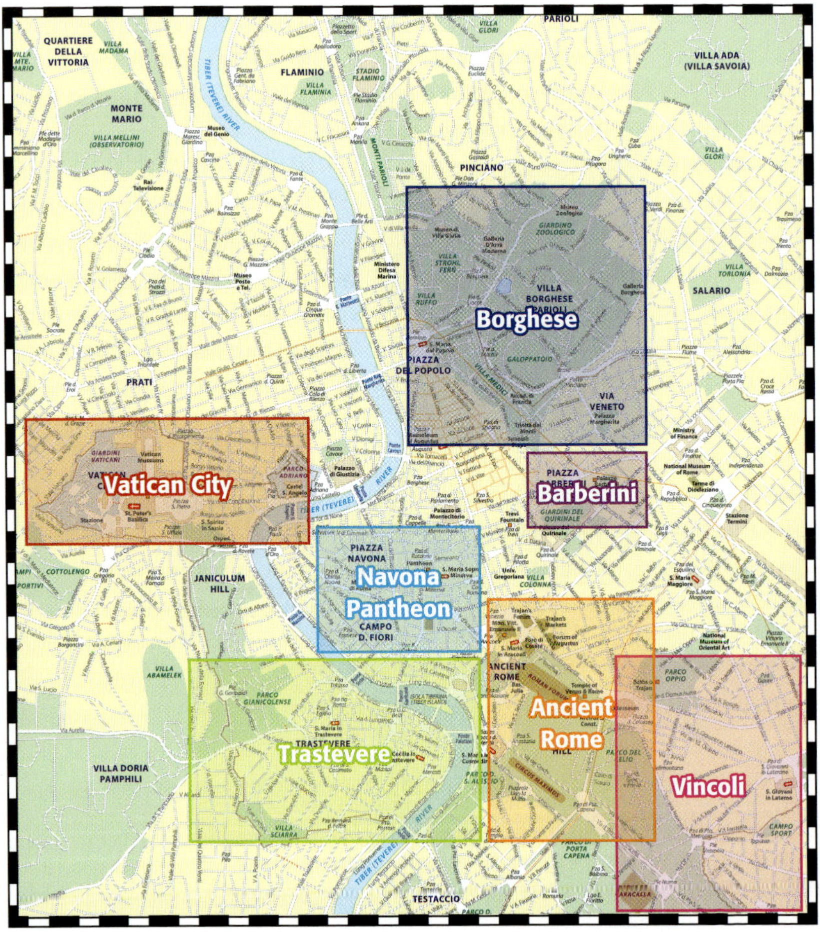

How to use UNABELLAVISTA·ROME

Unabellavista: Rome is organized into 8 sections: the cover and seven itineraries.

The **underlined** items in the itineraries are to note that additional sights are included inside the **underlined** church or museum. Below the **underlined** church or museum are the names of the masterpieces contained inside. This method is carried throughout **Unabellavista: Rome**

The pages of **Unabellavista: Rome** are arranged sequentially matching the itineraries. As Rome unfolds through an itinerary simply turn the page or listen to the audio and let **Unabellavista: Rome** bring life and meaing to the sights as you enjoy them. The audio track is arranged in the same way. You will find the track number of each site in **Unabellavista: Rome** before the name of the work.

Unabellavista: Rome includes:

- Food, wine, cheese, and dining tips for Rome.
- The list of all included works in the guidebook.
- Map of Rome illustrating the seven suggested color-coded itineraries
- The audio track guide - each track is arranged matching the itineraries. You will also find the track number in the content of the guidebook before the title of the masterpiece.
- Index of Sites Schedules - A high-level view.
- Index of Artists and their Masterpieces by location.
- Detailed Site Index providing location information and recommendations.

The Seven Itineraries:

A. Cover Section
1. Ancient Rome - Orange
2. Vatican - Red
3. Borghese - Dark Blue
4. Navona Pantheon - Light Blue
5. Barberini - Purple
6. Vincoli - Pink
7. Trastevere - Green

The Food of Rome and the Region of Lazio

One of the greatest things about going to Italy is the food. Rather than give you a list of restaurants to try I think it is better to find great dining experiences on your own. Wander around, get lost, and when you are ready just walk into a place that looks good. To really get a great dining experience let the server bring what he thinks is good. Many places will offer a misto ("mix") of antipasti or other courses so you can try a few different things. This type of request will bring you the finer things in the restaurant. More importantly it will bring a smile to your server's face. If the server feels you are willing to dig in to more than just the American basics you will have an incredible dining experience. Take your time, enjoy the wine, have an after dinner drink, and order something from each course. Remember the Italians don't rush any meal. They won't bring you the bill until you ask for it. * (On the next page I did include three places that you may want to fit in if you can. All three are excellent).

Dining Tips

- The portions are smaller than in the U.S.
- Service is slower because dining is an event in Italy not an interruption in a daily task list.
- Drink Prosecco (Italian Sparkling wine) to start your meal and Moscato (sweet, sparkling desert wine) to end it.
- Try a Vin Santo after dinner and don't forget to dunk the cookie in it.
- Cheese is often ordered as dessert.
- The house wine is often excellent.
- Limoncello is a great after dinner drink.
- Peaches are a great compliment to your wine and are often placed in the wine directly.
- NEVER put cheese on any dish that includes seafood of ANY kind.
- Order something from each portion of the menu - Antipasti, Primi, Secondi, Dolci.
- Water is ordered by the bottle and you will be charged. Tap water is rarely an option. You have the choice of with gas (sparkling) or without gas (flat).
- If you sit at a table in the cafe to drink your espresso you will be charged more.
- Caffe is Espresso, Caffe Americano is espresso with water.
- Italian breakfast is nothing like American breakfast. In Italy you will enjoy some bread, salami, cheese, chocolate croissant, and fruit. You will never get eggs (unless they are hard-boiled) for breakfast.

Some Dishes to consider while in Rome

"To dress a salad right you need four people: a wise man to put in the salt, a miser to add the vinegar, a wastrel to pour the oil, and a madman to mix and toss it."

Roman Saying

- **Fiori di Zucca Fritti** - Deep fried, stuffed Zucchini flowers.
- **Cacio e Pepe** - pecorino roman cheese and fresh crushed black pepper over spaghetti.
- **Spaghetti alla Gricia** - Guanciale (type of pork from the jowl of the pig) and red pepper.
- **Bucatini all'Amatriciana** - Pancetta (Italian Bacon), red peppers, and Pecorino Cheese.
- **Carciofi Romana** - Artichokes done in the Jewish Style.

Cheese from Lazio and Rome.

Give these a try if you see them on a menu in Rome

Caciotta Romana
Marzolino / Marzellino
Pecorino del Pastore
Ricotta Romana
Scacione / Caprone
Pecorino Toscano
Pecorino Romano (actually made in Sardegna)

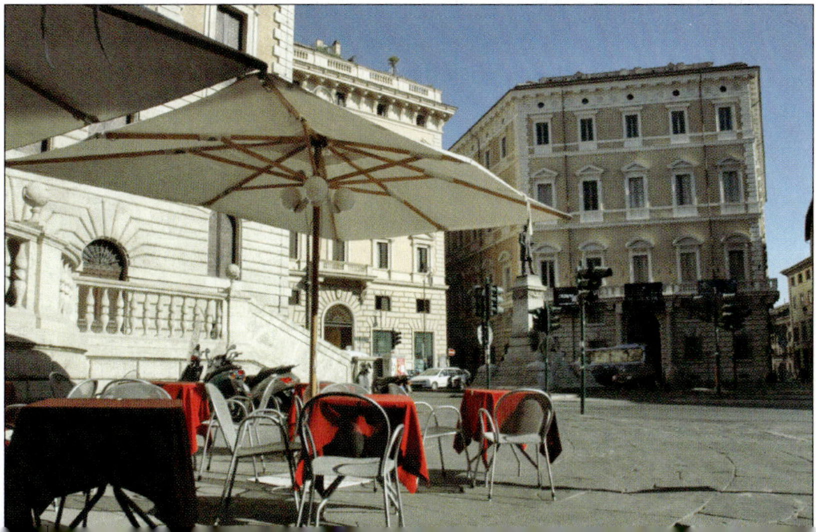

Restaurant Recommendations

La Campana

Vicolo della Campana 18
Near the Spanish Steps
and Piazza del Popolo

PHONE: 06-686-7820

Reservations Recommended
(have the concierge call)
They open at 7:30,
ask for an 8:30 or 9:00 reservation
The restaurant has been serving food since 1518

Recommended Menu Items :

- Antipasti - Carpaccio, the cold antipasti buffet, prosciutto (it is artisan made for La Campana) and melon, Fiori dei Zucchini Fritte
- Primi - Bucatini Amatriciana
- Secondi - Grilled fish or the roasted lamb
- Dolci - espresso with a sambuca and a gelato

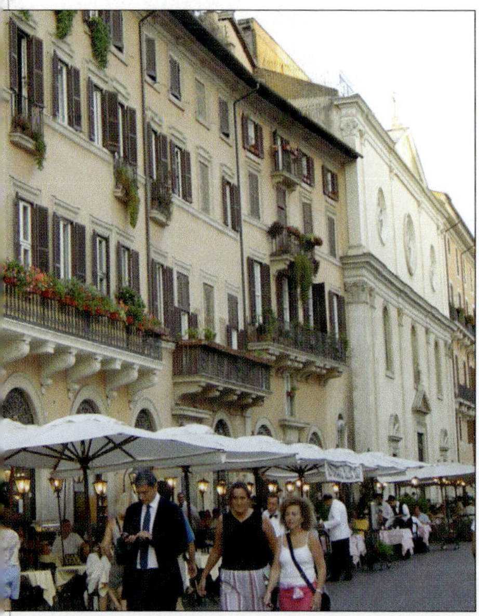

Vecchia Roma

Via della Tribuna di Campitelli
near Campo de' Fiori
and the Jewish Ghetto

PHONE: 06-686-46-4

Recommended Menu Items :

- Antipasti - The cold buffet is excellent
- Primi - Risotto of the day
- Secondi - Frutti de mare
- Dolci - The granita is incredible.

Cul-de-Sac

Piazza Pasquino 73
next to Piazza Navona

Cul-de-Sac specializes in wines, cheeses, and salami from all of the regions of Italy. You can't miss dining here.

Recommended Menu Items :

- Start with a glass of prosecco.
- Antipasti - Any of the salami plates. All are excellent
- Primi - Cacio e Pepe
- Secondi - Any of the fish or chicken dishes
- Dolci - One of the cheese plates

The wine list is fantastic at Cul-de-Sac. Order a different glass of wine for each course. Try to taste wine from 3 or 4 regions. End the meal with a Vin Santo or Muscato

The Drunken Ship is right next door to La Carbonara. After dinner one night, stop by and have a cocktail on one of the outside tables.
It is located in Campo dei Fiori

Wines from Lazio

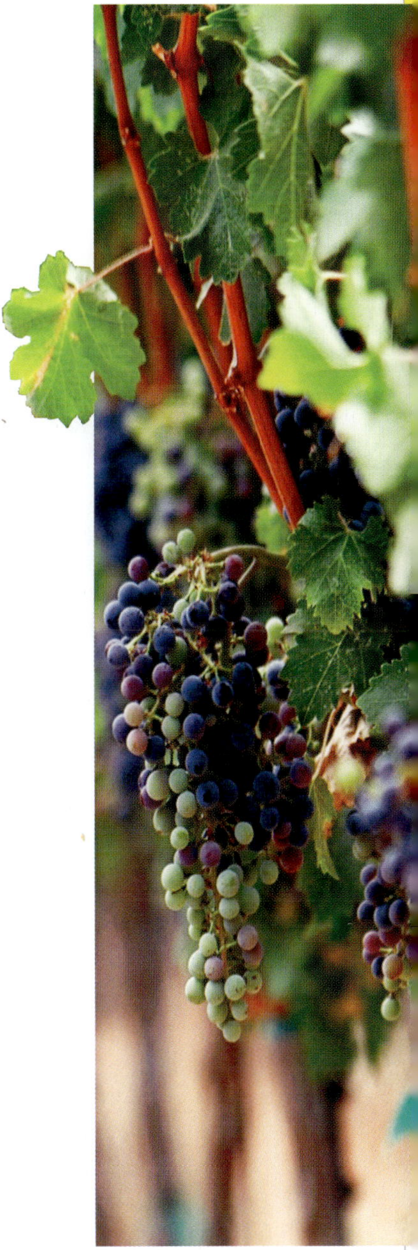

White Wines from Lazio

Aprilia
Bianco Capena
Castelli Romani
Cerveteri
Circeo
Colli Albani
Colli della Sabina
Colli Etruschi Viterbesi Colli Lanuvini
Cori
Est! Est! Est! di Montefiascone
Frascati,
Genazzano
Marino
Montecompatri-Colonna Orvieto
Tarquinia
Velletri
Bignanello
Zagarolo

Red Wines from Lazio

Aleatico di Gradoli
Aprilia
Castelli Romani
Cerveteri
Cesanese del Piglio
Cesanes di Affile
Cesanese di Olevano Romano Circeo
Colli della Sabina
Colli Etruschi Viterbesi
Cori
Genazzano
Tarquinia
Velletri

Rose Wines from Lazio

Atina
Cerveteri
Circeo
Colli della Sabina
Colli Etruschi Viterbesi
Tarquinia

DOC is an acronym that stands for Denominazione di Origine Controllata. This is how the Italians organize and protect their wines to insure that each maker creates wine by Italy's high standards. The DOC method has four major categories of certification. The ranking from lowest to best is:
VTD – Vin da Tavola
IGT – Indicazione Geographica Tipica
DOC – Denominazione di Origine Controllata
DOCG – Denominazione di Origine Controllata e Garantita

There are a lifetime of artistic and architectural treasures in Rome and no guidebook can hold the definitive guide on what you have to experience while there. It is the Eternal City and if you spent a lifetime there you couldn't possibly uncover all her treasures.

The following overview and detailed index will provide a way for you to make sure the sites you want to visit are open on the days you are in Rome. The index is cross-referenced to allow you to look up a sight by either artist name or name of the masterpiece.

The 20 Regions of Italy

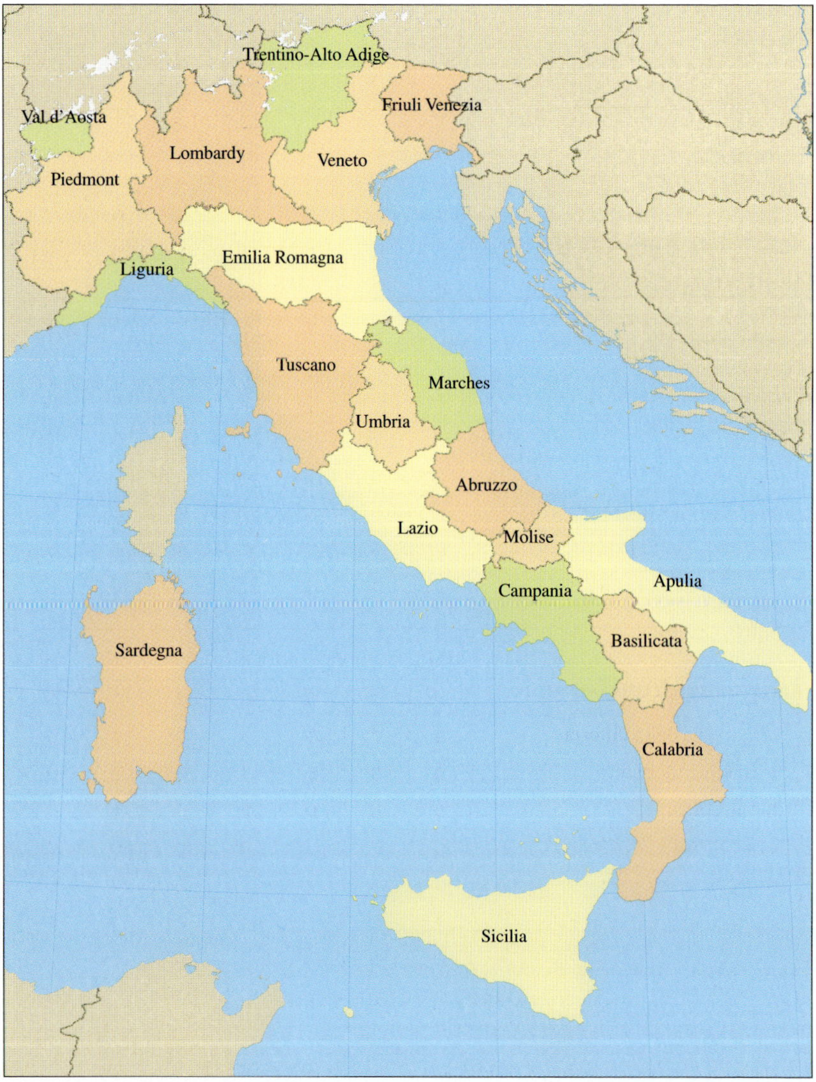

Index of Site's Schedules Overview

O = Open
X = Closed

Site	Mon	Tue	Wed	Thu	Fri	Sat	Sun
Capitoline Museums	X	O	O	O	O	O	O
Palatine Hill	O	O	O	O	O	O	X
Foro Romano	O	O	O	O	O	O	O
Arches of Titus & Contantine	O	O	O	O	O	O	O
Colosseo	O	O	O	O	O	O	O
Trajan's Forum	X	O	O	O	O	O	O
Trajan's Market	X	O	O	O	O	O	O
Trajan's Column	O	O	O	O	O	O	O
Vatican Museums[1]	O	O	O	O	O	O	X
Saint Peter's Basilica	O	O	O	O	O	O	O
Castel Saint Angelo	X	O	O	O	O	O	O
Ponte Saint Angelo	O	O	O	O	O	O	O
Santa Maria del Popolo	O	O	O	O	O	O	O
Borghese Palace	X	O	O	O	O	O	O
Spanish Steps	O	O	O	O	O	O	O
Fontana Barcaccia	O	O	O	O	O	O	O
Trevi Fountain	O	O	O	O	O	O	O
Palazzo Farnese[2]	O	O	O	O	O	O	O
Campo dei Fiori	O	O	O	O	O	O	O
Giordano Bruno	O	O	O	O	O	O	O
Piazza Navona	O	O	O	O	O	O	O
Fontana Quattro Fiumi	O	O	O	O	O	O	O
San Luigi dei Francesi 3	O	O	O	X	O	O	O
Pantheon	O	O	O	O	O	O	O
Santa Maria Sopra Minerva	O	O	O	O	O	O	O
Sant'Ignazio	O	O	O	O	O	O	O
Il Gesu	O	O	O	O	O	O	O
Palazzo Barberini	X	O	O	O	O	O	O
Santa Maria della Vittoria	O	O	O	O	O	O	O
San Pietro in Vincoli	O	O	O	O	O	O	O
Domus Aurea	O	X	O	O	O	O	O
Terme di Caracalla	O	O	O	O	O	O	O
San Francesco a Ripa	O	O	O	O	O	O	O
Trastevere	O	O	O	O	O	O	O
Villa Farnesina	O	O	O	O	O	O	X

1. Vatican Museums are closed on Sunday, except the last Sunday of the month
2. The viewing the inside of Palazzo Farnese is by appointment only. You can enjoy the exterior by Michelangelo daily.
3. San Luigi is open 7 days a week. It does not reopen for the afternoon on Thursdays.

Index of Artists and Their Masterpieces in Rome

This is a quick reference of the artists and their masterpieces in this guidebook.
Please see the Site's Hours Page for specific site's hours and daily schedule

O = Open
X = Closed

Artist	Masterpiece	Location	M	T	W	Th	F	S	S
Agesander, Polyorus, Athenodorus	Laokoon	Vatican Museum	O	O	O	O	O	O	X
Agrippa / Hadrian	Pantheon	Piazza della Rotondo	O	O	O	O	O	O	O
Antonio Canova	Pauline Bonaparte	Borghese Gallery	X	O	O	O	O	O	O
Apollonius	Belvedere Torso	Vatican Museum	O	O	O	O	O	O	X
Biagio d'Antonio	Passage of the Red Sea	Vatican Museum - Sistine Chapel	O	O	O	O	O	O	X
Caravaggio	Calling of Saint Matthew	San Luigi dei Francesi	O	O	O	O	O	O	O
Caravaggio	Martydom of Saint Matthew	San Luigi dei Francesi	O	O	O	O	O	O	O
Caravaggio	Entombment	Vatican Museum - Pinacoteca	O	O	O	O	O	O	X
Caravaggio	Crucifixion of Saint Peter	Santa Maria del Popolo	O	O	O	O	O	O	O
Caravaggio	Conversion of Saint Paul	Santa Maria del Popolo	O	O	O	O	O	O	O
Caravaggio	Saint John the Baptist	Borghese Gallery	X	O	O	O	O	O	O
Caravaggio	Sick Bacchus	Borghese Gallery	X	O	O	O	O	O	O
Caravaggio	Saint Jerome	Borghese Gallery	X	O	O	O	O	O	O
Caravaggio	Calling of Saint Matthew	San Luigi dei Francesi	O	O	O	O	O	O	O
Caravaggio	Martydom of Saint Matthew	San Luigi dei Francesi	O	O	O	O	O	O	O
Caravaggio	Entombment	Vatican Museum - Pinacoteca	O	O	O	O	O	O	X
Caravaggio	Crucifixion of Saint Peter	Santa Maria del Popolo	O	O	O	O	O	O	O
Caravaggio	Conversion of Saint Paul	Santa Maria del Popolo	O	O	O	O	O	O	O
Caravaggio	Saint John the Baptist	Borghese Gallery	X	O	O	O	O	O	O
Caravaggio	Sick Bacchus	Borghese Gallery	X	O	O	O	O	O	O
Caravaggio	Saint Jerome	Borghese Gallery	X	O	O	O	O	O	O
Caravaggio	Madonna dei Palanfrenieri	Borghese Gallery	X	O	O	O	O	O	O
Caravaggio	Boy with a Basket of Fruit	Borghese Gallery	X	O	O	O	O	O	O
Caravaggio	David with the Head of Goliath	Borghese Gallery	X	O	O	O	O	O	O

Index of Artists and Their Masterpieces – cont.

O = Open
X = Closed

Caravaggio	Narcissus	Barberini Palace	X	O	O	O	O	O	O
Caravaggio	Judith slaying Holofernes	Barberini Palace	X	O	O	O	O	O	O
Cosimo Rosselli	Last Supper	Vatican Museum - Sistine Chapel	O	O	O	O	O	O	X
Cosimo Rosselli	Sermen on the Mount	Vatican Museum - Sistine Chapel	O	O	O	O	O	O	X
Cosimo Rosselli	Handing over the Tablets of Law	Vatican Museum - Sistine Chapel	O	O	O	O	O	O	X
Domenico Ghirlandaio	Calling of the First Apostles	Vatican Museum - Sistine Chapel	O	O	O	O	O	O	X
Domenico Ghirlandaio/ Hendrik van den Broeck	Resurrection of Christ	Vatican Museum - Sistine Chapel	O	O	O	O	O	O	X
Gian Lorenzo Bernini	Fontana dei Quattro Fiumi	Piazza Navona	O	O	O	O	O	O	O
Gian Lorenzo Bernini	Elephant Obelisk	Santa Maria Sopra Minerva (outside)	O	O	O	O	O	O	O
Gian Lorenzo Bernini	Constantine	Saint Peter's Basilica	O	O	O	O	O	O	O
Gian Lorenzo Bernini	Saint Longinus	Saint Peter's Basilica	O	O	O	O	O	O	O
Gian Lorenzo Bernini	Baldacchino	Saint Peter's Basilica	O	O	O	O	O	O	O
Gian Lorenzo Bernini	Angel's of the Passion	Ponte Saint Angelo	O	O	O	O	O	O	O
Gian Lorenzo Bernini	David	Borghese Gallery	X	O	O	O	O	O	O
Gian Lorenzo Bernini	Apollo & Daphne	Borghese Gallery	X	O	O	O	O	O	O
Gian Lorenzo Bernini	Pluto & Proserpina	Borghese Gallery	X	O	O	O	O	O	O
Gian Lorenzo Bernini	Goat Amalthea Nursing Zeus	Borghese Gallery	X	O	O	O	O	O	O
Gian Lorenzo Bernini	Aeneas, Anchises, & Ascanius	Borghese Gallery	X	O	O	O	O	O	O
Gian Lorenzo Bernini	Fontana Barcaccia	Base of the Spanish Steps	O	O	O	O	O	O	O
Gian Lorenzo Bernini	Medusa	Capitoline Museum	X	O	O	O	O	O	O
Gian Lorenzo Bernini	Ecstasy of Saint Teresa	Santa Maria Della Vittoria	O	O	O	O	O	O	O
Gian Lorenzo Bernini	Blessed Lodovica	San Francesco a Ripa	O	O	O	O	O	O	O
Giavanni Battista Gaulli	Triumph in the name of Jesus	Gesu	O	O	O	O	O	O	O
Fra Andrea Pozzo	Glorification of Saint Ignatius	Saint Ignatius	O	O	O	O	O	O	O
Luca Signorelli	legacy & Death of Moses	Vatican Museum - Sistine Chapel	O	O	O	O	O	O	X

Index of Artists and Their Masterpieces – cont.

O = Open
X = Closed

Artist	Masterpiece	Location							
Luca Signorelli / Matteo da Lecce	Discussion Over the Body of Moses	Vatican Museum - Sistine Chapel	O	O	O	O	O	O	X
Michelangelo	Moses (& tomb of Julius II)	San Pietro in Vincoli	O	O	O	O	O	O	O
Michelangelo	Pieta	Saint Peter's Basilica	O	O	O	O	O	O	O
Michelangelo	Risen Christ	Santa Maria Sopra Minerva	O	O	O	O	O	O	O
Michelangelo	Ceiling	Vatican Museum - Sistine Chapel	O	O	O	O	O	O	X
Michelangelo	Last Judgement	Vatican Museum - Sistine Chapel	O	O	O	O	O	O	X
Pietro Cortona	Triumph of the Barberini	Barberini Palace	X	O	O	O	O	O	O
Pietro Perugino	Handing Over the Keys to Saint Peter	Vatican Museum - Sistine Chapel	O	O	O	O	O	O	X
Pietro Perugino	Journey of Moses	Vatican Museum - Sistine Chapel	O	O	O	O	O	O	X
Pietro Perugino	Baptism of Christ	Vatican Museum - Sistine Chapel	O	O	O	O	O	O	X
Raphael	Expulsion of Heliodorus	Vatican Museums - Raphael Rooms	O	O	O	O	O	O	X
Raphael	Liberation of Saint Peter	Vatican Museums - Raphael Rooms	O	O	O	O	O	O	X
Raphael	Mass of Bolsena	Vatican Museums - Raphael Rooms	O	O	O	O	O	O	X
Raphael	School of Athens	Vatican Museums - Raphael Rooms	O	O	O	O	O	O	X
Raphael	Parnassus	Vatican Museums - Raphael Rooms	O	O	O	O	O	O	X
Raphael	Disputa	Vatican Museums - Raphael Rooms	O	O	O	O	O	O	X
Raphael	Fire in the Borgo	Vatican Museums - Raphael Rooms	O	O	O	O	O	O	X
Raphael	Transfiguration	Vatican Museums - Pinacoteca	O	O	O	O	O	O	X
Raphael	Deposition / Entombment	Borghese Palace	X	O	O	O	O	O	O
Raphael	La Farnarina	Barberini Palace	X	O	O	O	O	O	O
Raphael	Galatea	Villa Farnesina	O	O	O	O	O	O	X
Sandro Botticelli	Punishment of Korah	Vatican Museum - Sistine Chapel	O	O	O	O	O	O	X
Sandro Botticelli	Events in the Life of Moses	Vatican Museum - Sistine Chapel	O	O	O	O	O	O	X
Sandro Botticelli	Temptation of Christ	Vatican Museum - Sistine Chapel	O	O	O	O	O	O	X
Sebastiano del Piombo	Polyphemus	Villa Farnesina	O	O	O	O	O	O	X
Titian	Sacred & Profane Love	Borghese Gallery	X	O	O	O	O	O	O

Sites and Works included in the UNABELLAVISTA·ROME Guidebook

Capitoline Museums

Campidoglio
Medusa
Marcus Aurelius
Colossus of Constantine
Doves
Dying Gaul
Commodus Hercules
Capitoline Wolf
Spinario

Palazzo Barberini

Ceiling
La Fornarina
Narcissus
Judith & Holofernes

Palazzo Borghese

Pauline Bonaparte as Venus
David
Apollo and Daphne
Rape of Proserpina
Aeneas, Anchises, and Ascanius
Deposition
Sacred and Profane Love
Young boy with a Basket of Fruit
Sick Bacchus
Saint Jerome
Madonna of the Palafrenieri
Goat Amalthea Nursing Zeus
Young Saint John
David with the Head of Goliath

Vatican Museums

Belvedere Torso
Laokoon
Entombment
Transfiguration

Raphael Rooms

School of Athens
Parnassus
Fire in the Borgo
Expulsion of Heliodorus
Liberation of Saint Peter
Mass of Bolsena
Disputa

Sistine Chapel

North Wall
South Wall
Alter Wall and Last Judgement
Ceiling
Entrance Wall

Saint Peter's Basilica

Constantine the Great
Pieta
Saint Longinus
Baldacchino
Exterior

Throughout Rome

Castel Saint Angelo
Ponte Saint Angelo
Colosseo
Domus Aurea
Fontana Barcaccia
Pantheon
Piazza Navona
Fontana dei Quattro Fiumi
Arch of Constantine
Arch of Titus
Baths of Caracalla
Campo dei Fiori
Statue of Bruno
Palatine Hill
Spanish Steps
Roman Forum
Trajan's Forum
Trajan's Market
Trajan's Column
Trevi Fountain

Villa Farnasina

Galatea
Polyphemus
Santa Maria Sopra Minerva
Risen Christ
Santa Maria del Popolo
Martydom of Saint Peter
Conversion of Saint Paul
Santa Maria della Vittoria
Ecstasy of Saint Theresa
San Pietro in Vincoli
Moses
San Luigi dei Francesi
Calling of Saint Matthew
Martydom of Saint Matthew
San Franceso a Ripa
Blessed Lodovica
Saint Ignazio
Glory of Saint Ignatius
Gesu
Triumph in the Name of Jesus

Roma Giornata – 1

Location/Masterpiece	Region of Rome	CD	Track #
Roman Forum *Arch of Titus*	Ancient Rome	1	10
Roman Forum *Arch of Constantine*	Ancient Rome	1	11
Colosseo	Ancient Rome		
Vatican Museum *Belvedere Torso*	Vatican City	1	14
Vatican Museum *Laocoon*	Vatican City	1	15
Vatican Museum – Pinacoteca *Entombment – Caravaggio*	Vatican City	1	16
Vatican Museum – Pinacoteca *Transfiguration – Raphael*	Vatican City	1	17
Vatican Museum – Raphael Rooms *Raphael Rooms Overview*	Vatican City	1	18
Vatican Museum – Raphael Rooms *Expulsion of Heliodorus – Room 5*	Vatican City	1	19
Vatican Museum – Raphael Rooms *Liberation of Saint Peter – Room 5*	Vatican City	1	20
Vatican Museum – Raphael Rooms *Mass at Bolsena – Room 5*	Vatican City	1	21
Vatican Museum – Raphael Rooms School of Athens – Room 6	Vatican City	1	22
Vatican Museum – Raphael Rooms *Parnassus – Room 6*	Vatican City	1	23
Vatican Museum – Raphael Rooms *Disputa – Room 6*	Vatican City	1	24
Vatican Museum – Raphael Rooms *Fire in the Borgo – Room 7*	Vatican City	1	25
Vatican Museum – Sistine Chapel *Ceiling – Michelangelo*	Vatican City	1	26
Vatican Museum – Sistine Chapel *Last Judgement – Alter Wall – Michelangelo*	Vatican City	1	27
Vatican Museum – Sistine Chapel *North, South, and Entrance Walls*	Vatican City	Details of walls included in written guidebook	
Saint Peter's Basilica *Constantine the Great – Bernini*	Vatican City	1	28
Saint Peter's Basilica *Pieta – Michelangelo*	Vatican City	1	29
Saint Peter's Basilica *Saint Longinus – Bernini*	Vatican City	1	30
Saint Peter's Basilica *Baldacchino*	Vatican City	1	31
Saint Peter's Basilica *Exterior – Michelangelo & Bernini*	Vatican City	1	32

Roma Giornata – 2

Location/Masterpiece	Region of Rome	CD	Track #
Borghese Palace *Pauline Bonaparte as Venus Victrix – Canova*	Borghese	2	1
Borghese Palace *David – Bernini*	Borghese	2	2
Borghese Palace *Apollo & Daphne – Bernini*	Borghese	2	3
Borghese Palace *Pluto & Prosperpina – Bernini*	Borghese	2	4
Borghese Palace *Goat Amalthea Nursing Zeus – Bernini*	Borghese	2	5
Borghese Palace *Aeneas, Anchises, and Ascanius – Bernini*	Borghese	2	6
Borghese Palace *Saint John the Baptist – Caravaggio*	Borghese	2	7
Borghese Palace *Sick Bacchus – Caravaggio*	Borghese	2	8
Borghese Palace *Saint Jerome Writing – Caravaggio*	Borghese	2	9
Borghese Palace *Madonna dei Palafrenieri – Caravaggio*	Borghese	2	10
Borghese Palace *Boy with a Basket of Fruit – Caravaggio*	Borghese	2	11
Borghese Palace *David with the Head of Goliath – Caravaggio*	Borghese	2	12
Borghese Palace *Deposition – Raphael*	Borghese	2	13
Borghese Palace *Sacred & Profane Love – Titian*	Borghese	2	14
Pantheon *Marcus Agrippa – Hadrian*	Navona Pantheon	2	22
Spanish Steps	Borghese	2	
Fontana della Barcaccia – Bernini	Borghese	2	15
Trevi Fountain	Borghese	2	16
Piazza Navona – Domitian	Navona Pantheon	2	18
Piazza Navona *Fontana dei Quattro Fiumi – Bernini*	Navona Pantheon	2	19

Roma Giornata – 3

Location/Masterpiece	Region of Rome	CD	Track #
San Luigi dei Francesi *Calling of Saint Matthew – Caravaggio*	Navona Pantheon	2	20
San Luigi dei Francesi *Martydom of Saint Matthew – Caravaggio*	Navona Pantheon	2	21
Santa Maria Sopra Minerva *Risen Christ – Michelangelo*	Navona Pantheon	2	23
Saint Ignazio *Glorification of Saint Ignatius – Pozzo*	Navona Pantheon	2	24
Gesu *Triumph in the Name of Jesus – Gaulli*	Navona Pantheon	2	25
Santa Maria del Popolo *Crucifixion of Saint Peter – Caravaggio*	Borghese	1	35
Santa Maria del Popolo *Conversion of Saint Paul – Caravaggio*	Borghese	1	36

Roma Giornata – 4

Location/Masterpiece	Region of Rome	CD	Track #
Castel Saint Angelo	Vatican City	1	33
Ponte Saint Angelo *Angels of the Passion – Bernini*	Vatican City	1	34
Palazzo Farnese *facade – Michelangelo*	Navona Pantheon		
Campo dei Fiori *Giordano Bruno*	Navona Pantheon	2	17
San Pietro in Vincoli *Moses & Tomb of Julius II – Michelangelo*	Vincoli	2	31

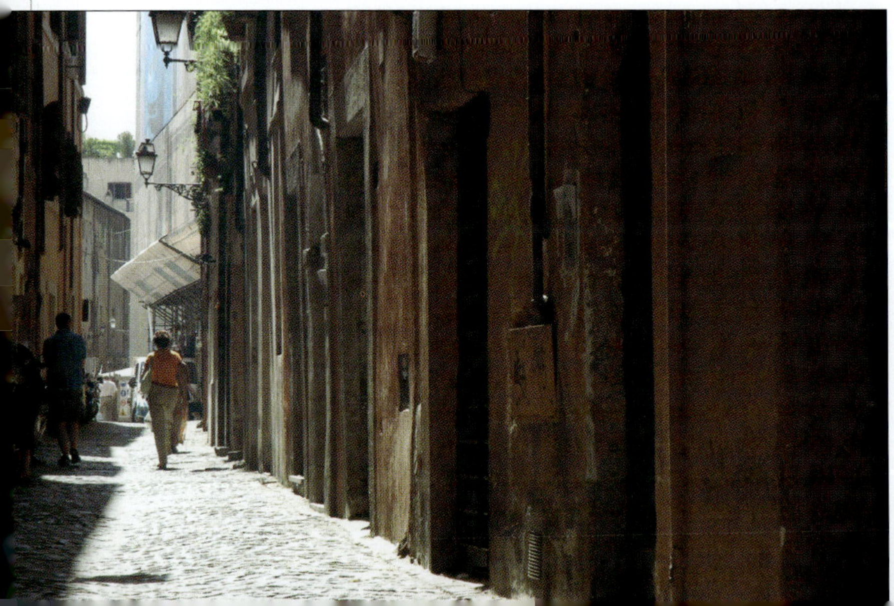

Roma Giornata - 5

Location/Masterpiece	Region of Rome	CD	Track #
Palazzo Barberini *Triumph of the Barberini - Cortona*	Barberini	2	26
Palazzo Barberini *La Fornarina - Raphael*	Barberini	2	27
Palazzo Barberini *Narcissus - Caravaggio*	Barberini	2	28
Palazzo Barberini *Judith Slaying Holofernes - Caravaggio*	Barberini	2	29
Santa Maria della Vittoria *Ecstasy of Saint Theresa - Bernini*	Barberini	2	30
Capitoline Museum *Overview*	Ancient Rome	1	1
Capitoline Museum *Marcus Aurelius*	Ancient Rome	1	2
Capitoline Museum *Capitoline Doves*	Ancient Rome	1	3
Capitoline Museum *Dying Gaul*	Ancient Rome	1	4
Capitoline Museum *Colossus of Constantine*	Ancient Rome	1	5
Capitoline Museum *Spinario*	Ancient Rome	1	6
Capitoline Museum *Capitoline Wolf*	Ancient Rome	1	7
Capitoline Museum *Medusa - Bernini*	Ancient Rome	1	8
Capitoline Museum *Commodus as Hercules*	Ancient Rome	1	9
San Franceso a Ripa *Blessed Lodovica - Bernini*	Trastevere	2	34
Villa Farnesina *Galatea & Polyphemus - Piombo & Raphael*	Trastevere	2	35

Roma Giornata - 6

Location/Masterpiece	Region of Rome	CD	Track #
Trajan's Forum	Ancient Rome		
Trajan's Market	Ancient Rome	1	12
Trajan's Column	Ancient Rome	1	13
Bath's of Caracalla	Vincoli	2	33

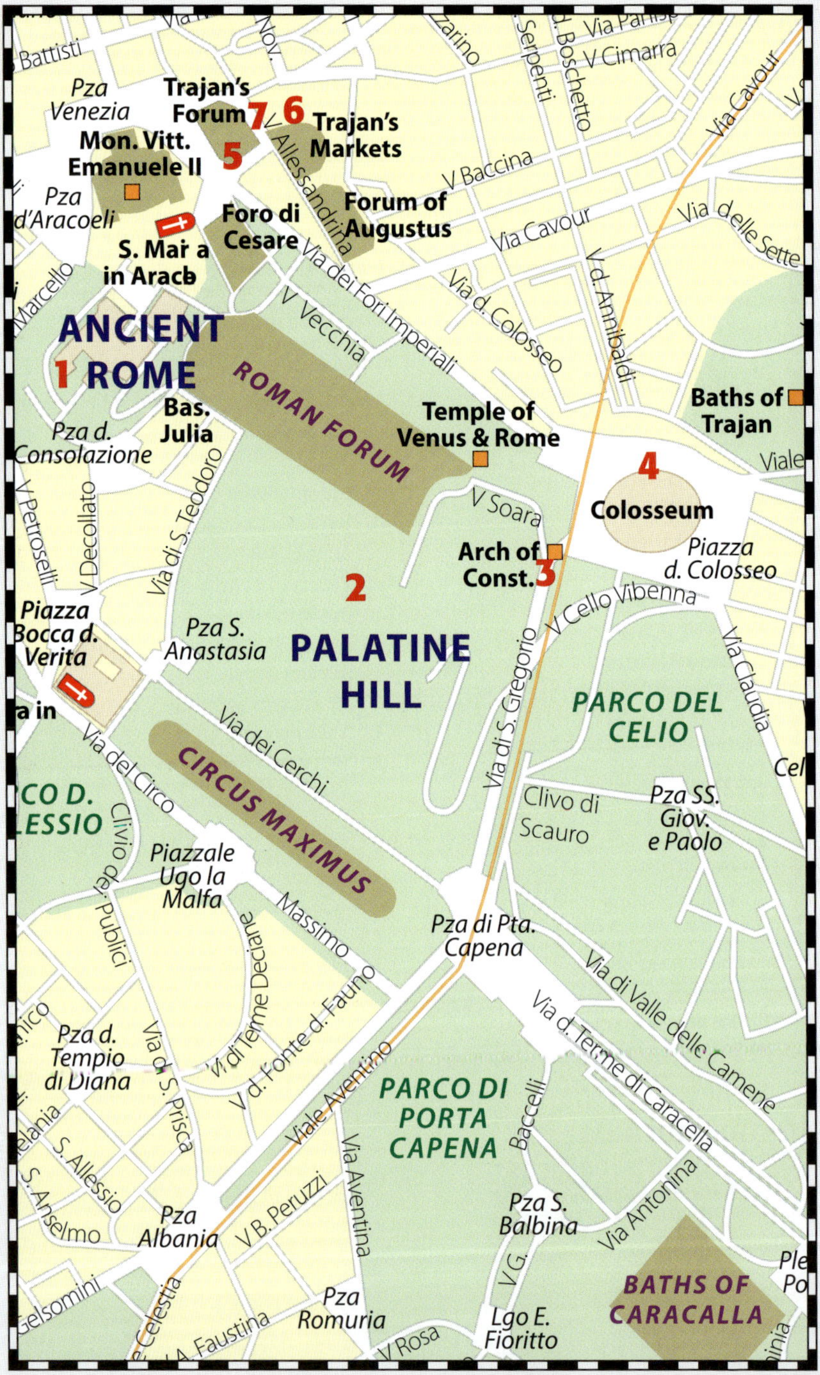

1. Capitoline Museums
2. Palatine Hill and Roman Forum
3. Arches of Titus and Constantine
4. Colosseo
5. Trajan's Forum
6. Trajan's Market
7. Trajan's Column

ANCIENT ROME

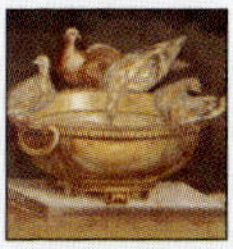

Site Hours, Daily Schedule, Address, Phone Numbers, and other important information

Site		Mon	Tue	Wed	Thur	Fri	Sat	Sun
Capitoline Museum Piazza Campidoglio 1 www.museicapitoline.org Buy tickets at http://www.pierreci.it/ Closed on May 1, January 1, December 25 Ticket office closes one hour before closing Special hours on December 24 & December 3 – 9:00 - 2:00 Reservations Recommended Adult tickets are 7,80 Euro (6,20 Euro + 1,60 Euro for exhibit access)	AM PM	X	9:00 to 8:00	9:00 to 8:00	9:00 to 8:00	9:00 to 8:00	9:00 to 8:00	9:00 to 8:00
Palatine Hill Piazza Santa Maria Nova 53 & Via di San Gregorio 30 Buy tickets at http://www.pierreci.it Closed December 25 & January 1 Ticket office closes one hour before closing Adult Tickets are 10 Euro (8 Euro + 2 Euro for exhibit access) This ticket grants access to the Palatine Hill and Colosseo	AM PM	8:30 to one hour before sunset	8:30 to one hour before sunset	8:30 to one hour before sunset	8:30 to one hour before sunset	8:30 to one hour before sunset	8:30 to one hour before sunset	X
Foro Romano & Arch of Titus Piazza Santa Maria Nova 53 & Largo Romolo e Remo 5/6 No tickets necessary Closed December 25 & January 1 Free Admission	AM PM	8:30 to one hour before sunset	8:30 to one hour before sunset	8:30 to one hour before sunset	8:30 to one hour before sunset	8:30 to one hour before sunset	8:30 to one hour before sunset	8:30 to one hour before sunset

Site		Mon	Tue	Wed	Thur	Fri	Sat	Sun
Colosseo & Arch of Constantine Piazza del Colosseo Buy tickets at http://www.pierreci.it Closed December 25 & January 1 Ticket offices close one hour before closing Adult tickets are 10 Euro (8 Euro + 2 Euro for exhibit access) This ticket grants access to Colosseo and Palatine Hill **Buy Colosseo ticket at the Palatine Hill ticket office to avoid the lines at the Colosseo**	AM PM	8:30 to one hour before sunset	8:30 to one hour before sunset	8:30 to one hour before sunset	8:30 to one hour before sunset	8:30 to one hour before sunset	8:30 to one hour before sunset	8:30 to one hour before sunset
Trajan's Forum & Trajan's Market Via dei Fori Imperiali & Via IV No tickets necessary Closed December 25 & January 1 Free Admission	AM PM	X	9:00 to 6:00	9:00 to 6:00	9:00 to 6:00	9:00 to 6:00	9:00 to 6:00	9:00 to 6:00
Trajan's Column Via del Foro di Traiano No tickets necessary Outdoor, 24 x 7 viewing	AM PM	24 x 7						

X = Closed

1 ▪ Piazza Campidoglio

with an overview to the Capitoline Museums

The Campidoglio rests on one of the most significant hills of Rome - The Capitoline Hill. It was religiously and politically important to the Ancient Romans because it was home of the temple of Capitoline Jove, the Tabularium (ancient archive), and mint of the Roman Empire.

The history of the hill is great having been touched by everyone from the Ancient Romans through to Michelangelo. Pope Paul III who commissioned Michelangelo to create the Last Judgement of the Sistine Chapel asked him to simultaneaously architect the piazza and buildings that make up the Campidoglio. Three buildings decorate the Capitoline Hill: The Palazzo dei Senatori (the first building you see when you walk up the ramp called the Cordonata), the Palazzo Conservatori (on your right as you enter the piazza from the ramp), and the Palazzo Nuovo (on your left). The Palazzo Conservatori is at an 80 degree angle to the Palazzo Senatori. The odd organization inspired Michelangelo to utilize the formation and create the Palazzo Nuovo at the same 80 degrees maintaining the harmony of the existing organization of the buildings.

In the center of Michelangelo's piazza is the decorated pavement and in it's center a statue of the emperor Marcus Aurelius. The emperor points toward the Palazzo Nuovo and was believed to be the Christian Emperor Constantine when Pope Paul III had the statue placed here. This is the only equestrian statue of an emperor to survive the Middle Ages. Pope Paul III ordered it moved to the hill and placed in the piazza against Michelangelo's wishes. The great artist hoped to create a statue of his own for the center of his oval pedastal.

The use of an oval pedastal was unique, but the great artist knew that it was necessary to keep the harmony of the piazza with the odd angle produced

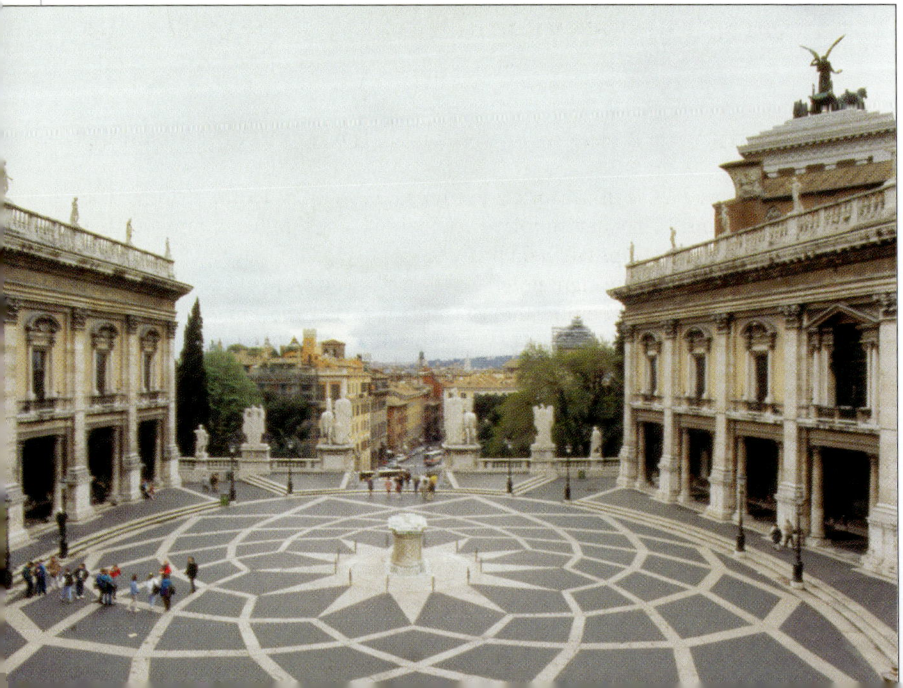

by the placement of the three buildings. After the piazza was finished the use of an oval pedastal became a popular option for statuary throughout Italy.

You enter the piazza up the gently graded cordonata. The Cordonata was graded this way to allow easier access for carts pulled by animals or men. The staircase on the Palazzo Senatori and the oval pedastal are the only design elements that remain from Michelangelo's original design. Other artists have made changes, additions, and improvements to the architecture of the buidlings and the piazza.

Pope Sixtus IV in 1471 gave the Roman people the bronze statuary currently found in the Lateran Palace. The statuary was gifted to the Romans as proof of their ancient greatness. This was the gift that initiated the creation of the Capitoline Museum. It is believed to be the oldest Art Collection in the Western World. Other Popes went on to contribute to the collection over the centuries. Pope Paul III had the piazza built, Pope Pious V contributed more Pagan centered art.

Finally, Pope Clement XII in 1734, had the museum inaugurated to the public. Many beautiful pieces of art are in the permanent collection of the Capitoline Musuem. You will find the bronze Spinario (the boy removing the thorn from his foot), the Dying Gaul, the Colossus of Constantine, Statues of River Gods, Remnants of the ancient building that make up this beautiful hill, the bust of the murdering emperor Commodus as Heracles, the famous Capitoline Wolf feeding Remus and Romulus, and the amazing micro-mosaic Doves found in Hadrian's Villa, the original statue of Marcus Aurelius thought to be Constantine at the time of its placement in the center of the Piazza, and a beautiful view of the Roman Forum

The Capitoline Museum and the Piazza Campidoglio

You will find maps to Palazzo Nuovo and Palazzo Conservatori in the following pages.

There are many pieces of art inside the museum that are worth visiting. The eight covered in your Unabellavista: Rome guidebook are significant and worth a little extra time. The write-ups will help bring the art to life.

The rooms containing the eight noted works are shown with an * on the map.

The museum is located behind the Monument to Vittorio Emanuele II. This monument is sometimes called the Wedding Cake. If you are facing the monument with Piazza Venezia to your back you will walk around the wedding cake to the right following Via del Teatro Marcello to the beginning of Michelangelo's Ramp.

The traffic is a little hairy around Piazza Venezia so be careful.

Capitoline Museum: Palazzo Nuovo

GROUND FLOOR

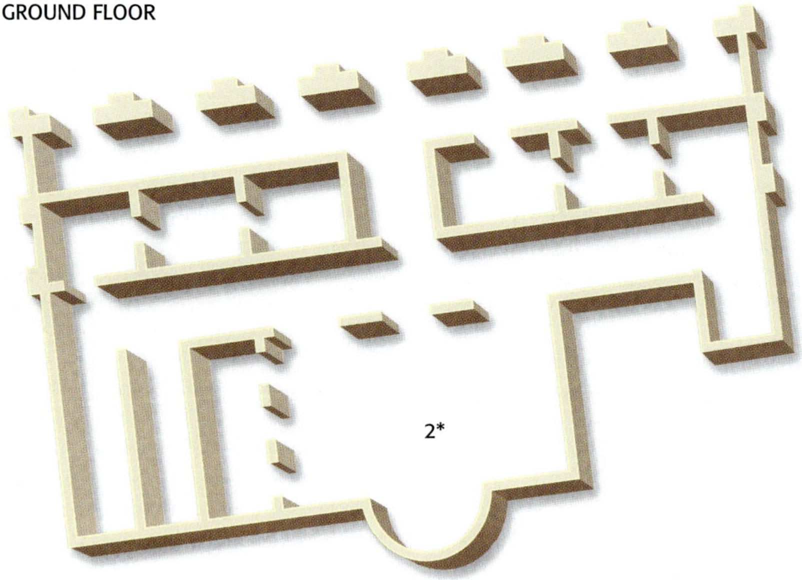

FIRST FLOOR

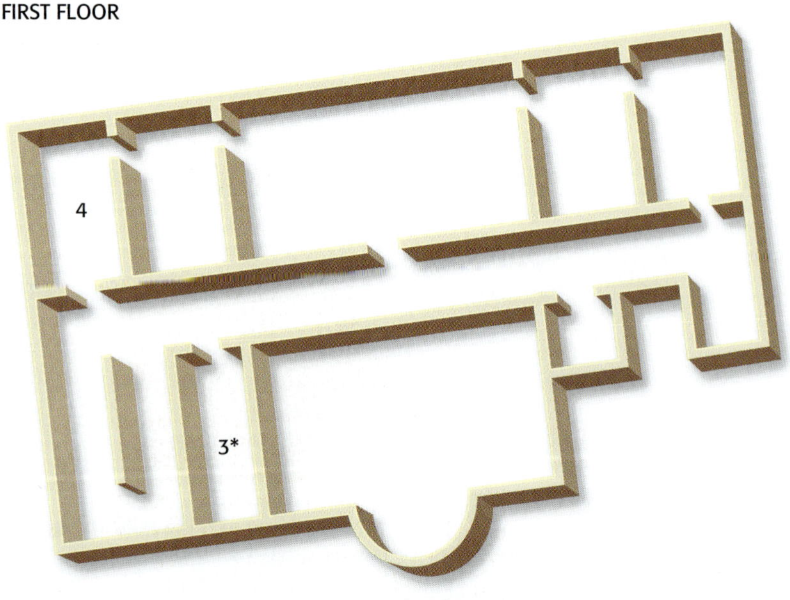

2 ▪ Marcus Aurelius
Campidoglio & Palazzo Nuovo Couryard

Surnamed Philosophus, Marcus Aurelius was known as the philospher emperor. He was benevolent, kind, and his people loved him. He was brought into power through the emperor Hadrian. When Hadrian selected an heir, he chose Aurelius Antoninus Pius, but as a condition of the selection, Antoninus Pius was to adopt Marcus Aurelius as his son.

His reign was not without difficulty. He fought his wars though he hated it. He dealt with pestilence and famine. He labored to keep his borders secure and his empire powerful.

The wife of Marcus Aurelius, Faustina, dishonored the emperor often with other men. He was oblivious to her scandals. Marcus Aurelius, promoted several of her lovers to posts of honor and profit. In his Meditations (his book of philosophy) he "thanked the Gods who had bestowed upon him a wife so faithful, so gentle, and of such a wonderful simplicity of manners." The Senate at his request made her a Goddess.

The magnificent bronze statue of the emperor is the only equestrian bronze of an emperor to survive to our day. The original stood in the center of the Piazza on Michelangelo's oval pedastal. It has been moved inside and replaced with a beautiful copy.

The statue survived and was placed in the piazza in a place of honor because Pope Paul III thought it was a statue of Constantine; the first Christian Emperor.

Marcus Aurelius died in 180 AD and left his empire to his son Commodus.

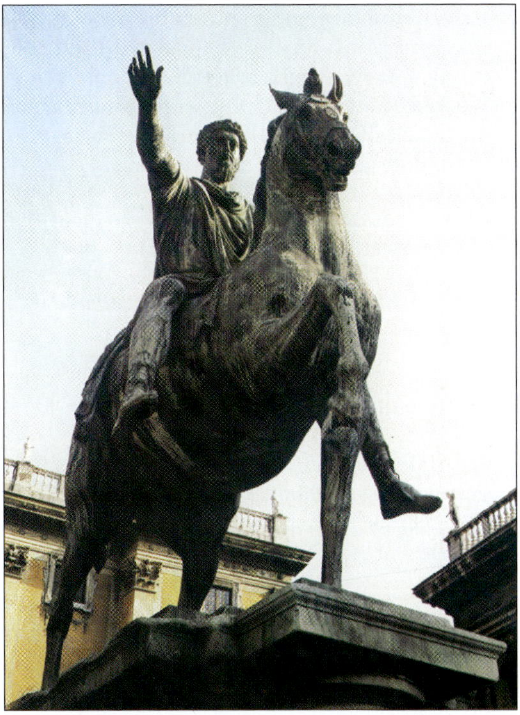

The Flavian and Antonine Emperors

- 69-79 AD Vespasian - began Colosseo
- 79-81 AD Titus - Completed Colosseo and ruled through the eruption of Vesuvius destroying Pompeii and Herculaneum
- 81-96 AD Domitian - Oversaw one of the largest construction campaigns of any emperor. He rebuilt 50 buildings throughout Rome (including the Temple of Jupitor on the Capital where the Capitoline Museum resides today) after a great fire and civil war.
- 96-98 AD Nerva - Took an oath not to slay any senators! Very few construction projects completed due to his short reign. Also the first emperor to select an heir by adopting who he thought should be the new emperor.
- 98-117 AD Trajan - Built the Roman Forum and the Trajan Market. He also constructed the first Imperial Bath. Beginning in the 4th Century new emperors were hailed with the chant, "felicior Augusto, melior Traiano" which means "luckier than Augustus, better than Trajan." He was well respected and his reputation grew stronger after his death.
- 117-138 AD Hadrian - Traveled to every province. He was the first emperor to consolidate the empire and build boundaries. His Pantheon still stands today. Hadrian rebuilt it and left the honor to Marcus Agrippa who was the advisor and architect of Augustus. He also built his Palace, which still stands today at Tivoli just outside of Rome. Hadrian was the central figure of the 5 good emperors starting with Nerva and ending with Marcus Aurelius. Hadrian is the emperor most responsible for the changing of the character and nature of the empire.
- 138-161 AD Antoninus Pius - Governed the empire capably and gently. His daughter Faustina married Marcus Aurelius
- 161-180 AD Marcus Aurelius - See previous page
- 180-192 Commodus - See details on page 13
- 193 AD Pertinax - Ruled for only 87 days
- 193 AD Didius Julianus - Won the "auction of the empire" after the death of Pertinax Disius Julianus outbid Flavius Sulpicianus with a final bid of 25,000 Sesterces per soldier. He only ruled for 2 months and the auction was the highlight of his reign.

3 ▪ Capitoline Doves

Palazzo Nuovo Hall of the Doves

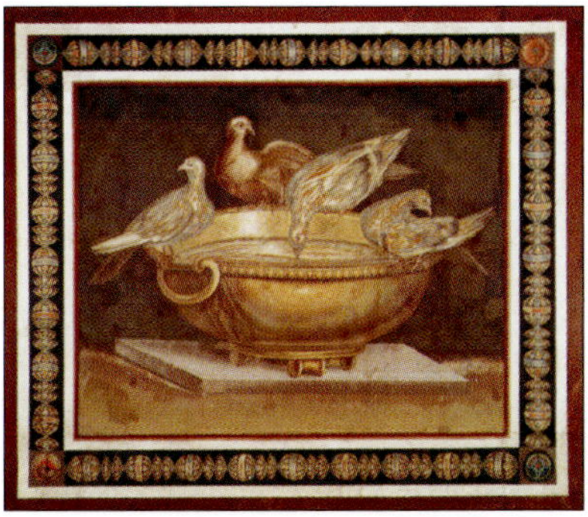

This incredible micro-mosaic was found at Hadrian's Villa in Tivoli just outside of Rome. Hadrian was a lover of all things Greek. He was one of the only emperors to travel to each province of his empire. The minute detail of this mosaic is incredible. Imagine how long it took the artist to create this masterpiece.

The Capitoline doves decorated the floor of Hadrian's Palace.

4 ▪ The Dying Gaul

Palazzo Nuovo Hall of the Galatian

This famous statue is an artistic rendering of a defeated Gaul at the hands of a Roman Soldier. Gaul was located where modern France is today.

The moustache and thick necklace were common among the barbarians from Gaul. In fact, the word Barbarian comes from the latin for beard - barba. The Romans did not wear beards while their enemies from the north did, so anyone wearing a beard became a Barbarian.

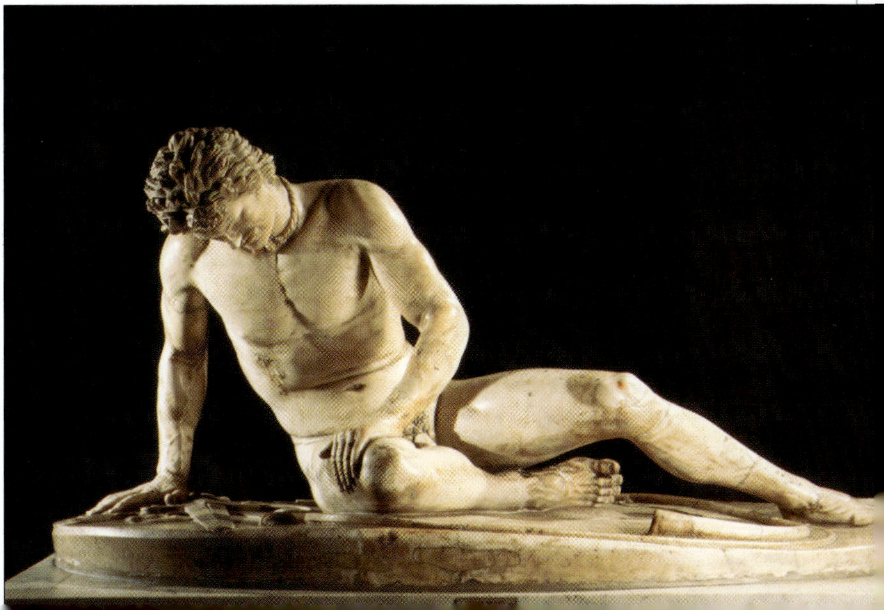

Palazzo dei Conservatori

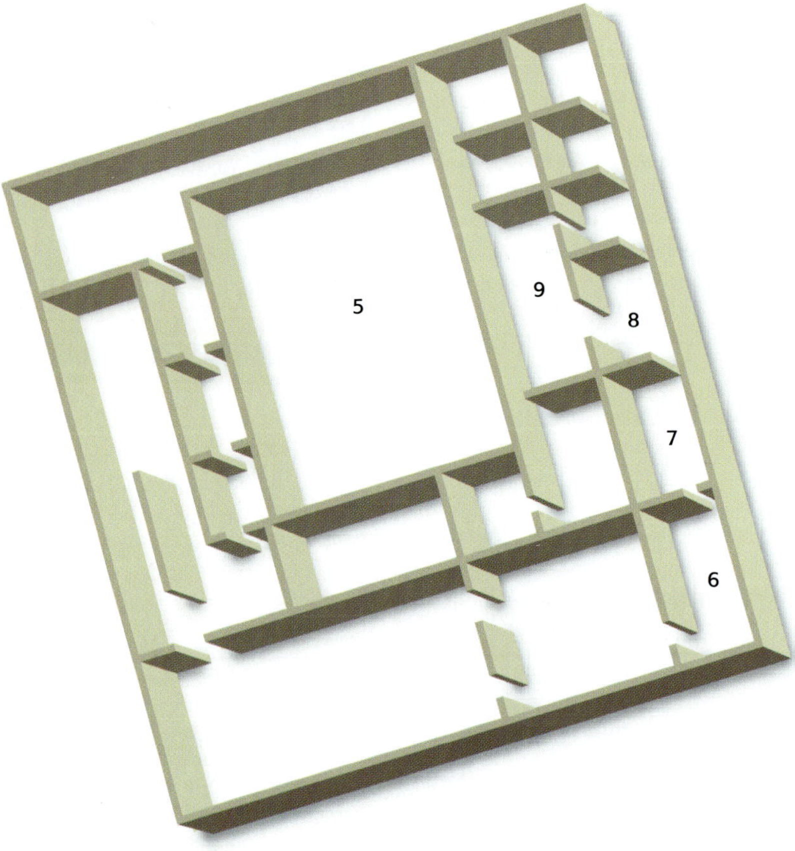

5 ▪ Colossus of Constantine

Palazzo dei Conservatori Courtyard

Constantine the Great made way for the acceptance of Christianity as a religion and ultimately the official religion of the empire.

The night before a battle against Maxentius in Rome Constantine had a vision of victory. In the vision he saw the symbol of Christ. His army marched under the banner of the Cross and each soldier had a cross painted on their sheild fulfilling the vision.

Constantine's army defeated a superior fighting force that greatly outnumbered them at the Milvian Bridge over the Tiber in Rome. Maxentius died in the battle.

After the victory Constantine drafted the Edict of Milan in 313 AD. The edict made the practice of Christianity legal in the Roman Empire and stopped the persecution of Christians. It also delivered back any land or property that was confiscated by the Empire.

Contantine honored his new religion by building Old Saint Peter's. The new Saint Peter's has since replaced Constantine's. The basilica was built where Constantine and Pope Sylvester (the 33rd Pope) thought Saint Peter, the first apostle and founder of the Roman Christian Community, was buried. Excavations have since proven that Saint Peter is buried under the Basilica.

The immense basilica is capable of holding up to 4000 worhshippers at once. The basilica also fulfills the words of Jesus Christ to Saint Peter, "Thou art Peter, and upon the rock I will build my church (Matthew 16:18). Peter was Rome's first bishop and the first pope.

The Colossus of Constantine stood 30 feet tall.

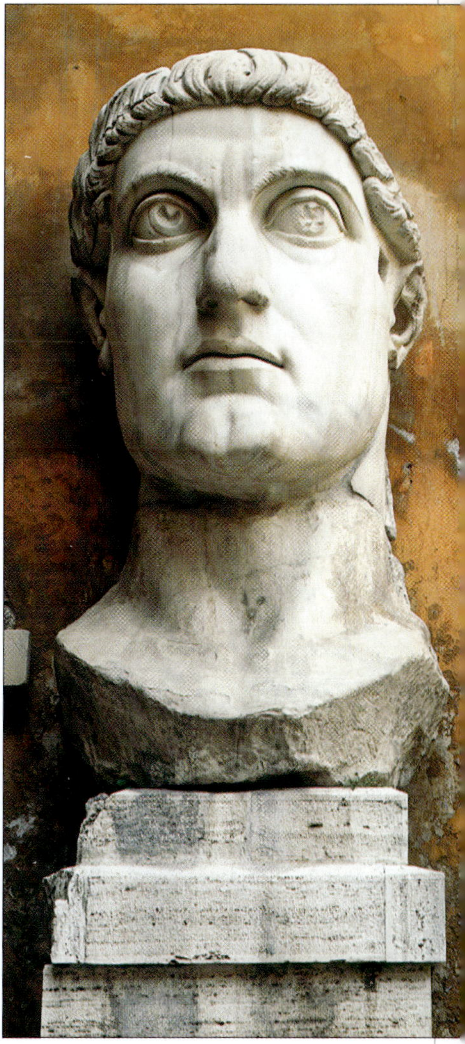

6 ■ Spinario

Palazzo dei Conservatori Hall of the Triumphs

The Romans, unlike the Greeks, captured everyday life in art. They chose to illustrate people as they really were versus in the ideal. This bronze is simple. It is of a boy removing a thorn from his foot. It is one of the original pieces gifted to the people of Rome by Pope Sixtus IV.

The Romans have many statues of people captured doing ordinary activities in the Capitoline Museum. You will find a drunken old woman and a wrinkly old man. When you look at the Spinario think of your childhood. Remember when all you had to worry about in life was taking a thorn out of your foot so you could keep playing? Do you remember the simple things in life. That is exactly what the artist was trying to illustrate...did he succeed?

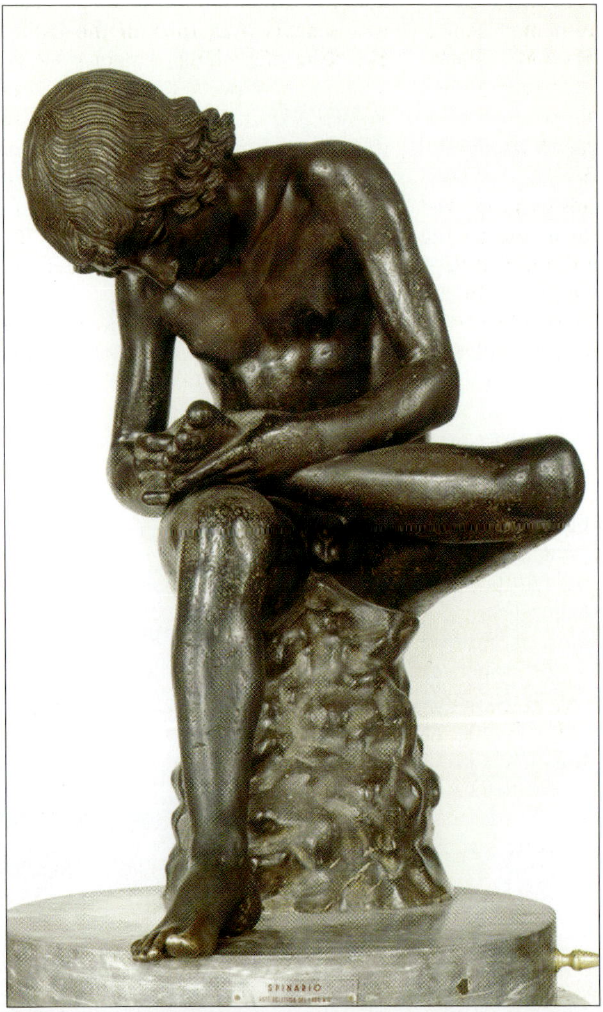

7 ▪ Capitoline Wolf with Remus and Romulus

Palazzo Conservatori The Hall of the She Wolf

The legendary founding of Rome has a rich history. It goes all the way back to the sacking of Troy by the Greeks. It is not a clear line from Troy to Rome, but the story is captured by Virgil in his epic poem; the Aeneid, written at the end of the first century for Augustus. The Aeneid glorified Augustus and Rome as Homer's Illiad and Odyssey did for the Greeks.

Accroding to the poem, Aphrodite, the Goddess of love and beauty seduced Anchises bearing a son named Aeneis. As Troy fell to the Greeks Aeneis, his father Anchises, and his son Ascanius escaped bearing the Gods of Troy. It was upon Aeneis to find a new home for the Trojans and their Gods.

The escape of Aeneis was captured in art by Michelangelo in the Sistine Chapel, by Raphael in the famed Raphael Rooms in the Vatican, and by Bernini in sculpture at the Palazzo Borghese. Another tie to legendary founding of Rome is in the Belvedere Courtyard in the Vatican Musuem - the Laokoon.

As Aeneis continues his own odyssey he lands at Carthage, located in northern Africa. The Queen Dido offers him her hand in marriage, but he declined. Thus beginning the hatred between the Rome and Carthage which stretches throughout history.

Upon his departure from Carthage Aeneis sailed to the mouth of the Tiber River. There a great king took him and the Trojans in. The King's name was King Latinus ruler of the Latins. The King offered his daughter Lavinia's hand to Aeneis. At once Aeneis became the mortal enemy of Turnus who was also courting Lavinia. The hatred resulted in a war between Turnus and Aeneas. Turnus fell and Aeneas went on to marry Lavinia finding a home for the Trojans and their Gods where modern day Rome stands today.

The official founding of Rome came centuries later. Numitas, the last of the Alban Kings of Latium had a daughter

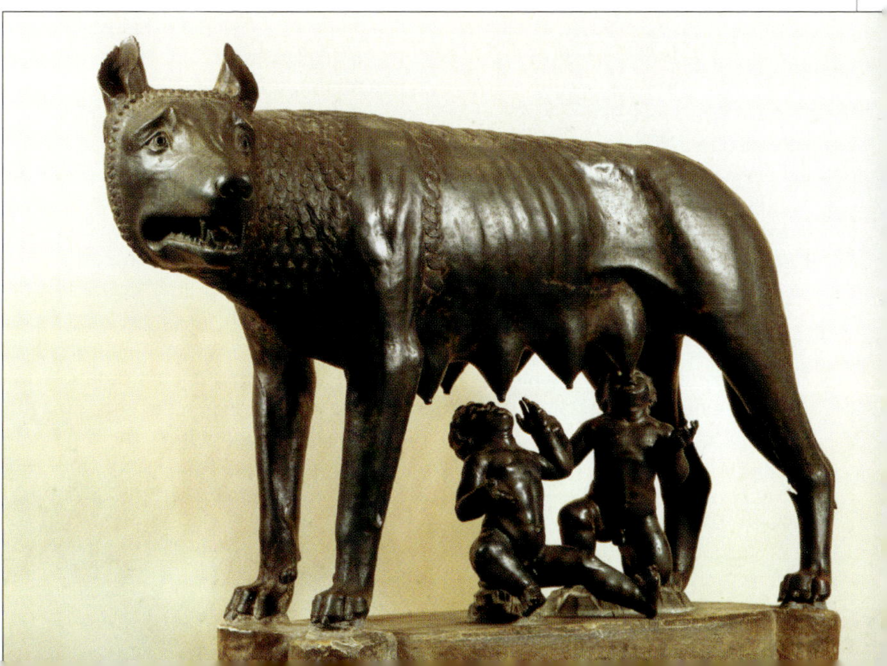

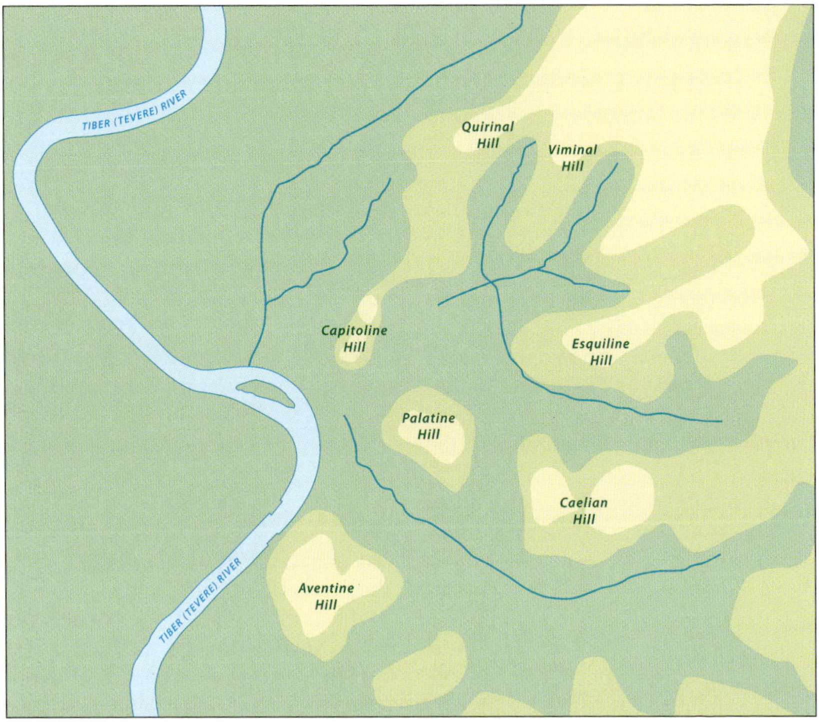

named Rhea Silvia. She was a Vestal Virgin. The Vestals were the priestesses of Vesta coming into the role between the ages of 6 to 10. They had to be without personal blemish (read virgin), of free respectable families whose parents were still alive and living in Italy. After their election each vestal served for 30 years. At the end of the term the Vestels could enter private life and marry, but few did. They watched over the sacred, eternal flame of Vesta. Should one of the priestesses let the flame go out, or violate her vow of chastity she was burried alive in the Field of Transgression and her seducer was scourged to death. The Vestals enjoyed distinct favor. They held a place of honor at public games and it was death to he or she that injured a Vestal. If a criminal being dragged to their punishment met a Vestal en route the criminal was immediately pardoned.

Rhea Silvia, the Vestal Virgin daughter of Numitas was seduced by the God of War - Mars. She bore the twins Remus and Romulus. A new King usurped the throne from King Numitor and ordered the newly born twins to die in the Tiber River. They were set adrift in a basket. The basket washed ashore and the twins were suckled to life by the Capitoline Wolf. A few days later the twins were found by the new kings shepherd named Faustulus. The twins were immediately recognized for who they were and sent to a safe home away from the wrath of the king.

As the twins grew the tension between Remus and Romulus became great. They fought and Remus was killed by his brother Romulus. Romulus went on to found Rome in 753 BC. The infant city of Rome was populated by too many men. The Roman men tricked the Sabians and stole their woman. A war broke out between Rome and Sabia that ultimately resulted in peace and finally Rome was ruled by Romulus and thus founded within the seven hills of Rome today.

8 ▪ Medusa

Palazzo dei Conservatori The Hall of the Geese

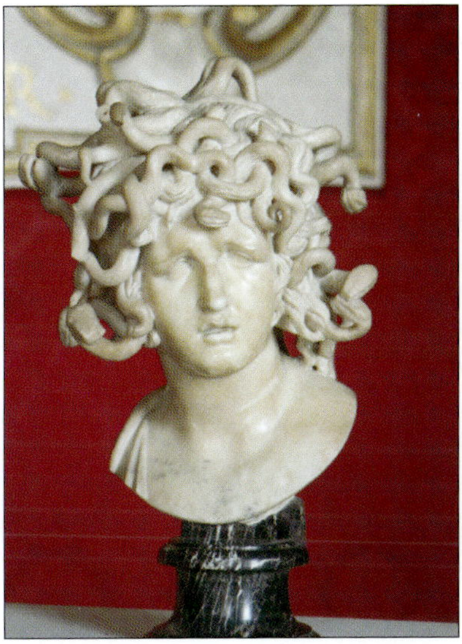

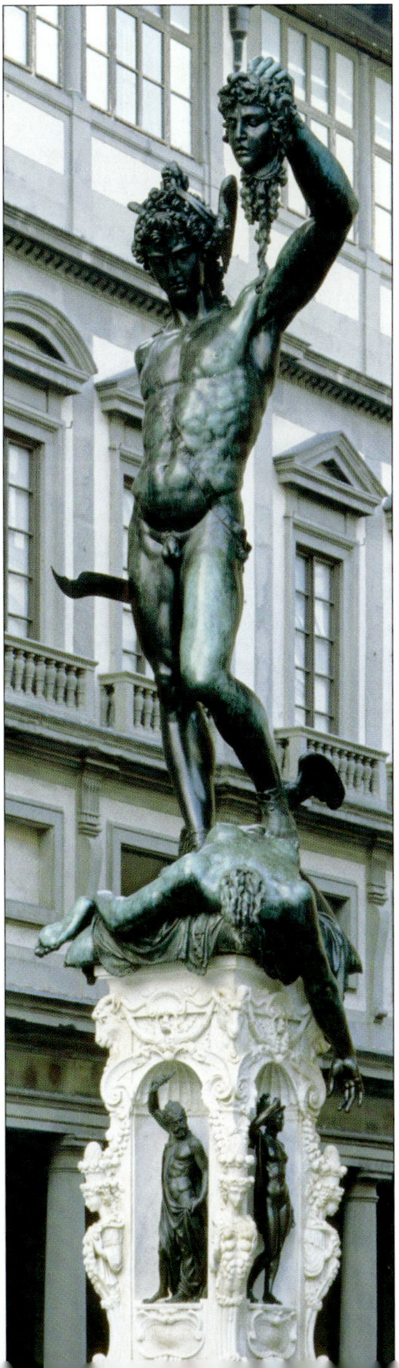

The only mortal of the three Gorgons, Medusa was beheaded by Perseus. Her site so hideous that one glimpse of her turned the viewer to stone. Medusa's hair was live, writhing snakes and only Bernini could capture the frightening movement in stone. Bernini is the master of capturing motion through sculpture. Medusa appears alive and her snakes evil.

Perseus beheaded her and gave her head to Athena. Athena placed Medusa's head on her shield. The use of a frightening figure on a shield to inspire fear is called an Aegis. You can see many instances of a frightening figure in armor, under banners of arms, or on a shield all pointing to Athena's use of the mythological Gorgon.

The statue to the right is Celini's bronze Perseus bearing the head of Medusa located in Florence in the Loggia in Piazza Signoria.

9 ■ Commodus Hercules • Gladiator Emperor

Palazzo dei Conservatori   Hall of the Tapestries

Marcus Aurelius who was one of Rome's most benevolent emperors, fathered a son named Commodus. At the age of 14 Commodus was admitted to full imperial power. His father ruled wisely, and though Rome had her wars during the reign of Marcus Aurelius the political stability of the empire was secure and Commodus had few enemies and no real competition for the imperial throne.

His father was a wise and just ruler who prized education and philosophy, but Commodus took on few of his father's admirable traits. He was born weak. He was a slave to his attendants and servants unable to make a decision or lead the empire on his own after his father's death. Gradually his mind became corrupted. His cruelty originally came from the dictation of others, but over time became his habit. In the Decline and Fall of the Roman Empire it reads, "the pride of one requires the submission of the multitude," to describe the reign based in fear and uncertainty of Commodus.

Then it happened...the assasination attempt. As the assassin neared Commodus he yelled, "the Senate sends you this!" In actuality his own sister Lucilla (not the senate) plotted the assassination to gain the Empire for herself. The attack failed, but to Commodus suspician equaled proof. Many innocent senators died at the hand of Commodus as a result of the attempt at his life. To be sure he quashed all who were involved and to insure no retribution for those he killed, he extended his scourge to all of the murdered senators supporters numbering in the thousands.

Commodus ruled his empire in oblivian. It was certain death to bring him unwelcome news. Civil wars raged in the streets of Rome and none would alert the emperor for fear of death. He spent his days in the company of 300 concubine. He luxuriated in his wealth and omnipotence considering himself to be descended from Hercules. The lion skin and club he wears in this sculpture are the mythological symbols of Hercules. The lion skin comes from the Nemean Lion killed by Hercules, and the club is Hercules weapon of choice. One of Hercules' twelve labors was to kill the Nemean Lion. The lion's skin was impenetrable by arrows so Hercules cut a club and chased the lion into a tunnel. Sealing up one end of the tunnel and crawling in the other Hercules strangled the lion in his grip. This is how the lion skin and club are the symbols of Hercules.Commodus went so far as to have a lion skin draped and a club leaned against his throne. This sculpture was created at his demand.

Commodus, as emperor, entered the gladiatorial games. He came to the arena as a secutor armed with a helmet, sword, and buckler. He chose to fight a naked enemy armed with only a net and trident. He fought in the arena 737 times. At his gladiatorial school many of his training opponents were delivered mortal wounds. He grew acustomed to the arena and gave up his favor of Hercules and thought himself the better hero. He became known as Paulus the Secutor.

Commodus killed Roman nobles and his domestic help at his whim. This would prove his downfall. For fear of death his concubine, slaves, and chamberlain plotted his murder. Marcia, his favorite concubine, brought a draft of poisened wine to Commodus as he lay in his bed chamber. Commodus drank the wine and while he slept in his poisoned state he was strangled to death by a wrestler.

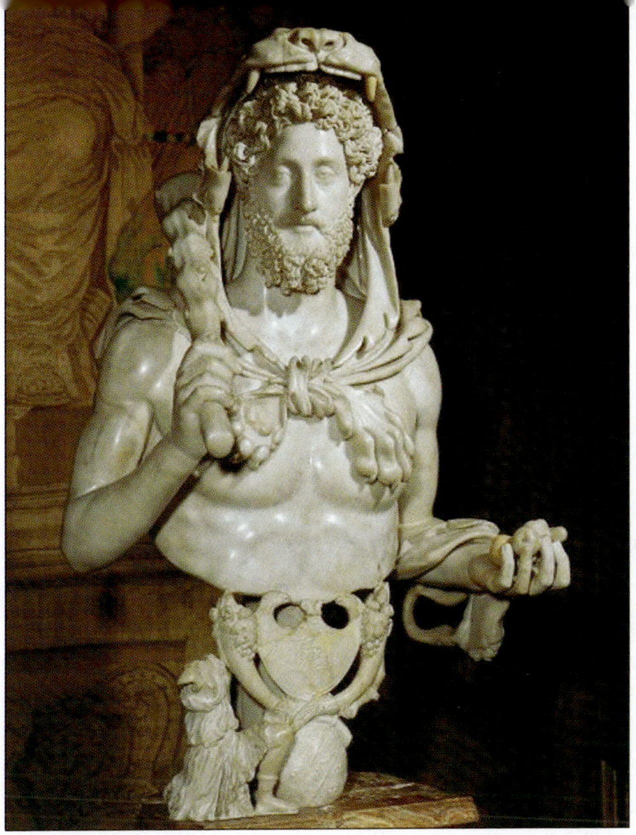

Hercules also died by poison.

Hercules is most famous for his 12 labors. One of the twelve labors was to kill the hydra – a multiheaded water serpent. When Hercules killed the hydra he dipped the tips of his arrows in it's blood. The Hydra's blood was a lethal poison capable of killing the strongest of men.

Hercules and his bride were traveling to a city named Trachis near the famous city Thermopylae. On the way they had to cross the river Evenus where a centaur named Nessus escorted Deianira while Hercules easily swam across. As they were crossing the centaur tried to rape the wife of Hercules. Enraged Hercules shot Nessus with one of his poisoned arrows. As he died he instructed Deianira to collect his blood, a powerful love potion should she ever need it.

As Hercules prepared a sacrifice in honor of his father he put on his cloak. However, Deianira, wanting to seduce Hercules after the sacrifice applied the poisenous love potion to the inside of the cloak. It was prophesied that no living man could kill Hercules and the prophesy was about to be fulfilled.

As Hercules went through the process of the sacrifice to Zeus he began to sweat with his cloak on. The sweat mixed with the blood of Nessus that was poisoned by the blood of the Hydra. The poison took its effect. Soon after, Hercules was dead by the killed centaur Nessus fulfilling the prophesy.

In Hercules last breath he created a funeral pyre. As he lay dying, no one dared light it. A passing shepherd named Philoctetes finally dared to do so. As a gift of thanks Hercules gave Philoctetes his bow and poisoned arrows. Philoctetes would go on to play an important role in the Trojan War.

The death of Commodus by poison is his last association to Hercules. In no way is the association honorable. Hercules was a hero. Commodus was a killer.

Palatine Hill & Roman Forum

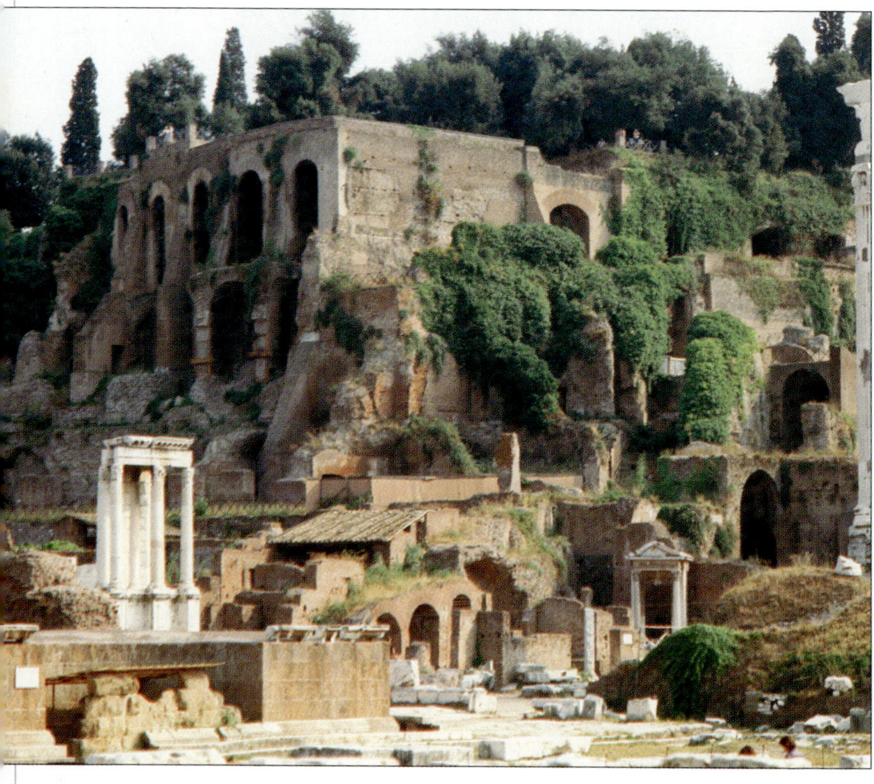

Rising above, and to the South of the Forum, is the Palatine Hill (Collo Palatino). It is the oldest inhabited site in Rome. The hill was home to the Ceasars. Augustus was born on the Palatine Hill and as he rose in power he bought the surrounding estates and transformed them into his private home. It is now the home to some of Rome's greatest views of the Forum and the Colosseum.

The Roman Forum lies in what was once a marsh between the Capitoline Hill and the Palatine Hill. The Forum was the political, religious, and commercial epicenter of Rome. What you see today is a fragment of what the Forum once was.

No guidebook will do the Forum (Trajan's or Roman) and Hill justice. The best way to enjoy and appreciatte the Forum and Hill is by way of a guided tour. I HIGHLY recommend a walking tour with one of my partners noted on the Tips page of www.unabellavista.com. Reach out to one of them to plan your walking tour of the Palatine Hill and Forums.

Roman Forum and Palatine Hill

THE ROMAN FORUM:

The Roman Forum has the highest concentration of ancient Rome's archeological treasures.

The area of the Roman Forum started as a market and a burial place situated in a marshy valley between the Palatine Hill and the river Tiber. Building there required the installation of the *Coaca Maxima*, an extensive drainage system which drew off the water from the valley, thus permitting the construction of several public buildings. Basilicas, temples, porticos, and arches were erected and many remain, even today.

One of the peak periods of urban architecture on this site was during the 2nd century B.C. when the whole city changed with the addition of imposing basilicas, market areas, and law courts.

The 1st century B.C. saw the installation of the Roman State Archive, the *Tabularium* in Latin, which was situated on one slope of the Capitol Hill and gave the Forum a magnificent background. Over time, the Roman Forum came to be considered the heart of the religious, political, commercial and judicial center. With all of these major activities being concentrated on one site, it is easy to see how the Forum transformed the valley into Rome's own downtown, the heart of the Empire. Further, considering it's importance to Rome, it can easily be argued that the Forum was the heart of the civilized world during a period when Rome was considered *Caput Mundi*, literally "head of the world."

Through to the beginning of the 1st Century AD, Julius Caesar and Augustus completed a new design in the valley. Throughout this period, the Forum became an instrument of imperial propaganda and a demonstration of dynastic prestige. The last single column erected was in the 7th century opposite the Curia, and was dedicated to Emperor Phocas.

Centuries later, abandonment of the valley left the Forum filled with silt due to flooding. Construction on the site did not begin again until the 14th century, after the return of the Popes from Avignon, France at which point the Roman Forum became a stone quarry.

It was't until the 17th century that any real attention was paid to the forum. The first excavations took place in 1788. Since then archeologists have been consistently uncovering and studying the ruins of the Forum.

The best way to see the treasures of the Forum is to approach from the Colosseum and the Arch of Constantine, and head towards the Arch of Titus along the Via Sacra, the Main Street. It is still paved with the original basalt stones and was used

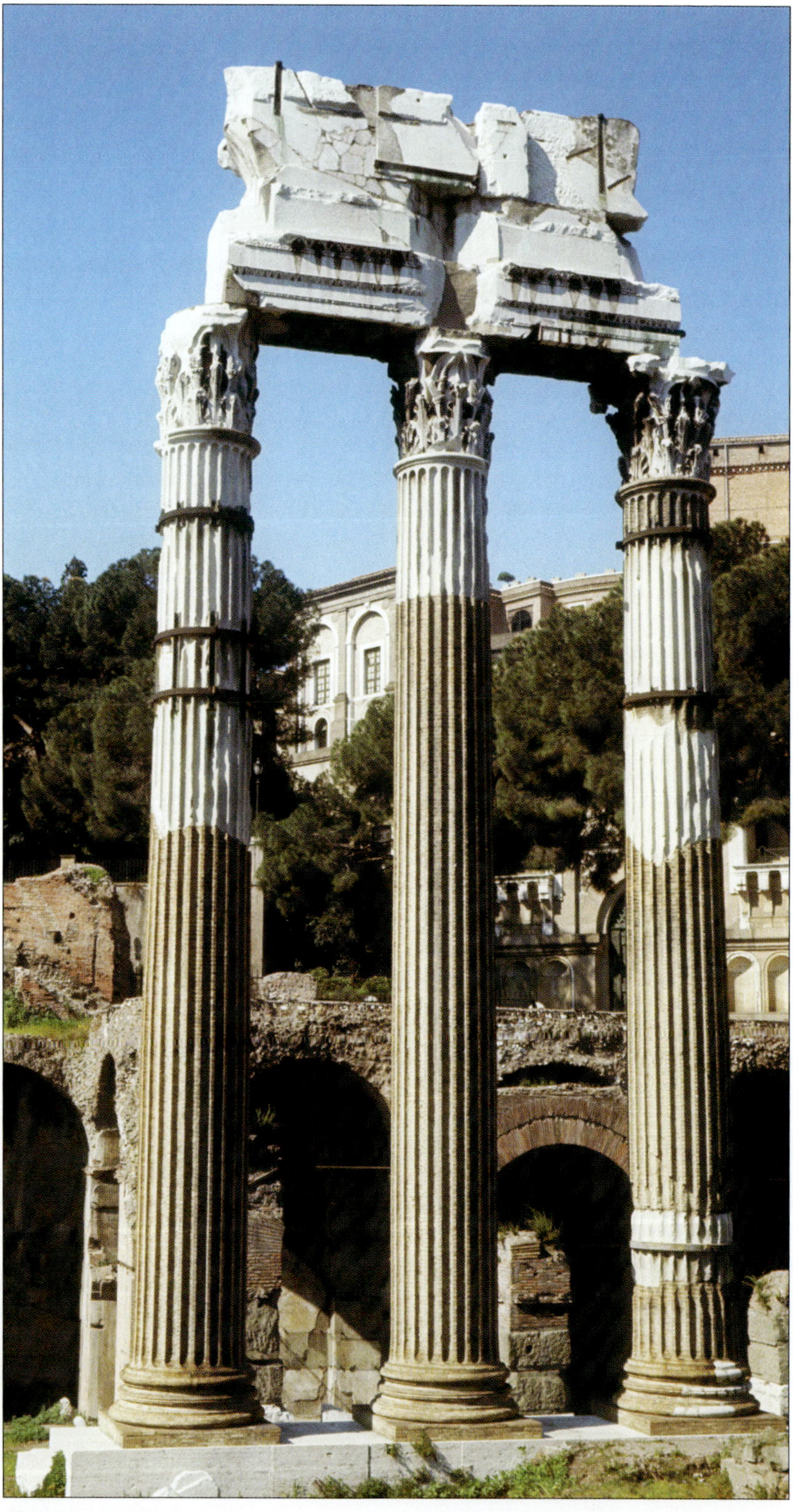

by the Emperors during their triumphal parade which consisted of generals, soldiers, looted treasures, animals, and prisoners of war (in chains, of course) all passing along, and then across, the valley to the opposite Arch where they then marched to the top of Capitol Hill and to the Temple of Jupiter, Juno and Minerva, to whom the victory was dedicated.

Reminder: *Try to use your imagination to add colors, decorations, and bronze to the ruins around you. Ancient Rome was not black and white, but filled with color.*

Key Forum Monuments:

The smallest and most ancient triumphal arch was erected to commemorate the victories of Titus and his father Vespasian in the province of Judea. It depicts the Emperor leading the parade followed by Nike, the Goddess of Victory.

The Basilica started by Maxentius and finished by Constantine is the largest and one of the finest buildings in the Forum. Imposing and impressive, it was originally as long as a football field and contained a colossal, seated statue of Emperor Constantine. One has to imagine it with the colorful marble columns, statues, floors, walls and ceilings it possessed in its prime to truly understand the majesty of this monument. Now, its remains are in the Capitoline Museums. Only one column is still preserved. It stands in front of the Basilica of St. Mary Major.

As you walk through the Forum you encounter six gigantic (each is 50 feet tall) columns in *Cipollino* (onion) marble in front of the Basilica of St. Mary Major. The original temple was built more than 1800 years ago. Emperor Antoninus Pius ordered the building in honor of his wife Faustina. A beautiful frieze goes around the top of the Basilica with winged griffins, acanthus and candelabras showing one of the best examples of Roman art and architecture. Looking at the green door of the church (built above and inside much later) you can see the level reached by the dirt and silt. It covered the entrance of the church.

The Temple of Vesta housed the sacred fire kept burning by the Vestal Virgins. These women were chosen very young and dedicated 30 years of their lives to serve Vesta in exchange for great privileges and respect.

In the middle of the Roman Forum one should make sure to visit Julius Caesar's burial place. After Caesar's death, Emperor Augustus ordered a temple built dedicated to god Julius, making him the first Roman who became a god after death. To this day flowers are brought to honor the great general, writer, and one of Rome's most famous rulers.

Each side of the valley is occupied by Law courts, called Basilica in Latin, where they administered the justice and public affairs of the empire. This architecture can be seen throughout the world, imitated by every major religion when building their Cathedrals and Basilicas.

The valley ends with the Curia, built by Julius Caesar, completed by Augustus, and renovated by Domitian. It was once considered the most important political symbol of Rome and was where the senators met. For the record, this is not where

Julius Caesar was killed. This building was not completed in the year 44 B.C. At the time of Ceasar's death the Senatorial meetings were held in a different area of Rome.

The final Arch has detailed inscriptions related with Emperor Septimus Severus and his son Caracalla. Nearly 1800 years old it celebrates the 10th anniversary of the Emperor and his victories. It shows in relief how the Roman soldiers took the prisoners in chains.

PALATINE HILL:

Too many people limit their visit to only the Forum and miss the Palatine Hill which is a MUST see for anyone truly looking to get a glimpse back in time. It reveals the history of Rome from its beginning to the Severi Emperors of the 3rd century A.D. It illustrates the evolution from simple wooden huts to the marble masterpieces to imperial palaces.

A terrace overlooking the Roman Forum gives the opportunity to understand the layout of the valley and provides a superb view for pictures of the *Colosseum*, the *Capitoline Hill* as well as six of the seven most famous of Rome's hills. The opposite corner has remnants of the Iron Age period as well as the residence of Emperor Augustus.

On the Palatine Hill you will find the remains of an Iron Age settlement believed to be the house of Romulus.

During the Republican period the Palatine Hill became the favorite residential area for the Roman upper class. It allowed them to showcase their villas, gardens and fountains to everyone else who shared 'the best address in the city'. It was such an impressive place to live that the first Emperor Augustus and his wife Livia chose the Palatine as their residence.

After Augustus, other Emperors (Tiberius, Nero, the Flavians, the Severi) followed suit and built their palaces on Palatine Hill. Each created their own magnificent complex. Much later churches, monasteries, and even a fortress were added. In the 16th century the noble Farnese family added their own spectacular gardens.

Recently Rome has opened the underground passage built for Nero's Palace, named Criptoportico. It was used as a service and delivery area and can now be enjoyed by those walking the Hill.

From the Hill, you can gaze on the *Circus Maximus*, the largest entertainment complex in the empire, from above. Charioteers would race seven laps around its outskirts. The Circus Maximus is so large that its crowd capacity was three times that of the Colosseum.

The Palatine Hill Museum is worth a visit for statues, frescoes, terracotta and models of the Iron Age huts.

It is difficult to effectively describe the Palatine Hill and Forum in a few short pages. While you are certainly encouraged to explore at your own pace, it is worthwhile to consider hiring a private tour guide to help you visualize the beauty and complexity at this center of Rome.

10 ▪ Arches of Titus and Constantine

The Arch of Titus was erected by his brother Vespasian in the honor of Titus on the sacred way in the Roman Forum. It follows an earlier style and utilizes only one archway. Originally it was covered with guilded bronze statuary at the top.

The columns are engaged in a composite form utilizing a combination of the Ionic and Corinthian style.

The relief is an illustration of the victory of Titus at Jerusalem. In it the Romans carry the Golden Menorah, the Showbread table, and trumpets.

The inscription reads :

SENATVS
POPVLVSQVEROMANVS
DIVOTITODIVIVESPASIANIF
VESPASIANOAVGVSTO

THE SENATE
AND THE PEOPLE OF ROME
DEIFIED TITUS VESPASIAN AUGUSTUS
SON OF DEIFIED VESPASIAN

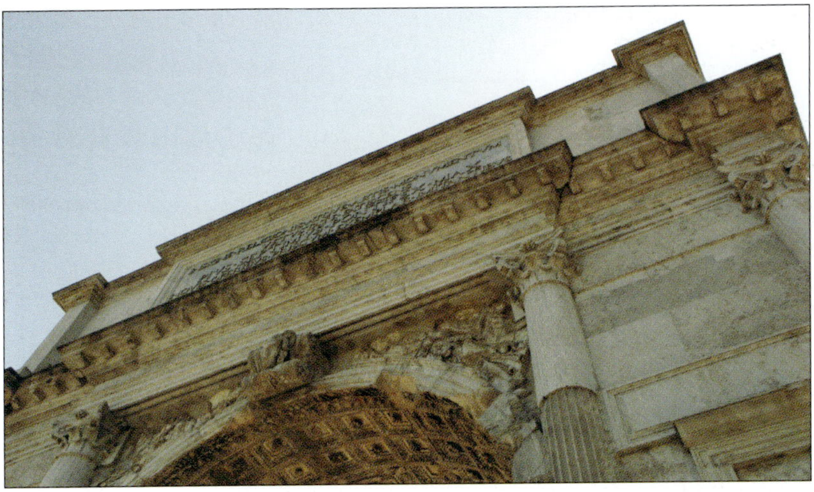

Triumphal arches were built to showcase military victories, the creation of roads, and the creation of bridges.

The Arch of Constantine was built to honor Constantine's victory over Maxentius at the Milvian Bridge.

Constantine's arch utilizes three archways and is near the Colosseum. Much of the decoration used on the Arch was taken from other public works built by Trajan, Hadrian, and Marcus Aurelius.

The columns used are from an earlier era. The features of Constantine were simply updated. The emperor wanted the arch up quickly and asked his artists to simply utilize an existing narrative. They did just that and recarved Constantines features over the previous emperors.

The artists added new labels to the arch:

FUNDATOR QUIETUS
BRINGER OF PEACE

LIBERATOR URBIS
LIBERATOR OF THE CITY

The labels represent the downfall of Maxentius and the end of the civil war that raged until Constantine's victory.

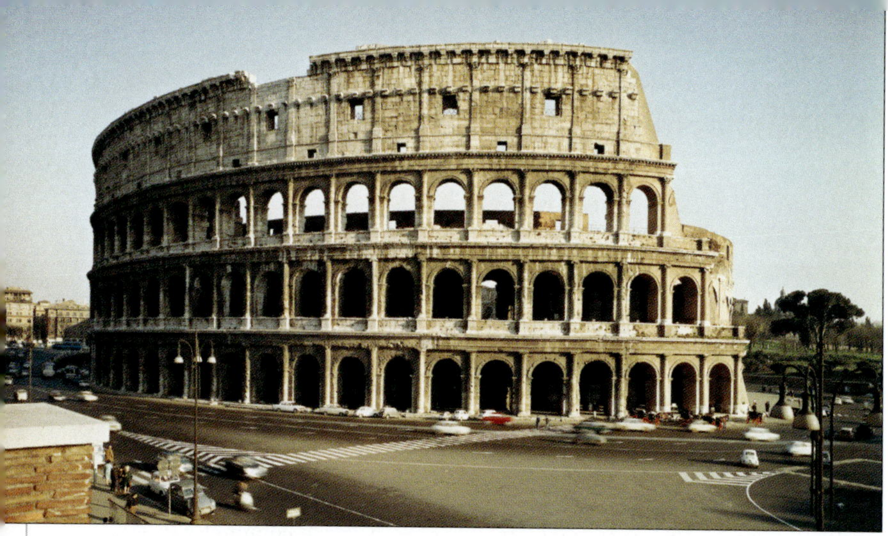

11 ▪ Colosseo

Originally named Flavian's Ampitheater after Vespasian's (The builder of the Colosseum) family name. The creation of the Colosseo was shrewd. Vespasian had to win back the mob after the previous emperor Nero turned every Roman against the empire by building his enormous Golden House. The artificial lake in Nero's Golden House stood where the Colosseo now stands today. With the creation of the new ampitheater Vespasian reclaimed the land for the citizens of Rome and won back the Romans.

The Colosseo takes it's name not from its size, it could hold up to 50,000 spectators, but from the huge statue of Nero that once stood near the entrance to the former Golden House.

The ampitheater was completed in 80 A.D. and formally dedicated by Titus (Vespasian's son and new Roman Emperor after his father died). The opening games were held for 100 days at an incredible expense. The highlight of the games were the naval battles that took place in the Colosseo after it was flooded and filled with ships. The seating area rests over a complex system of corridors covered by concrete barrel vaults. This concrete skeleton reveals itself today. In the centuries following the fall of Rome the Colosseo served as a quarry for ready-made building material. Almost all of it's marble seats were hauled away. Hidden in antiquity, but visible today the arena substructures where the gladiators and animals waited to enter the arena through machinery that lifted them up through a trap door and into the fight. On top of the Colosseo was set a huge sail called a velarium. It was used to protect the spectators from the sun and elements. It was weilded by members of Rome's navy.

The exterior is travertine and is 160 feet high (16 stories). It has 76 numbered entrances designating seating and social rank. The facade was purely for decoration and has three orders of columns from the ground up: Doric, Ionic, and Corinthian. The sequence is based on aesthetic and is not functional.

The Colosseo still stands as the powerful symbol of the Roman Empire and illustrates to all the power of the Romans.

Trajan's Forum

No guidebook will do the Forum (Trajan's or Roman) and Hill justice. The best way to enjoy and appreciatte the Forum and Hill is by way of a guided tour. I HIGHLY recommend a walking tour with one of my partners noted on the Tips page of www.unabellavista.com.

The Forums are the world's largest, outdoor, ancient museums. It was one of Trajan's major building efforts coming in at twice the size of the Forum of Augustus that was built a century before.

Trajan's Forum was paid for by the spoils of his victory over the Dacians (modern day Romania). Trajan had his architects follow forum archictural rules.

The temple for the forum was completed after his death and was dedicated to Trajan the God. His temple was set behind the Basilica. The temple stood at the rear of the forum in it's own courtyard with two libraries and a giant commemorative column (see Trajan's Column).

One entered Trajan's Forum through a gateway like a triumphal arch with a statue of Trajan driving six horses being crowned by the Goddess Victory.

The basilica built by Trajan is called the Basilica Ulpia after Trajan's family name.

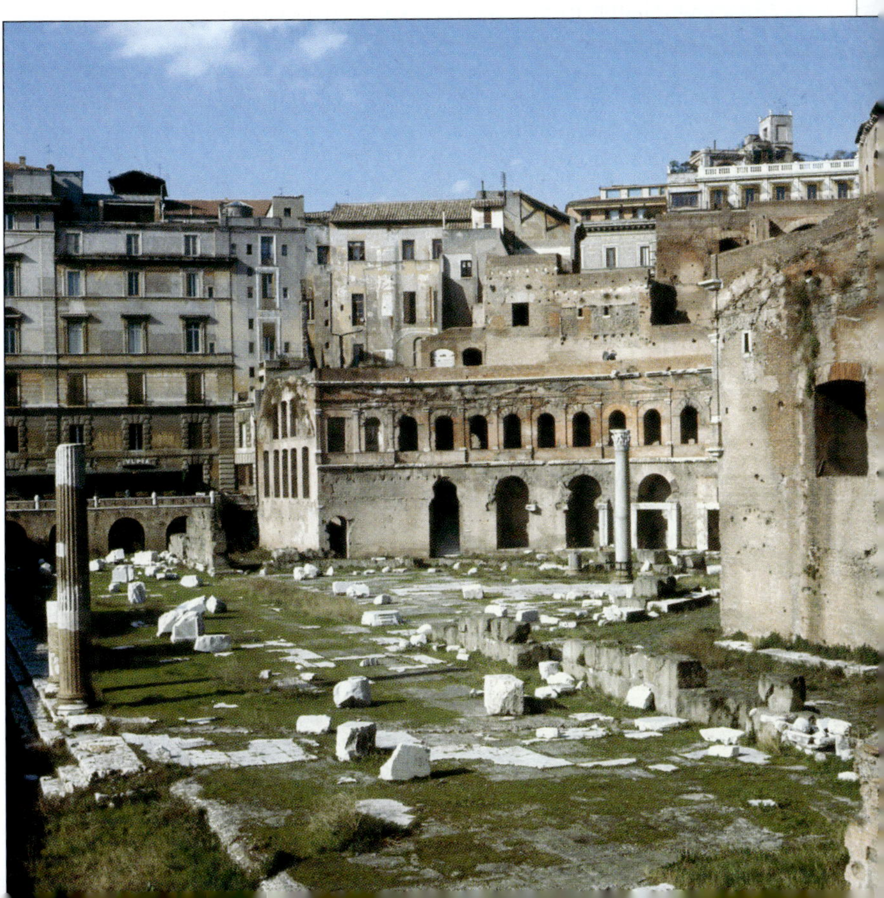

Trajan's column created by Apollodorus of Damascus

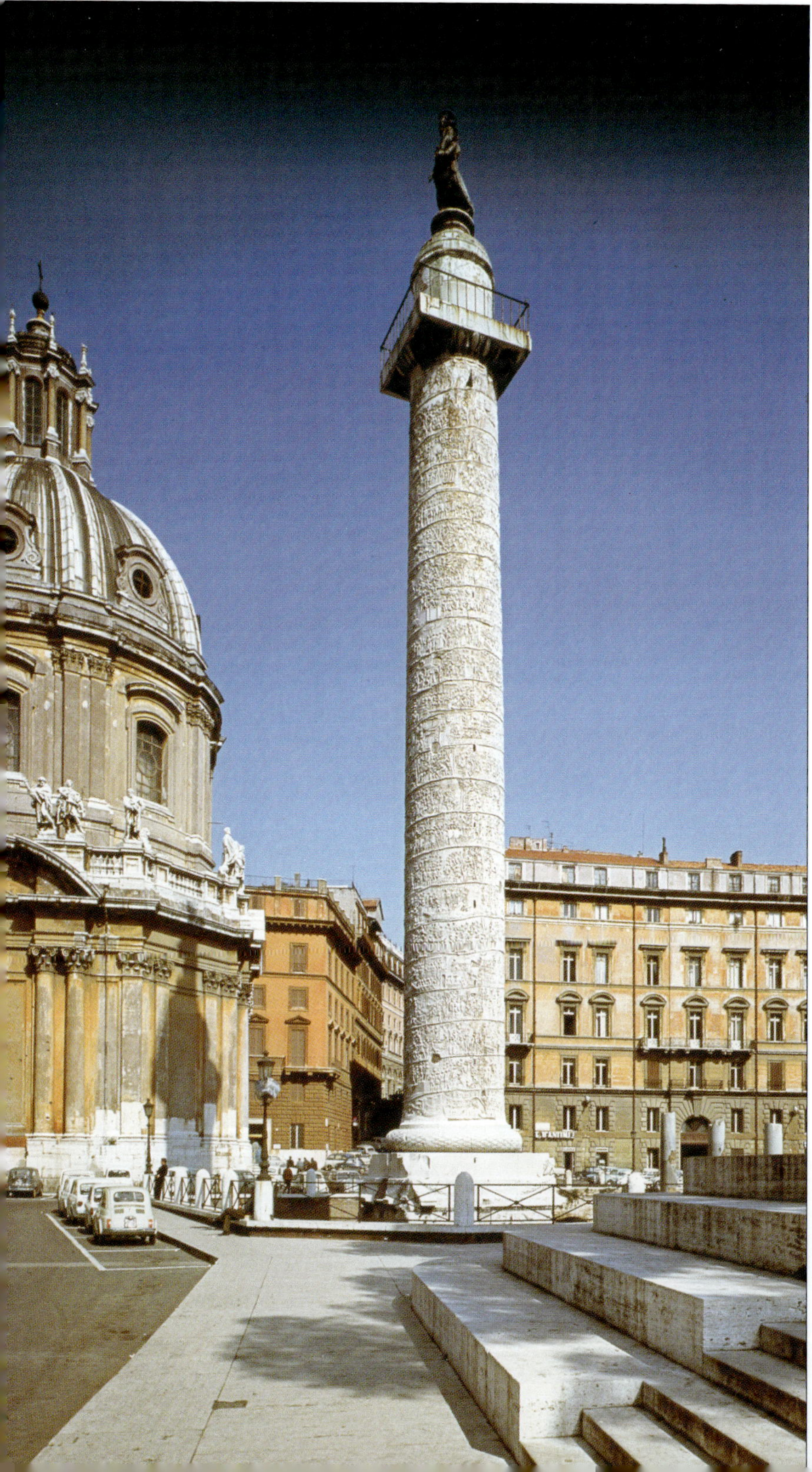

12 ▪ Trajan's Market

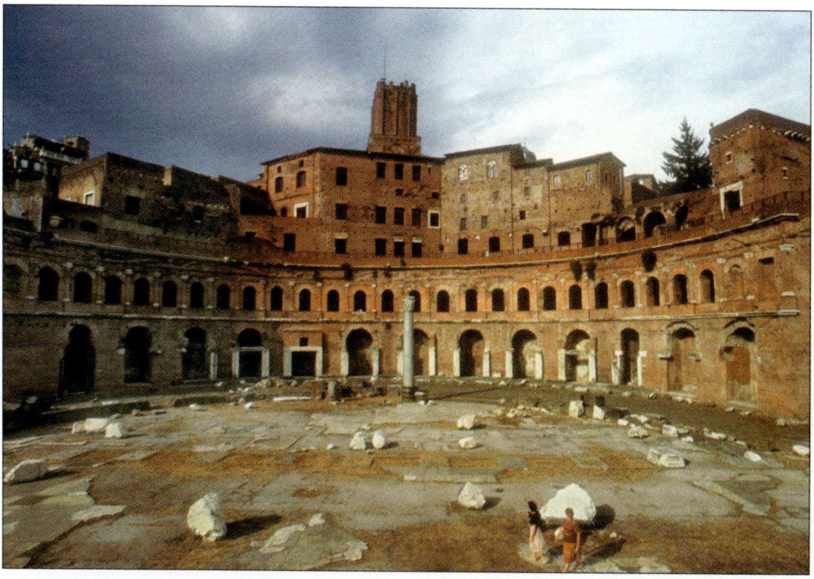

Trajan's Market overlooks the forum. His famous architect Apollodorus of Damascus built the market as he did Trajan's column.

The markets are made of concrete and built on a natural slope that allows for a tiered marketplace. The base unit was called the taberna which is a single-roomed shop covered by a barrel vault. Above the wide doorway of the taberna is a window that illuminates the attic storage space.

The markets had shops on several levels and opened to either a hemispherical facade, the street, or an indoor marketplace.

The market was a place for the Romans to come and purchase a variety of items the same way we shop our malls today.

13 ▪ Trajan's Column

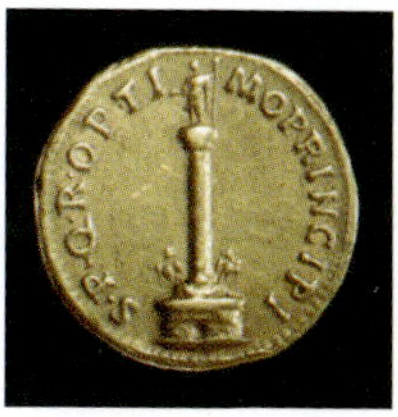

Coin showing the Column of Trajan

128 Feet Tall
625 Feet of Narrative
150 Episodes illustrated
2500 figures
2 successful campaigns

Battle scenes cover 25% of the column. The other 75% is covered with battle preparation and fortification. The battles illustrated are against the Dacians, modern day Romania. The narrative grows in width higher up the column. This is to provide easier viewing from the base. The statue at the top today is Saint Peter. Originally it was a statue of a naked Trajan.

The base is the resting place of Trajan and his wife Plotina.

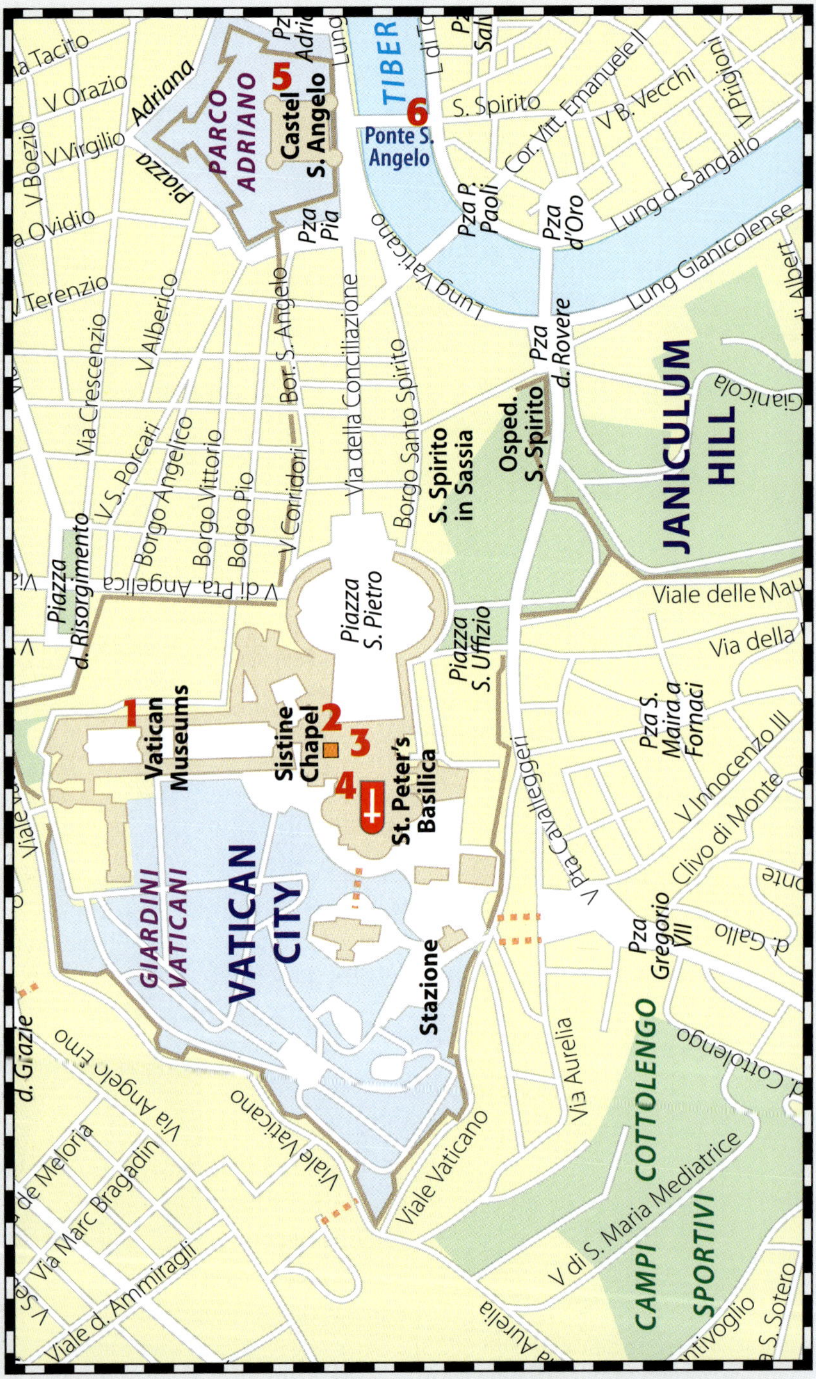

1. Vatican Museums
2. Raphael Rooms
3. Sistine Chapel
4. Saint Peter's
5. Castel Saint Angelo
6. Ponte Saint Angelo

VATICAN CITY

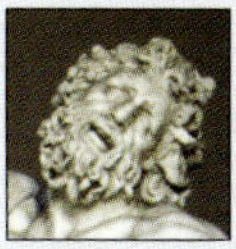

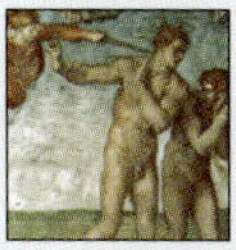

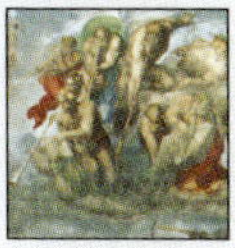

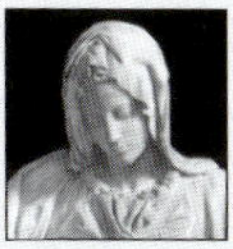

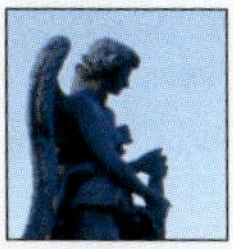

Site		Mon	Tue	Wed	Thur	Fri	Sat	Sun
Vatican Museums Viale Vaticano http://mv.vatican.va/ Cannot prepurchase tickets. Tickets are cash only Adult tickets are 12 Euro Open last Sunday of the month with free admission	**entrance** varies by time of year **exit** varies by time of year	The Vatican Museums allow entry from 8:45 to 12:20 or 8:45 to 3:20 The Vatican Museums close at 1:45 or 4:45. Please visit www.unabellavista.com/tips for the current Vatican schedule.						X
Castel Saint Angelo Lungotevere di Castello 50 Closed December 25 & January 1 Adult tickets are 7 Euro (5 Euro + 2 Euro for exhibits) Ticket office closes one hour before closing	AM PM	X	9:00 to 8:00	9:00 to 8:00	9:00 to 8:00	9:00 to 8:00	9:00 to 8:00	9:00 to 8:00
Ponte Saint Angelo Lungotevere de Castello 50 No tickets necessary. Outdoor, 24 x 7 viewing	AM PM	24 x 7						
Saint Peter's Basilica Piazza di San Pietro http://mv.vatican.va. No tickets necessary. Free Admission. Free one hour English guided tours available at Centro Serviczi	AM	April - Setptember 7:00 - 7:00	April - Setptember 7:00 - 7:00	April - Setptember 7:00 - 7:00	April - Setptember 7:00 - 7:00	April - Setptember 7:00 - 7:00	April - Setptember 7:00 - 7:00	April - Setptember 7:00 - 7:00
	PM	October - March 7:00 - 6:00	October - March 7:00 - 6:00	October - March 7:00 - 6:00	October - March 7:00 - 6:00	October - March 7:00 - 6:00	October - March 7:00 - 6:00	October - March 7:00 - 6:00

X = Closed

Vatican Museum & Sistine Chapel Hours – example calendar

January – Gennaio							
M	L	1	8	15	22	29	
T	M	2	9	16	23	30	
W	M	3	10	17	24	31	
T	G	4	11	18	25		
F	V	5	12	19	26		
S	S	6	13	20	27		
S	D	7	14	21	28		

February – Febbraio							
M	L		5	12	19	26	
T	M		6	13	20	27	
W	M		7	14	21	28	
T	G	1	8	15	22		
F	V	2	9	16	23		
S	S	3	10	17	24		
S	D	4	11	18	25		

March – Marzo							
M	L		5	12	19	26	
T	M		6	13	20	27	
W	M		7	14	21	28	
T	G	1	8	15	22	29	
F	V	2	9	16	23	30	
S	S	3	10	17	24	31	
S	D	4	11	18	25		

April – Aprile							
M	L		2	9	16	23	30
T	M		3	10	17	24	
W	M		4	11	18	25	
T	G		5	12	19	26	
F	V		6	13	20	27	
S	S		7	14	21	28	
S	D	1	8	15	22	29	

May – Maggio							
M	L		7	14	21	28	
T	M	1	8	15	22	29	
W	M	2	9	16	23	30	
T	G	3	10	17	24	31	
F	V	4	11	18	25		
S	S	5	12	19	26		
S	D	6	13	20	27		

June – Giugno							
M	L		4	11	18	25	
T	M		5	12	19	26	
W	M		6	13	20	27	
T	G		7	14	21	28	
F	V	1	8	15	22	29	
S	S	2	9	16	23	30	
S	D	3	10	17	24		

July – Luglio							
M	L		2	9	16	23	30
T	M		3	10	17	24	31
W	M		4	11	18	25	
T	G		5	12	19	26	
F	V		6	13	20	27	
S	S		7	14	21	28	
S	D	1	8	15	22	29	

August – Agosto							
M	L		6	13	20	27	
T	M		7	14	21	28	
W	M	1	8	15	22	29	
T	G	2	9	16	23	30	
F	V	3	10	17	24	31	
S	S	4	11	18	25		
S	D	5	12	19	26		

September – Settembre							
M	L		3	10	17	24	
T	M		4	11	18	25	
W	M		5	12	19	26	
T	G		6	13	20	27	
F	V		7	14	21	28	
S	S	1	8	15	22	29	
S	D	2	9	16	23	30	

October – Ottobre							
M	L	1	8	15	22	29	
T	M	2	9	16	23	30	
W	M	3	10	17	24	31	
T	G	4	11	18	25		
F	V	5	12	19	26		
S	S	6	13	20	27		
S	D	7	14	21	28		

November – Novembre							
M	L		5	12	19	26	
T	M		6	13	20	27	
W	M		7	14	21	28	
T	G	1	8	15	22	29	
F	V	2	9	16	23	30	
S	S	3	10	17	24		
S	D	4	11	18	25		

December – Dicembre							
M	L		3	10	17	24	31
T	M		4	11	18	25	
W	M		5	12	19	26	
T	G		6	13	20	27	
F	V		7	14	21	28	
S	S	1	8	15	22	29	
S	D	2	9	16	23	30	

Entrance (Ingresso) 8:45 - 12: 20	Exit (Uscita) 1:45 / 13:45
Entrance (Ingresso) 8:45 - 13:20 (1:20)	Exit (Uscita) 2:45 / 14:45
Entrance (Ingresso) 8:45 - 15:20 (3:20)	Exit (Uscita) 4:45 / 16:45
Entrance (Ingresso) 8:45 - 12:20 *FREE	Exit (Uscita) 1:45 / 13:45
Closed	

1. Vatican Museums are closed every Sunday except the last Sunday of the Month
2. Free admission on the last Sunday of every month
   Cash Only (Euro 12,00) • No Reservations Accepted

Map to Vatican Museums • Pinacoteca

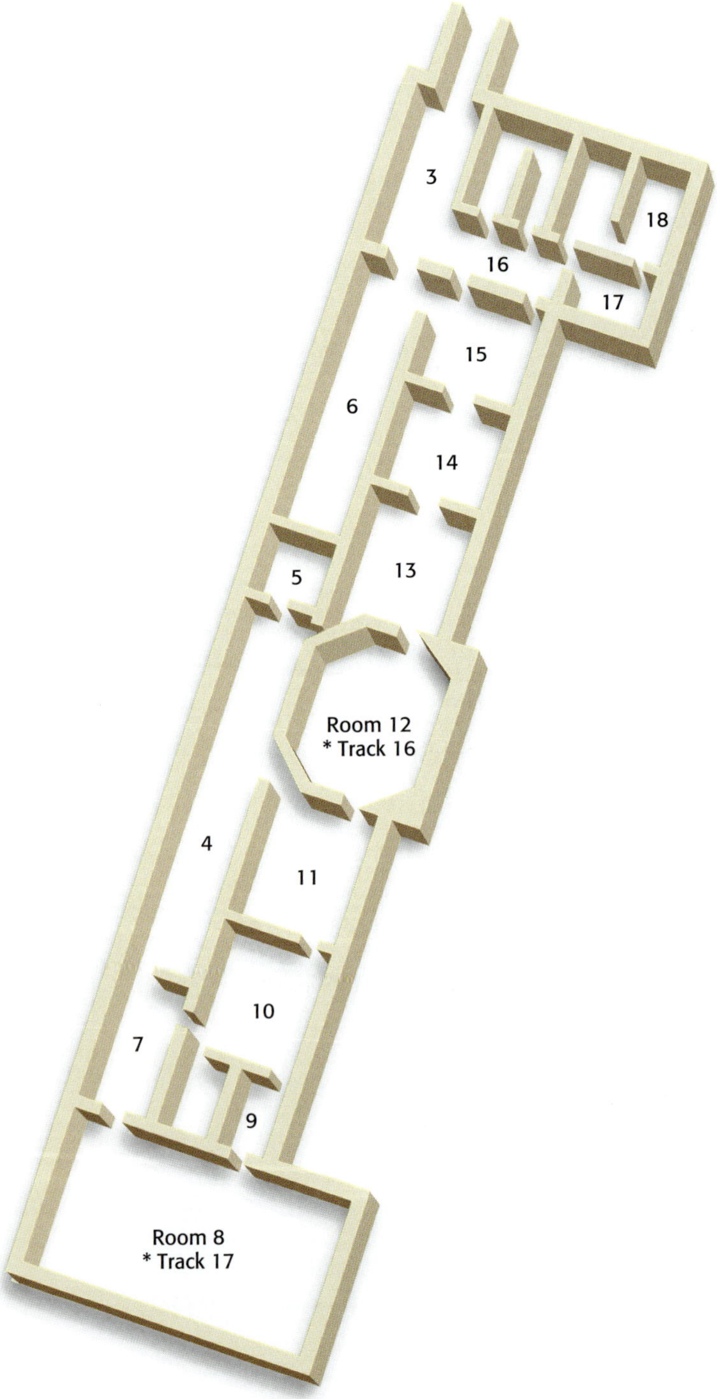

Each of the rooms contains treasures beyond your imagination and should be given ample time to enjoy. The graph below contains a short description of the era and names of the masters you will see in each room. Included in the Vatican Pinacoteca pages are write-ups on the Transformation by Raphael and the Deposition by Caravaggio found in rooms 8 and 12 both marked in RED. The rooms marked in BLUE contain masterpieces worth extra time enjoying.

Room 1 - I	12 th - 15th centuries
Room 2 - II	Giotto, Simone Martini: 13th - 15th centuries
Room 3 - III	Beato Angelico: 15th century
Room 4 - IV	15th - 16th centuries
Room 5 - V	15th century
Room 6 - VI	15th century
Room 7 - VII	Perugino, Pinturicchio: 15th - 16th centuries
Room 8 - VIII	Raphael: 16th cenury
Room 9 - IX	Bellini, Leonardo da Vinci: 15th - 16th centuries
Room 10 - X	Titian, Giulio Romano, Veronese: 16th century
Room 11 - XI	Barocci: 16th century
Room 12 - XII	Caravaggio, Domenichino: 17th century
Room 13 - XIII	Pietro da Cortona: 17th century
Room 14 - XIV	Carlo Maratta, Baciccia: 17th century
Room 15 - XV	Francesco Mancini: 18th century
Room 16 - XVI	Wenzel Peter: 19th century
Room 17 - XVII	Gian Lorenzo Bernini: 17th century
Room 18 - XVIII	Russian Art: 15th - 19th centuries

14 ▪ Belvedere Torso
The Inspiration of Michelangelo

This is considered one of the most beautiful blocks of marble in Rome. It so inspired Michelangelo that he spent his life trying to outdo it not only in sculpture, but in painting. It is a statue of Heracles with his arms, legs, and head missing.

The statue is attributed to Apollonius of Athens in the 1st Century BC.

It is identifiable as Heracles by the lion's paw dangling from the back side of the statue. The statue takes its name from its location in the Belvedere Courtyard in the Vatican Museums.

With the exception of the missing limbs this statue is perfect; every muscle is flexed. You can feel the struggle of Heracles as he gathers his strength to knock out another one of his labors.

Remember the flexed contortion of Michelangelo's inspiration as you look up at the ceiling or the alter wall in the Sistine Chapel.

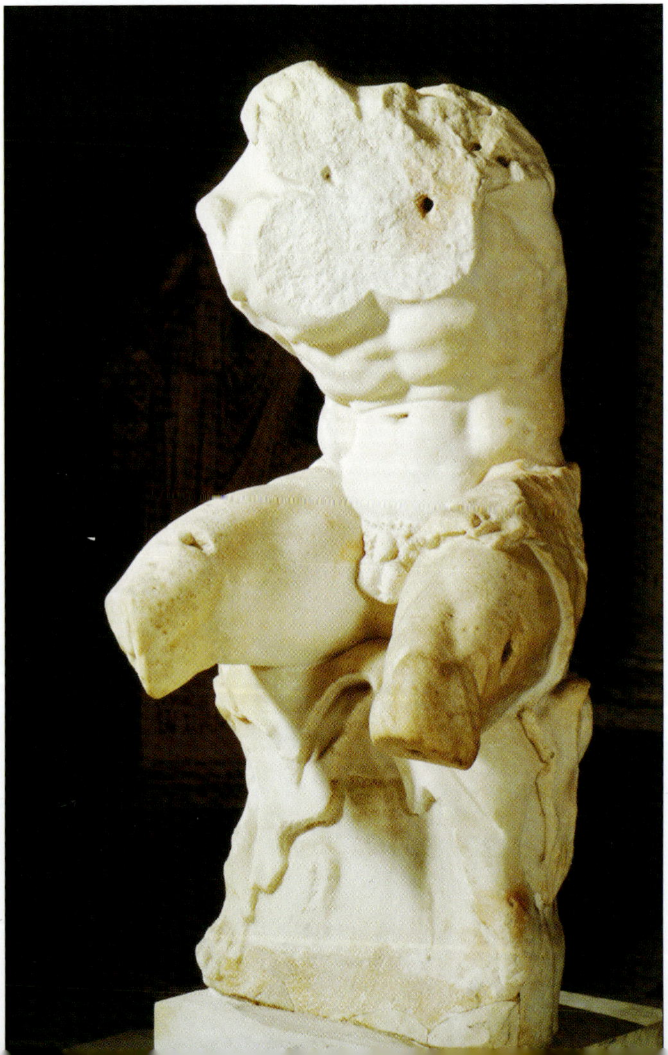

15 ▪ Laocoon
The Vatican Museum

The Laocoon was carved in 25 BC by a team of three sculptors living on the island of Rhodes in Greece. The names of the artists are Agesander, Polydorus, and Athenodorus. The work tells the story of the priest of Apollo, Laocoon, and his two sons being taken by serpents sent by the Gods to prevent the saving of Troy.

The Greeks appeared departed from Troy in order to convince King Priam that he had been successful in holding off the Greeks. The Trojan victory was supposedly honored by the Greeks through the gift of a large wooden horse. The wooden horse was the idea of Odysseus, the smartest of the Greeks.

As the Trojans accepted the gift of the Greeks they would inadvertantly bring the enemy within their walls, as the Greeks were stowed away within the belly of the horse. During the night, as the Trojans slept, the Greeks climbed down and razed the city. Laocoon was the Trojan Priest of Apollo who warned the Trojans of treachery and muttered the famous words, "beware of Greeks bearing gifts." The warning incited the Gods to bring Laocoon and his children to death by sending serpents to drag them into the sea.

The sculpture was transported to Rome by the emperor Titus in 69 AD. The beautiful statue was lost for centuries amid Rome's rubble and ruins. In 1506 the group minus Laocoons right arm was unearthed in a vineyard on the Esquiline Hill in Rome. Michelangelo was present at the excavation to help confirm its identity. Ecstatic at the find, Pope Julius II (the pope who decorated the Sistine Chapel and the famous Raphael Rooms) purchased the statue from the vineyard owner for 600 gold ducats per year for life.

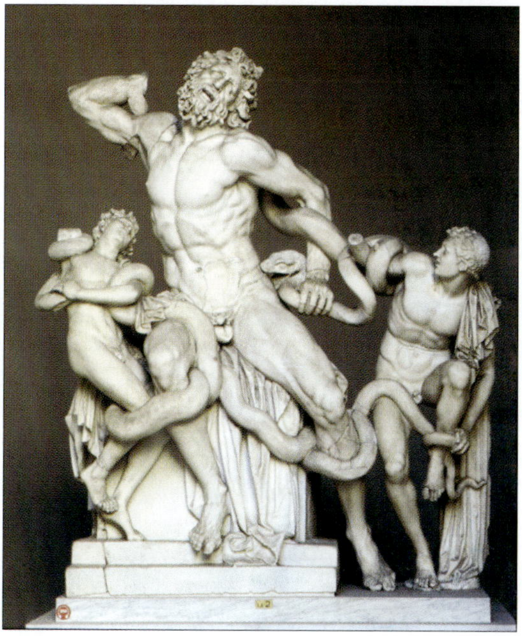

16 ▪ Michelangelo Merisi Caravaggio

Entombment   Vatican Museums • Pinacoteca

Originally this painting was set above the alter at Cappella della Pietro in Santa Maria in Vallicella. The church is also called Chiesa Nuova even though it was built in the 16th century. Chiesa Nuova was set to be enlarged. The plan was to have each of the twelve naves and transepts dedicated to the mysteries of Mary.

The commission was Caravaggio's most important public commission to date. He was to replace the Pieta that was in the Vittrice Chapel. The work was to be the scene of the Entombment. It seems an odd choice because there is no record of Mary being present at the burial. This departure from Biblical text would have had to be approved by the Oratory fathers as Chiesa Nuova was dedicated to the Oratorians in Rome. The approval came and allowed Caravaggio to add Mary to the Entombment scene. It is ironic that the Oratorians would allow the change since they were charged with keeping the accuracy of sacred images throughout Rome.

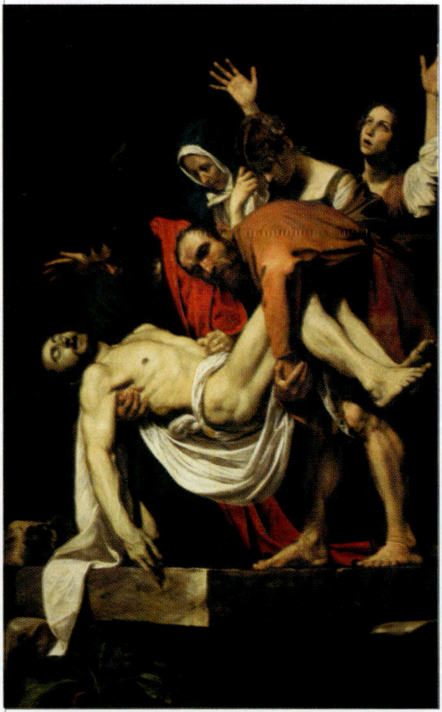

The commission was granted to Caravaggio by Girolamo Vittrice who was the nephew of the patron who donated the money to do the work on the church and, coincidentally, the owner of another Caravaggio named The Fortune Teller that is in the Louvre in Paris.

The painting was placed above the alter of the transept and the action of the scene goes to the edge of the work. The work is set at the burial of Christ at Calvary. Saint Joseph of Arimathea who carries Jesus' legs engages the viewer. Saint John holds Christ's upper body while the Virgin Mary has her arms outstretched behind the two Saints mirroring the crucifixion of her son.

The scene being placed above the alter would come to life over the priest's head during mass. It was a constant reminder that Christ died for our sins, our redemption. Congregants looked up from darkness into God's light. As the priest raises the Eucharist above his head it becomes the Body and Blood of Christ against the magnificently painted scene and recalls the event of our salvation and our right to enter Heaven. The Eucharist is actually raised above Christ's tomb truly symbolic of his salvation.

The cloth around and under Jesus is the shroud of Turin.

17 ▪ Raphael Santi

Transfiguration Vatican Museums • Pinacoteca

This was Raphael's final masterpiece. The work was essentially completed by the time of his death on April 6, 1520. According to Vasari, Raphael worked continously on this piece until he could work no more. It was done in his own hand which meant he did not just design the work and pass it along to one of his assistants to complete. Vasari also writes, "the shared judgement of the craftsman is that this work is his most celebrated, the most beautiful, and the most divine, so that who wishes to know the depiction in painting of Christ transfigured to divinity, sees him in this work. Christ dressed in the color of snow shows the essence and the Godhood of all three Persons (of the Trinity), tightly united in the perfection of the art of Raphael; who it seems so greatly bound himself to his power in order to demonstrate the force and the valor of art in the visage of Christ, that finishing it, as the last thing that he had to do, never again touched brushes, death taking him."

The Transfiguration was done in competition with Sebastiano del Piombo's Raising of Lazarus. As he had done previously Michelangelo assisted Piombo with the design of his work. Both pieces were done for the Cathedral of Saint Juste in Narbonne. The Cardinal Giulio de' Medici who commissioned the artists had to know that they would compete and that Michelangelo would assist Piombo. The two paintings are the same dimensions and meant to be placed next to each other or across the nave from one another.

Raphael held off on beginning his work while Piombo started and finished. When Piombo's work was completed Raphael urged the patron to have it sent to France for framing. This would remove the masterpiece from view of

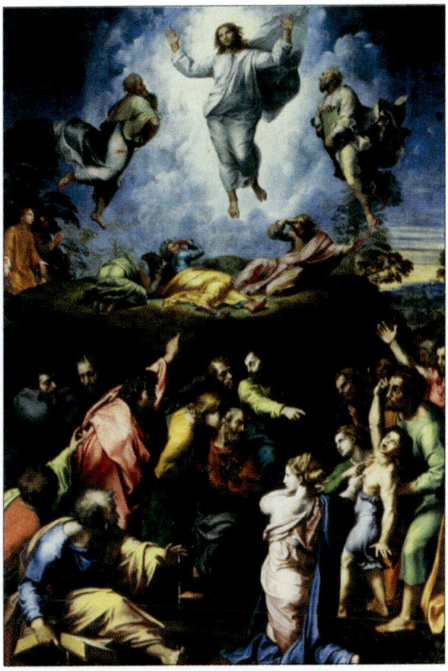

the Roman audience and prevent his work from being compared directly with the beautiful painting. When Raphael completed his Transfiguration it was commonly thought of as the more beautiful of the two works. The success of his final work made him victorious, not only over Piombo, but over the great Michelangelo as well.

The victory allowed Raphael to take one more commission away from Piombo even after his death. Piombo sought to paint the room in the Vatican that is now known as the Sala de Constantino. Instead this room was given to Raphael's assistants to paint after Raphael's death.

The Transfiguration with its use of light was to Caravaggio what the cartoons Battle of Cascina (Michelangelo) and Battle of Anghiari (Leonardo da Vinci) were to Raphael.

This beautiful painting was displayed at the head of Raphael at his memorial in the Pantheon of Rome.

18 ▪ Stanza di Raffaelo

Raphael Rooms The Papal Apartments of Pope Julius II and the Fine Works of Raphael Sanzio

Pope Julius II was preceeded by the hated Borgia Pope Alexander VI. When Pope Julius II became the Vicar of Christ he decided to relocate the living quarters in the Vatican from the Borgia Apartments where Alexander lived to the now named Raphael Rooms. The Raphael Rooms are where Julian Della Rovere known as Pope Julius II lived during his papacy.

Before moving into his living quarters, Julius II called on his trusted architect and friend Bramante to discuss who to commission to decorate the rooms. Bramante was from Urbino and knew of a young, up and coming artist named Raphael Sanzio. Bramante quickly recommended young Raphael. By helping Raphael gain the commission, Bramante successfully prevented his enemy Michelangelo from earning the work and also brought fame and Papal favor to another citizen of Urbino.

The young Raphael was blessed by God. He was beautiful and charming. He was given the natural gift of painting, not only in his style, but he could exactly imitate the style of other masters.

Raphael accepted the invitation by Pope Julius II to work on the Papal Apartments.The artist was instructed to create scenes illustrating the content of the books that were to be shelved under each wall. Under the School of Athens books on Philosphy were shelved. Under Parnassus books on Poetry.

As he worked on his walls Michelangelo worked on his ceiling next door. The walls are beautiful beyond words. They capture the essence of the classical form and the human spirit by bringing together elements from the Ancients, the Bible, and contemporary men of the age.

Here lies Raphael while he lived Mother Nature feared to be outdone and when he died she feared to die with him

The tomb of Raphael in the Pantheon, Rome

How generous and kind Heaven sometimes proves to be when it brings together in a single person the boundless riches of its treasures and all those graces and rare gifts that over a period of time are usually divided among many individuals can clearly be seen in the no less excellent than gracious Raphael Sanzio of Urbino.

Giorgio Vasari, The lives of the Artists, 1568

Map to the Raphael Rooms

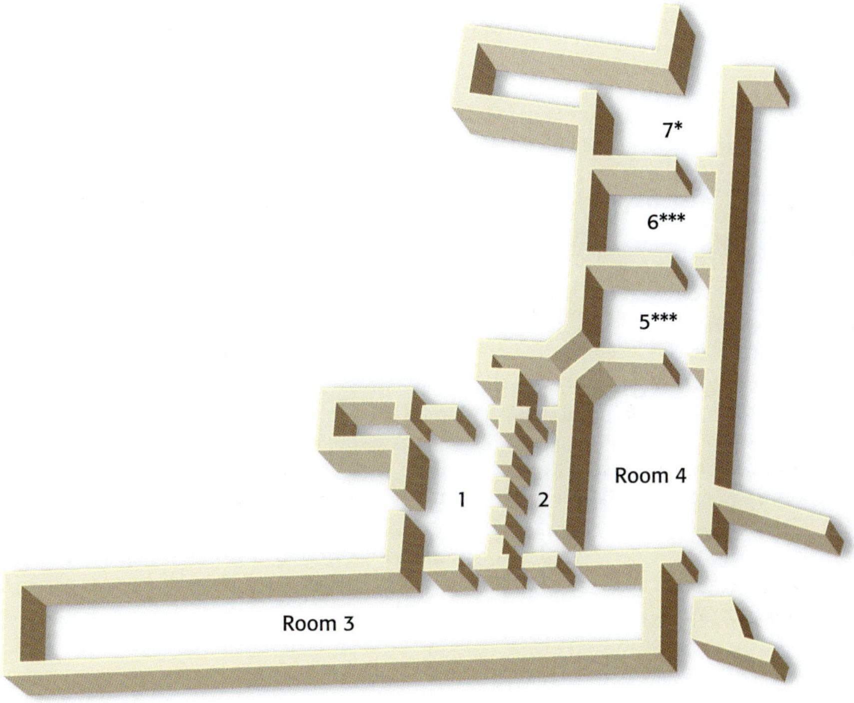

1. Camera dei Paramenti (Sala vecchia degli Svizzeri)
2. Camera del Pappagallo (Sala del Palarenieri)
3. Loggie di Raffaello
4. Sala di Costantino
5. **Stanza di Eliodoro**
   Expulsion of Heliodorus
   Liberation of Saint Peter
   Mass at Bolsena
6. **Stanza della Segnatura**
   School of Athens
   Parnassus
   Disputa
7. **Stanza dell'Incendio**
   Fire in the Borgo

Stars equal number of frescoes detailed in this guidebook contained in the room.

Stanza di Eliodoro ▪ Room # 5

1. Expulsion of Heliodorus
2. Liberation of Saint Peter
3. Repulse of Attila from Rome by Leo I
No write-up for this masterpiece included
4. Mass at Bolsena

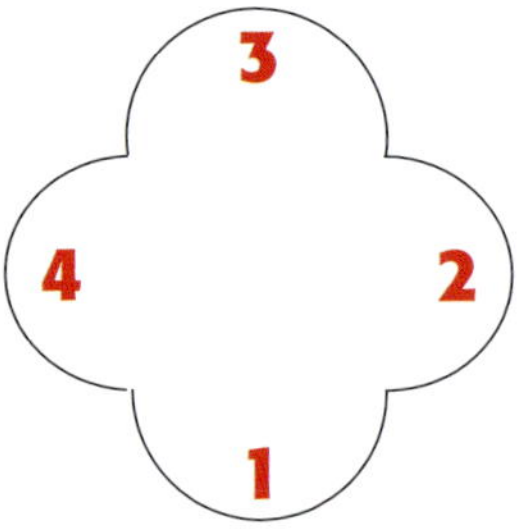

19 ▪ The Expulsion of Heliodorus

Raphael Rooms East Wall • Fresco 1 • Room 5

The Expulsion is based on the narrative found in the second book of Maccabees and gives rise to the name of the room itself. Raphael's interpretation closely follows the events.

Because of his hatred for the High Priest Onias, Simon the Benjamite (overseer of the temple and "betrayer of the money and his country"), told the King of the riches that were held in the temple. Heliodorus was sent by the King to steal the treasures. Prayers of the faithful drove out Heliodorus from the temple saving the treasure. He was driven out by "a horse with a terrible rider striking Heliodorus with his forefeet as others scourged him to the brink of death."

Note Julius II in the Red Papal garb being carried on a litter to the bottom left of the work. Artists often painted the person who commissioned the work into the painting to bring immortality and fame to the patron.

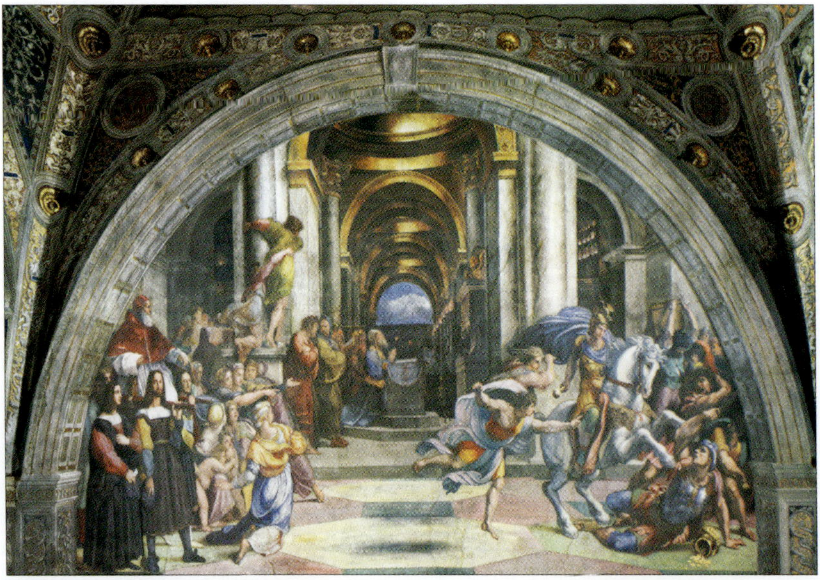

20 ▪ Liberation of Saint Peter

Raphael Rooms North Wall • Fresco 2 • Room 5

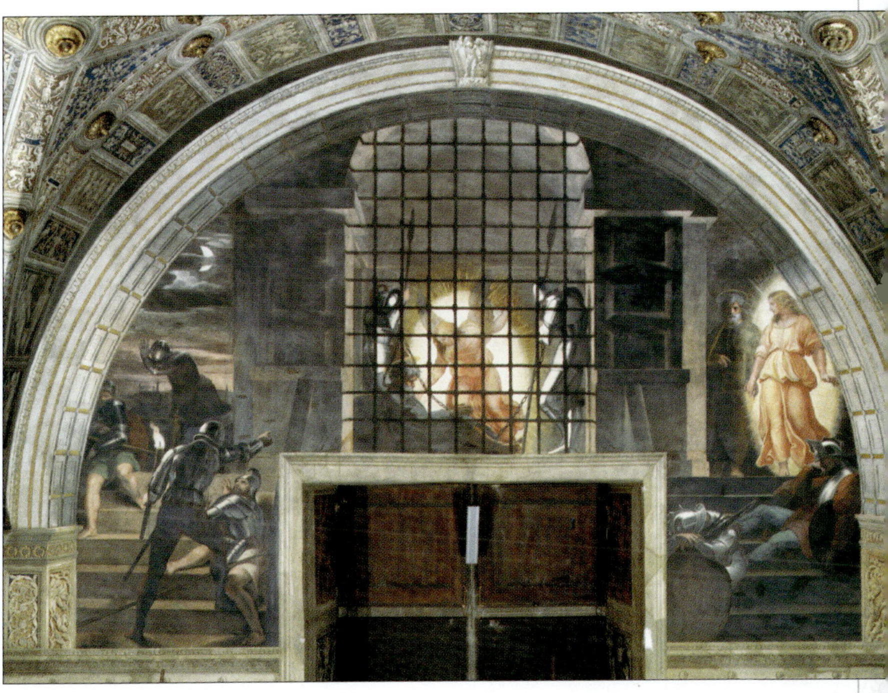

The liberation of Saint Peter from prison has textual origins in the Bible; The act of the freeing of Saint Peter ties directly to Pope Julius II. Julius was the Cardinal in charge of the church in Rome named San Pietro in Vincoli, which translates to Saint Peter in Chains. It is the church that houses the chains that bound Peter in the scene illustrated by Raphael. You can still see the chains encased in glass above the alter. San Pietro in Vincoli is also the home of Michelangelo's famous Moses and the tomb of Julius II. Some have interpreted the Liberation of Saint Peter by Raphael as the illustration of Pope Julius II freeing the Papal State and reclaiming lands lost to previous Papacies. The story of the freeing of Saint Peter goes as follows. Saint Peter was bound and sleeping between two soldiers. An angel of the Lord came to Saint Peter and a light shone on him through the walls of the prison. As the light shone, the soldiers slept. Saint Peter fell free of his chains to freedom.

21 ▪ Mass at Bolsena

Raphael Rooms South Wall • Fresco 4 • Room 5

The image of Pope Julius II kneeling at the right of the alter in the red Papal garb commemorates a 13th century miracle connected with the feast of Corpus Domini. A traveling priest who had been troubled by doubts about transubstantiation (the changing of bread and wine into the body and blood of Christ) was given proof of the Eucharist when the alter cloth used for mass became stained with blood from the host. The relic was brought to Orvieto Cathedral where it was venerated by Julius II's uncle Pope Sixtus IV (This is the Pope that the Sistine Chapel is named after). Julius paid homage to the relic cloth during one of his military campaigns which earned him the name Papa Terribile (The terrible Pope). The relic is still preserved in a special alter to this day at the church in Orvieto.

The fresco is a tribute to the alliances Pope Julius II found important. On the bottom right are the Swiss Guards that were the hired mercenary force used by Julius during his military campaign to reclaim the Papal Territories. Due to their savage fighting tactics, the Swiss were a feared fighting force. As a result of their success in fighting for the Pope, he deemed them Protectors of the Church and they have owned that title since the early 1500's. You can still see them today in Vatican City. They are still responsible to protect the Pope and the lands of the Church. The Swiss Guards still wear the uniform you see in the Mass of Bolsena at the bottom right.

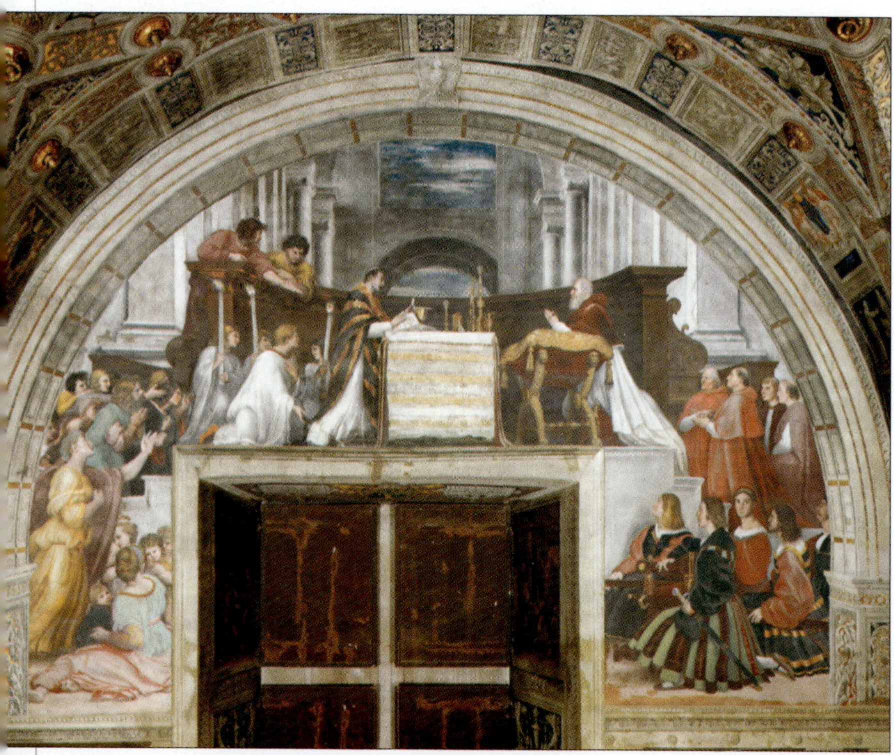

Stanza della Segnatura ▪ Room #6

1. School of Athens
2. Parnassus
3. Disputa
4. Fortitude Prudence Temperance

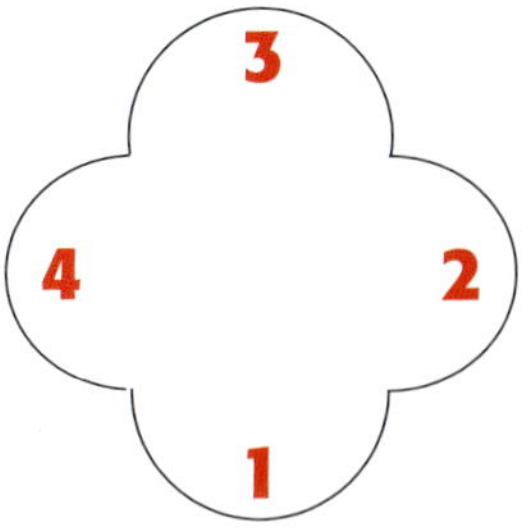

22 ▪ The School of Athens: Scuola di Athena

Raphael Rooms East Wall • Fresco 1 • Room 6

The School of Athens is a depiction of Philosophy and Reason.

The two central figures are Plato and Aristotle. Plato is pointing skyward holding his book Timaeus. Aristotle to Plato's left is pointing downward holding his book Ethics. The two philosophical masters are pointing towards the core of their philosophical teachings.

The grouping of men on the left of Plato are men who represent the ultimate mysteries of the world. Their beliefs transcend earth and human affairs. To the right of Aristotle those pictured represent men who are interested in nature or issues related to human affairs and the rational.

The niches in the background of the scene are filled with two pagan gods that represent the nature of the intellectuals depicted in the scene. Apollo on the left represents the arts and Athena on the right, the patroness of wisdom.

The figure of Plato is represented with the look of Leonardo Da Vinci(1). Moving from the extreme left you see Epicurus(2) crowned with laurel holding his discourse on hedonism. Lower down to the right is Pythagoras(3) and behind him, his assistant Averroes(4). The youth in white behind the group is Francesco Maria della Rovere, the duke of Urbino(5). Moving up the stairs in profile you see Socrates(6) in a brown robe with a piggish face debating with the loved and hated Alcibiades(7) in armor. Sitting on the steps leaning on his left elbow is Heraclitus(8) in the likeness of Michelangelo. Michelangelo was added after Raphael had seen a partial unveiling of the Chapel ceiling forced

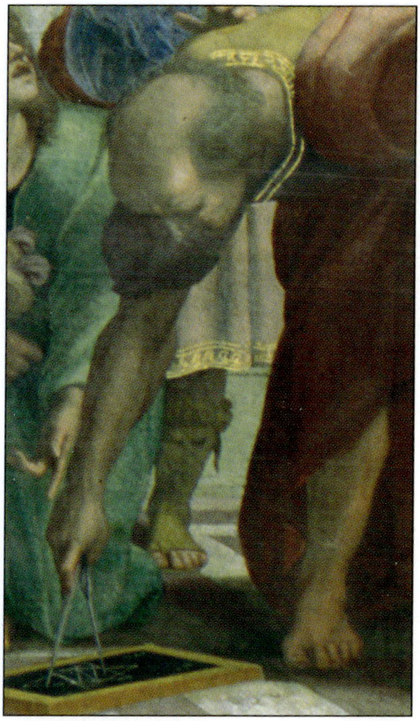

upon Michelangelo by Pope Julius II. Immediately after viewing the work, Raphael went back to his completed School of Athens, chipped away a giornata and added the master Michelangelo. (A giornata is a days work for an artist to apply wet plaster and paint over the fresh plaster in one day before it dries.) Note that Raphael used Michelangelo's style to add the master. See how the style is a bit different than the other figures. You can truly make out the muscles and movement know as terribilita. Michelangelo is the only figure in the entire work to be dressed in the clothes of the Renaissance. All the others are dressed in Classical garb.

The philosopher lying on the steps in the blue toga is the cynic Diogenes(9). Moving to the right is Euclid (10) who bears the face of the architect Bramante. Euclid is bending over a slate as he demonstrates with a compass one of his theories to his pupils. Bramante was the connection to Pope Julius that helped Raphael earn the work to decorate the Papal Apartments. Bramante was also from Urbino as was Raphael.

Standing behind Euclid is Zoroaster (11) holding a celestial globe, while Ptolemy (12) wearing the orange toga holds a terrestrial globe.

In the bottom right corner, the only figure in the entire work looking directly at the viewer, is a self-portrait of Raphael (13). He has placed himself on the scientific side. Next to Raphael in the white toga and hat is Sodoma (14). He has been painted in the image of Raphael's master Pietro Perugino.

Raphael has signed and dated the work in the neckband of Euclid's robe.

Finally, the large man in the orange toga to the right side of Aristotle (15) is Cardinal Bibbiena (16).

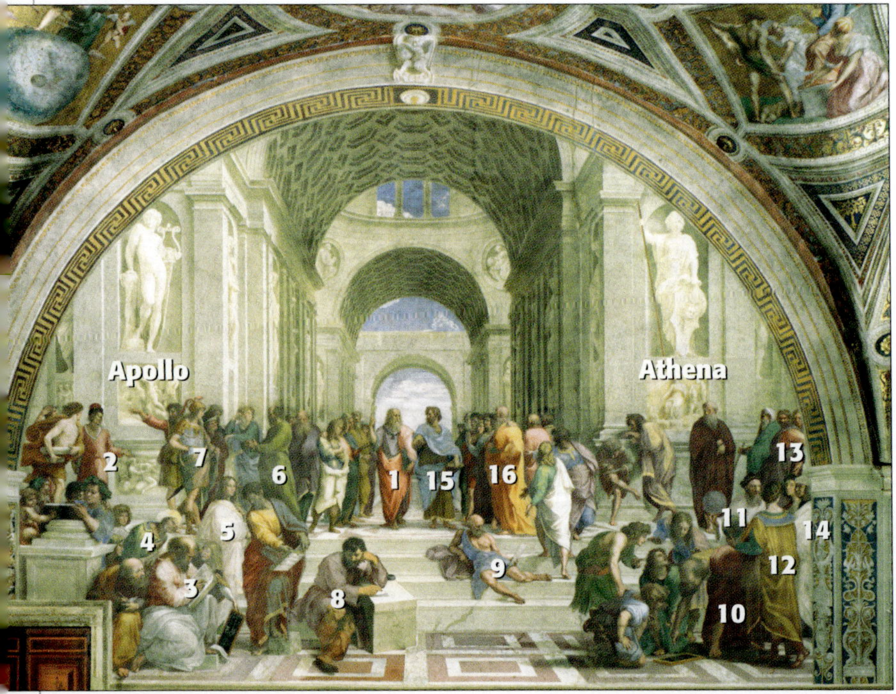

23 ▪ Parnassus

Raphael Rooms North Wall • Fresco 2 • Room 6

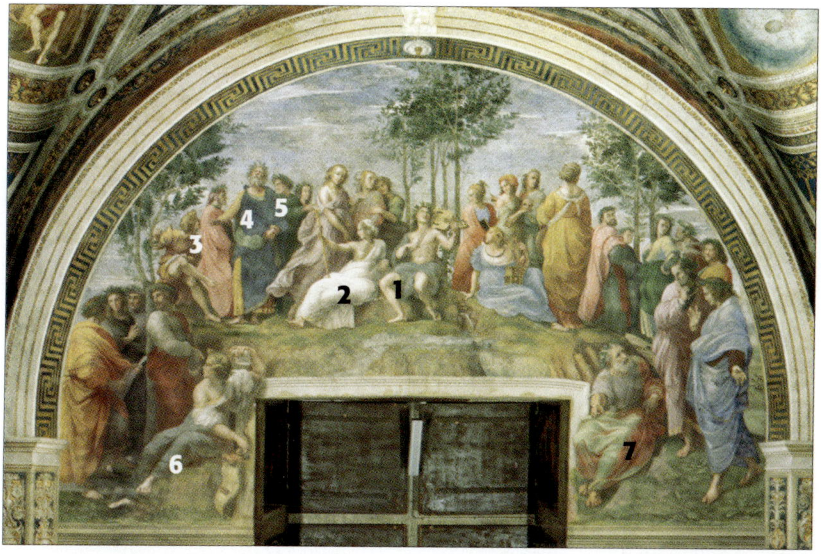

Mount Parnassus is in central Greece about 100 kilometers from Athens. The mystic town of Delphi is on Mount Parnassus and is home to the Delphic Oracle of Apollo. Delphi was one of the most sacred sites in the Hellenistic World. The temple at Delphi was for two Gods - Apollo and Dionysis. The Greeks considered Delphi the navel of the earth. A monument called an Ompholos marks the exact center of the earth at Delphi.

Mount Parnassus is the second highest mountain in Greece after Olympus. One of the four major Olympic Games were held at Delphi and included athletic, poetry, and acting events. The Olympic Poetry competition is how the fresco ties to Mount Parnassus, Apollo, and Delphi. Apollo, was the god of poetry and fine arts and every four years a major poetry competition was held at Delphi to honor him. Each of the figures in the Parnassus by Raphael are poets or bards.

In the center of the fresco sits Apollo(1) representing Poetry. He is joined by the classical worlds most famous poets. Poets are represented by contemporaries of Raphael. First, the nine classical muses are represented along side Apollo balanced by Erato(2) on the left side of Apollo. All of them act to inspire poets to write or orate. Note that Apollo is playing a modern instrument rather than the lyre.

On the left side of the fresco are Dante(3) and Homer(4). On Homer's left is Virgil(5) who wrote the Aeneid on the founding of Rome. He was also Dante's guide through the Divine Comedies. In the Aeneid you discover how Troy fell to the Greeks. The other poets are Petrarch, Bocaccio, and Ariosto on the bottom left. Also on the bottom left near the door is the female poet Sappho(6). On the opposite side of the door is Horace(7)

24 ▪ Disputa: The Disputation over the Sacrament

In the Stanza Della Segnatura on the opposite wall from the School of Athens • Room #6 wall #3 on the map of the Stanze

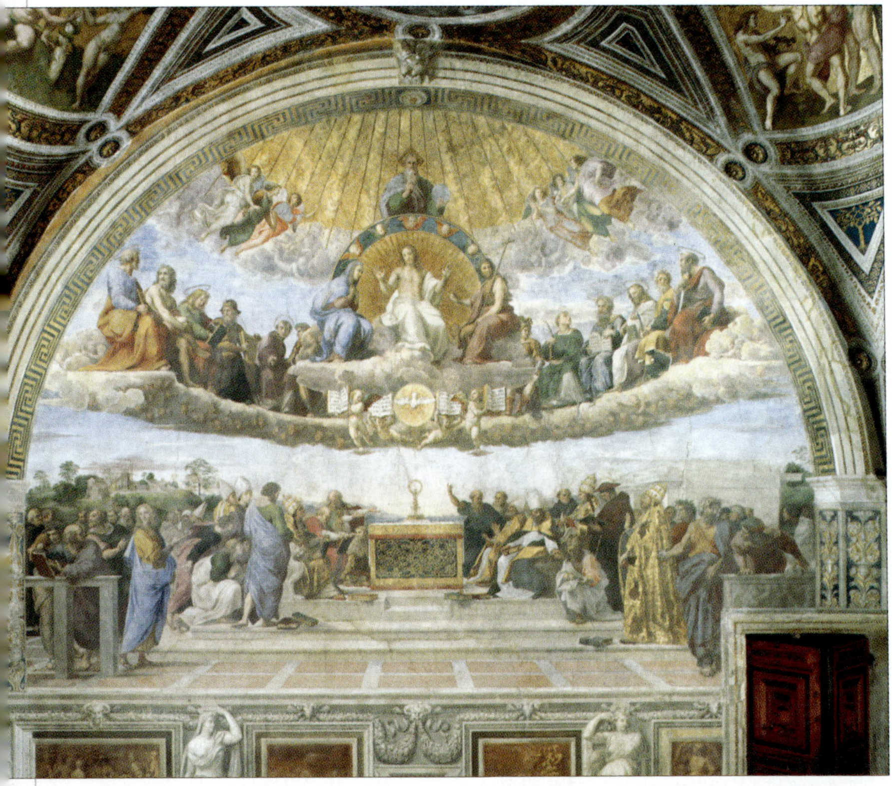

The Disputa sets the standard, along with the School of Athens as the highest achievement for multi-figured painting in the world.

The work is the amplification of the Eucharist. The four principle personalities are Saint Gregory as the seated Pope in the Golden robes and Saint Jerome in the red garments with the lion underfoot -both on the left.

Saint Ambrose is depicted seated to the right of the alter with both hands in the air as he looks skyward and Saint Augustine shown seated next to Ambrose pointing to his left.

Also gracing the Disputa are Saint Thomas Aquinas shown standing behind Saint Augustine in the brown robe, then Pope Innocent III directly behind the seated figure wearing the Papal tiara, and Saint Bonaventure in Franciscan Robes reading. Dante is also pictured wearing the laurel wreath recognized by his long nose and jaw. Finally Bramante is pictured standing in front of Dante.

Along the top of the masterpiece Jesus is surrounded by a host of heavenly Saints.

Stanza dell'Incendio ▪ Room # 7

1. Oath of Leo III
2. Coronation of Charlemagne
3. Fire in the Borgo
4. Battle of Ostia

No write-ups for 1, 2, or 4

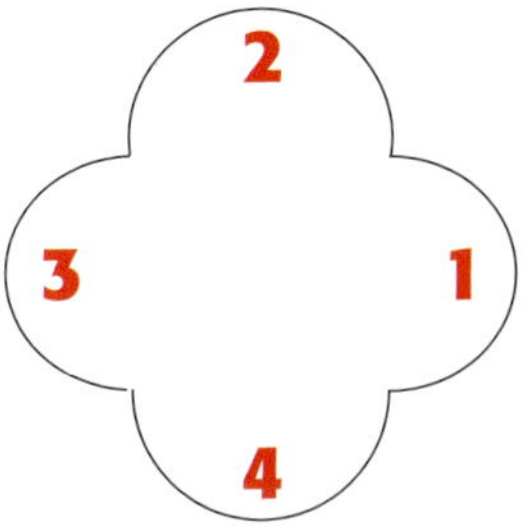

25 ▪ The fire in the Borgo

Raphael Rooms South Wall • Fresco 3 • Room 7

The room where this fresco lay takes its name from the work. The fresco illustrates the fire that broke out in the Borgo of Rome during the reign of Pope Leo IV near Saint Peter's Basilica. Pope Leo, with a blessing, seen in the background of the fresco on the balcony, put out the flames. The figure carrying the old man on his back with the child following behind quotes Michelangelo's figures in the flood scene in the Sistine Chapel. The configuration also illustrates a passage from Virgil's Aeneid as Aeneas carries his father Anchises and his son Ascanius out of Troy as they escape the Greeks and go on to found Rome.

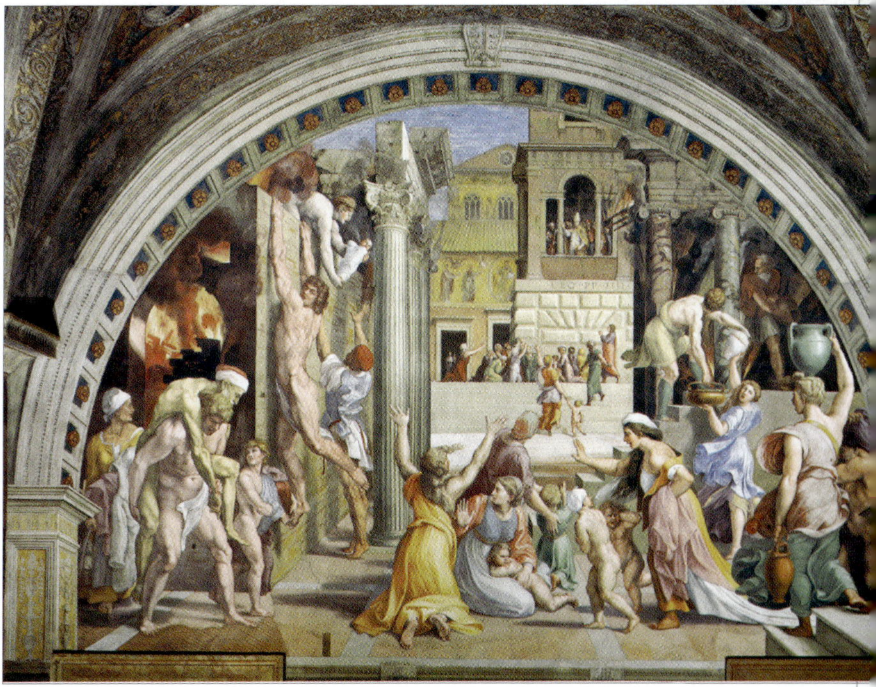

26 ▪ Sistine Chapel

Vatican Palaces and Museum   Rome

The Sistine Chapel was built by Pope Sixtus IV and bears his name. He had it constructed to the exact size of the Temple of Solomon in Jerusalem - 130′ x 43′ x 65.′ The chapel is twice as long as it is high and three times as long as it is wide. At the time of the chapel's construction a war between Rome and Florence was ending. As a show of peace Lorenzo de' Medici of Florence sent a number of painters to Rome to work on decorating the chapel walls for Pope Sixtus. The leader of the group of artists was thirty-one year old Pietro Perugino, Raphael's master. The other artists in the group were Sandro Botticelli, Cosimo Rosselli, Piero di Cosimo, and Michelangelo's master Domenico Ghirlandaio.

The walls of the chapel were divided by the artists into six panels. Each panel is 20′ x 12.′ The artists decided that on one wall the life of Moses would be depicted and on the other wall the life of Jesus. On the original ceiling it was blue with gold stars.

Pope Julius II came to the Papacy in the year 1503. His uncle Pope Sixtus IV created the chapel and decorated its walls. Pope Julius II would bring fame to the chapel beyond anyones imagination by hiring the the great Michelangelo to decorate the ceiling.

After Pope Sixtus IV died, three Popes held the Papacy before his nephew Giuliano della Rovere became Pope Julius II. The Popes that held the Papacy between the blood-line are Innocent VIII, Alexander VI - the hated Spanish Borgia Pope, and Pius III. None of the three Popes did any work on the chapel and this suited Julius, as he would be able to complete the work his uncle began and bring fame and glory to himself and his family name.

The discussions began about decorating the ceiling between the Pope and his advisors. Bramante from Urbino was the Papal Architect and had the confidence of Julius. Discussions continued about who to hire to decorate the ceiling. Bramante and Michelangelo were enemies and Bramante thought this was a perfect opportunity to bring shame and humiliation to Michelangelo. So, Bramante offered Michelangelo to the Pope as the artist of choice to work on the ceiling. Bramante knew well that Michelangelo was a sculptor and was not a painter. Michelangelo did not like painting, nor had he done any major work in the medium. Bramante knew that Michelangelo could not refuse the Pope for fear of being excommunicated or worse. Bramante also knew that should Michelangelo accept the work that it could very well turn out poorly and be a disgrace to the already celebrated artist. Pope Julius II summoned Michelangelo and offered him the ceiling. Michelangelo flatly refused and offered the ceiling to Raphael who was already at work on the Papal Apartments. But, Pope Julius was stubborn and insisted that Michelangelo accept his offer. The great artist held out as long as he could and finally agreed to take on the commission.

Bramante offered to build the scaffolding where Michelangelo would stand to do the work on the ceiling. When Bramante finished the scaffolding Michelangelo found it difficult to use and noticed that it left holes in the wall as it was moved. Michelangelo spoke to Pope Julius and offered to create the scaffold himself. The one created by Michelangelo was not only functional, but easier to use. It provided access to the ceiling and did not damage the walls as it was moved. In Bramante's scaffold he used ropes. Michelangelo did not need the rope and gave it to an asisstant. There was so much rope that the man was able to sell it all and pay the dowry for his two daughters.

Michelangelo had to learn how to prepare the ceiling to receive the plaster and the paint. He had to learn how to mix his colors. He had to learn how to create fresco cartoons. He had to figure out how to deal with the perspective of the viewers being sixty feet below the ceiling.

Pope Julius II was a very ambitious man and knew well the power of art as the means to immortality and fame. Through art and visual imagery he would include himself in the Church's history and be seen among the Saints. He was also the first Pope to wear a beard. Julius earned the nickname Papa Terribile because he would march at the front of the Papal armies as they went to war. Julius was not afraid to use force to gain what he wanted or to take back what he lost. He had a terrible temper and tolerated little with regard to the Papacy, its lands, his power, or his family. Papa Terribile was a brilliant strategist and won wars before they began and gained back many of the Papal lands without a single day of fighting due to his reputation and political alliances.

The scaffolding placed Michelangelo within arms length of the ceiling. He painted the entire work standing up contrary to the popular belief that he painted it on his back. You can see an illustration of how Michelangelo stood as he painted on the previous pages within the letter Michelangelo wrote to show a friend his pain and torment at creating the ceiling.

Pope Julius had already decided on a scene to be painted by Michelangelo. As the artist reviewed the work, he began to feel that he could create a better, more glorious scene and thus sought permission to create a scene on his own. The Pope granted Michelangelo this boone. Michelangelo went on to design the book of Genesis from the separation of light and dark, to the Drunkeness of Noah, including the ancestors of Jesus. Michelangelo depicted scenes of David and Goliath, Judith and Holofernes, the Crucifixion of Hanaan, and the Brazen Serpent. Michelangelo tied the Classical world together with the Biblical world through the Sibyls and prophets. He also created illustrations of other important Biblical events in the shields within the central section.

Michelangelo's ceiling delivered sculpture through painting. It is a glorious masterpiece that won Michelangelo fame beyond all recollection.

As Michelangelo prepared the ceiling for the fresco, he had to remove the old scene. This is where he used his assistants. It took time and tiring labor to scrape down the old and lay the first layer of the new ceiling. During this time, Michelangelo mastered the creation of plaster and its application. But even the great Michelangelo suffered losses. As he painted his first sections, he mixed the plaster too wet and as it dried, mold grew over his completed work. This enraged Michelangelo. He tried to get himself thrown off of the project by complaining to the Pope that the mold was proof that this was not his art. But Julius didn't budge and forced Michelangelo to continue. The Pope did, however, call in an expert to fix Michelangelo's plaster problem. Michelangelo learned how to properly mix the plaster so it would not be applied too wet. This stopped the mold from growing and allowed the work to continue.

As he learned how to mix plaster, he learned how to mix colors. This was work usually left to assistants, but Michelangelo was a perfectionist with an artist's temper. He insisted on mixing his own colors so they would be exactly what he expected.

Fresco means fresh. It is the painting on wet plaster so that as the plaster dries it locks in the paint and its colors. First, a layer of plaster is applied to a prepared surface. This first layer is called an intonaco. The intonaco is a smooth paste made from lime and sand. The artist would create cartoons of the painting on paper, then tap holes into the paper outlining the drawn design. Then the cartoon was placed onto the wet intonaco. The artist would apply the outline to the plaster in one of two ways. The first way was called Spolvero. Spolvero involves perforating the lines of the drawing with little holes then a bag of charcoal was bounced on the Spolvero leaving on the plaster the design created by the artist. The second style was simpler. The artist would trace the outline of the cartoon onto the plaster with a stylus leaving the marks on the wet plaster. Once the tracing was complete the painting could begin.

To make things more difficult only one days work could be traced onto the plaster at a time. These daily renderings are called Giornata.

The artist would race against the clock to get the painting done before the plaster dried, and if he didn't, the days work was a waste. It would have to be removed and begun again.

Once the work was complete artists would often go back to the work and add paint dry. This dry work is called Secco.

All of the steps in the process were new to Michelangelo. And after the ceiling was made ready he fired his assistants and worked alone giving strict orders that no one was to be allowed in the chapel to see his work. The Pope and a select few were allowed in if Michelangelo was in good spirits.

On May 10, 1508 Michelangelo began his work on the ceiling. It took him fours years to complete.

He chose to begin on the Flood scene. Michelangelo felt this would be a good place to start because it would be less noticable among the rest of the ceiling and he would be able to hide any mistakes.The Flood scene took him thirty-eight giornata. It is the most dense scene with the most activity, overloaded with people trying to escape the rising waters.

As Michelangelo gained confidence, and painting ability, he portrayed fewer people in the style of Michelangelo's famous contraposto. Contraposto is the twisting of a body to show activity and emotion. Michelangelo was able to portray emotion through the human form better than anyone. And, as he completed each section he was better able to use his talents of sculpure in the painting. When you get to the Creation of Man where Adam arrogantly relaxes his finger and God works to touch him, you see the perfect creation of emotion through activity. In the scene of the Creation, under God's arm is Eve and the unborn Jesus.

Michelangelo was a different kind of man. He liked to be alone. He prefered the company of only a few people in his life. He trusted no one. He always felt that one conspiracy or another was working against him by the Pope or powerful Dukes throughout Italy.

When Michelangelo was a young student in Ghirlandaio's workshop a fellow apprentice grew jealous of him and his sharp tongue. Each time Michelangelo added words of criticism or offered words of advice the other apprentice grew more agitated. Then one day the other apprentice could stand it no longer and punched Michelangelo in the face. This single punch rendered Michelangelo marked for life. His nose was badly broken and never returned to normal. The name of the apprentice who punched him was Torrigiani.

Michelangelo was prone to headaches and didn't eat or sleep much. He was convinced that too much sleep gave him the headaches. And his stomach was weak so he could only eat a little. He often ate only bread and did so as he worked. He rarely drank wine and only ate or drank when he needed sustenance.

He often slept in his clothes and wore the same clothes for weeks at a time. In fact, when he did remove his boots his skin would peel away like a snake's skin.

Michelangelo never married. He writes, "I already have a wife who is too much for me; one who keeps me unceasingly struggling on. It is my art, and my works are my children.

His father and uncle worked tirelessly to dissuade young Michelangelo from becoming an artist. He was brutally punished in an attempt to force him to take on a career that was considered proper for a man. Thankfully, Michelangelo was as stubborn a child as he was a man and forged ahead with his art. Only after Lorenzo "the Magnificent" Medici discovered young Michelangelo's talent did his father relent and allow him to work in the arts.

He wrote poetry and sonnets, but his passion was sculpture. He became a great painter and architect. At one point in his life he laid down his tools for almost ten years and completed no works at all.

When he signed his letters to his patrons, friends, or family he would sign them Michelangelo, the sculptor. As a child, Michelangelo's father sent him to a wet-nurse. The wet-nurse was married to a stonemason and her father was a stonemason. Michelangelo attributes his gift of sculpture and working with stone to his wetnurse.

Back to the ceiling. Take a look at the figure of Jonah. On the ceiling it is written as Ionas. It is the figure at the top of the alter wall where his Last Judgement is painted. It appears that Jonah is falling away from you as the viewer. In reality, Jonah is painted on a forward arch and through perspective Michelangelo was able to make it appear that Jonah was falling away.

The ceiling is the finest example of fresco the world will ever know. It is the culmination of sculpture and painting creating by the worlds only Master. Every other artist of the past and the future can only hope to be Michelangelo's student.

Michelangelo was touched by God.

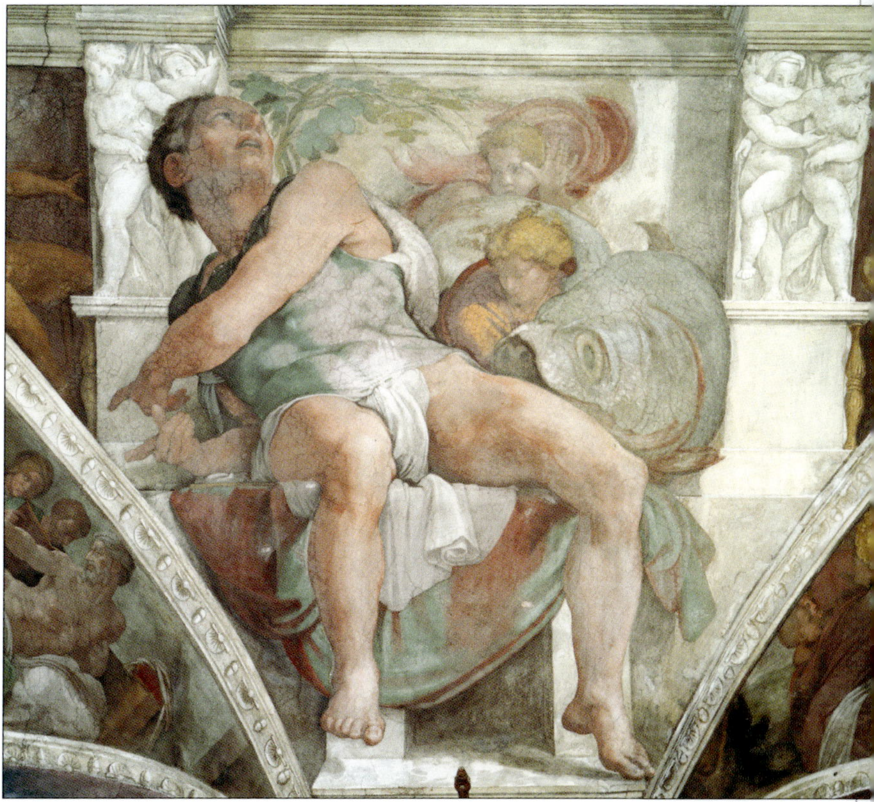

Sistine Chapel ▪ Overall Layout

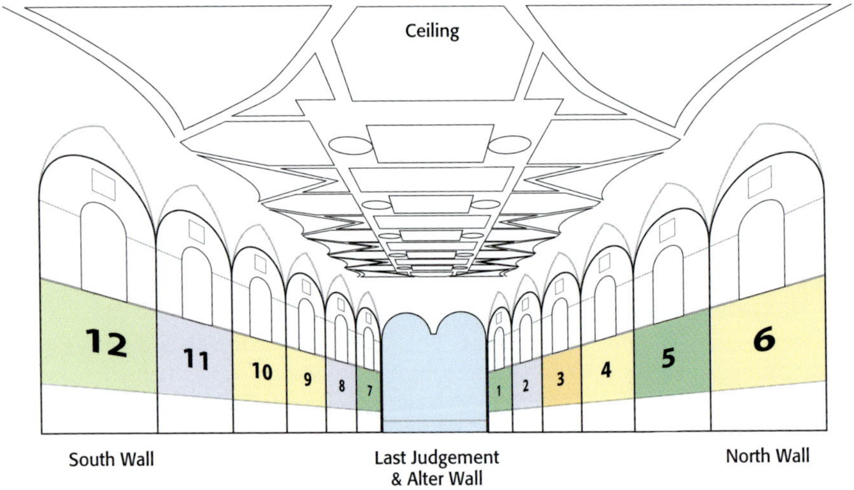

Perugino	Botticelli	Ghirlandalo
Rosselli	Signorelli	Michaelangelo

1. Baptism of Christ in the Jordan
2. Temptations of Christ
3. Calling of St. Peter and St. Andrew
4. Sermon on the Mount
5. Handing over the Keys to St. Peter
6. Last Supper
7. Journey of Moses into Egypt
8. Events in the Life of Moses
9. Passage of the Red Sea
10. Handing over the Tablets of Law
11. Punishment of Korah, Dathan, and Abiron
12. Legacy and Death of Moses

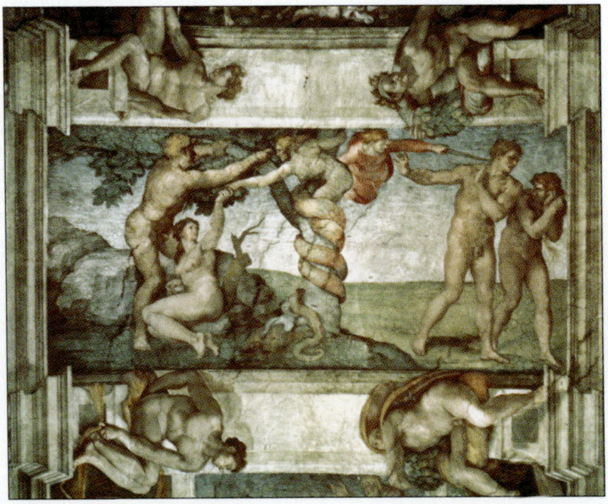

Sistine Chapel ▪ Ceiling

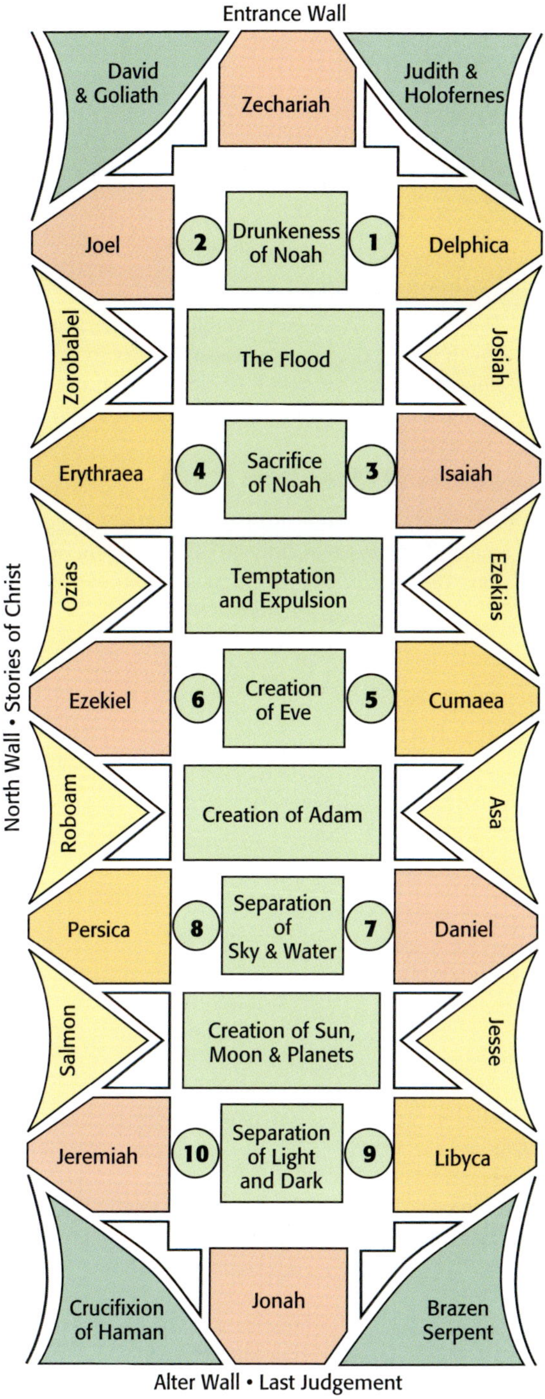

Sistine Chapel Shields

1. Death of Razis
2. Antiochus Epiphanes Falls from his Chariot
3. Expulsion of Heliodorus
4. Mattathias Pulls Down the Altar
5. Alexander the Great before the High Priest of Jerusalem
6. Death of Nicanor
7. Death of Absalom
8. Elisha Cures Naaman of Leprosy
9. Abraham's Sacrifice of Isaac
10. Ascension of Elijah

Guide to the Walls of the Sistine Chapel

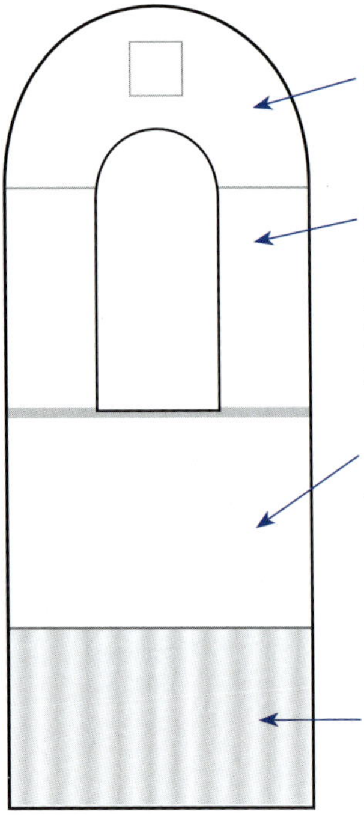

Prophets and Ancestors of Christ

Pontiffs

The Popes alternate in chronolgical order from the North wall to the South wall. So in order to view the Popes in order of their Pontificate you must alternate your viewing from wall to wall.

Stories of Moses and Christ

The stories of Moses and Jesus originally began on the wall where Michelangelo's Last Judgement is today. The painted stories end on the entrance wall.

Drapery

Popes painted on the Walls

1. Saint Peter
2. Saint Linus
3. Saint Anacletus
4. Saint Clement
5. Saint Evaristus
6. Saint Alexander I
7. Saint Sixtus I
8. Saint Telesphoros
9. Saint Hyginus
10. Saint Pius I
11. Saint Anacletus
12. Saint Soter
13. Saint Eleutherus
14. Saint Victor I
15. Saint Zephirinus
16. Saint Callistus I
17. Saint Urban I
18. Saint Pontian
19. Saint Anterus
20. Saint Fabian
21. Saint Cornslius
22. Saint Lucius
23. Saint Stephen
24. Saint Sixtus II
25. Saint Dionysius
26. Saint Felix I

Entrance Wall

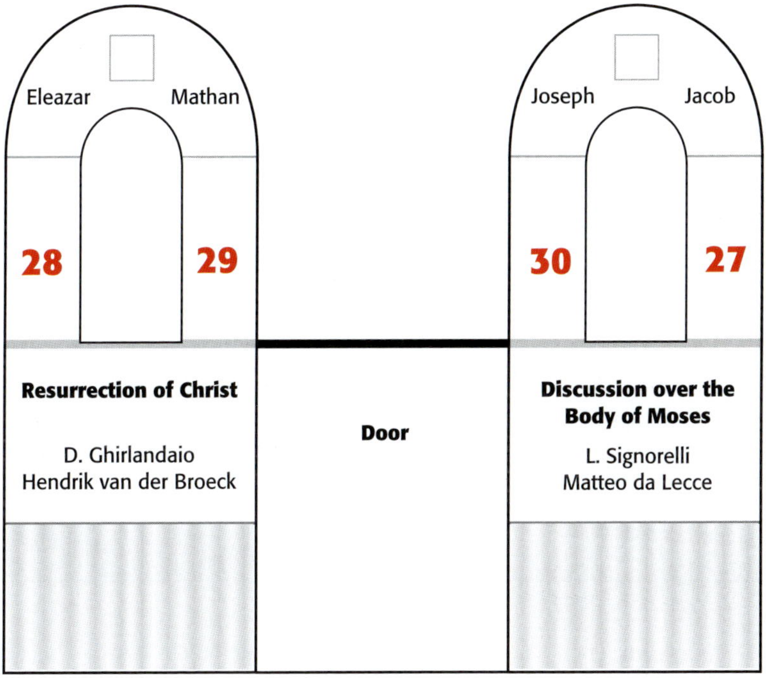

28. St. Caius

Saint Caius had a twelve year Pontificate. Other than the duration and that his term was peaceful very little is know of him or his term.

29. St. Marcellinus

Saint Marcellinus was removed from the list of Popes by the following Pope for lapsing in faith during the persecutions of Emperor Diocletian. He was also accused of handing over the Sacred Scriptures to Diocletion.

30. St. Marcellus I

Saint Marcellus I is best known for his vigorous and merciless punishment of those that waivered in faith during the persecution of Emperor Diocletian. His cruelty and retribution was so severe that the Emperor Maxentius had him banned from Rome for disturbing the peace. He was the Pope to remove Saint Marcellinus from the list of Popes. He died outside of Rome, but was buried in Rome.

27. St. Eutychianus

Saint Eutychianus was the last Pope to be buried in the cemetary of Callistus on the Appian Way.

Sistine Chapel ▪ North Wall ▪ Stories of Jesus

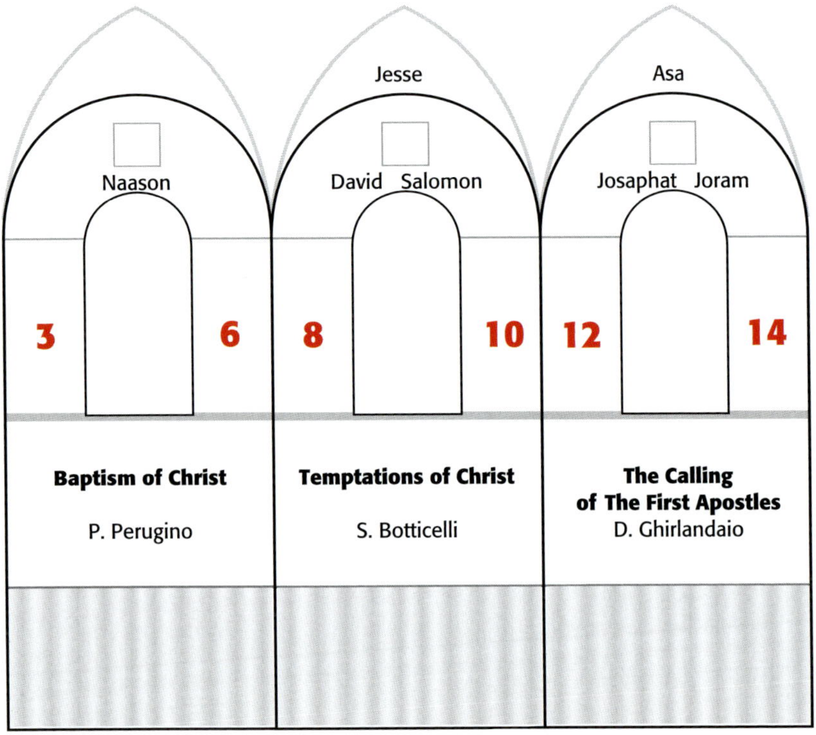

3. St. Anadetus (76 – 88)
Second successor of Saint Peter. He divided Rome into 25 parishes. He died during the reign of Emperor Diometian.

6. St. Alexander I (105 – 115)
Fifth successor of Saint Peter Saint Alexander is attributed with the insertion of the Eucharistic institution narrative from the last supper into the Canon of the Mass. He is also credited with the blessing of houses with salt and Holy Water

8. St. Telesphoros (125 – 136)
Very little is known of his Pontificate.

10. St. Pius I - 10 (140 – 155)
The first Pope to function as the sole Bishop of Rome. Prior to his Pontificate Rome was governed by a council of Presbyters. Those regarded as Pope prior to Saint Pius I may have just been the most influential member of the council of Presbyters.

12. St. Soter (166 – 175)
Easter introduced as liturgical feast in Rome.

14. St. Victor I (189 – 198)
Known for his firm resolution on the controversy over the celebration of Easter. The denomination called the Quartodecimans celebrated Easter on the 14th day of the Jewish month of Nison. The Roman Church originally did not celebrate the Easter Feast because every Sunday was a celebration of the resurrection of Christ. Saint Victor worked with the Imperial house of the Roman Emperor and through the Emperor's mistress was given the names of Christians in prison camps on the island of Sardinia. Saint Victor secured their release. The Emperor's mistress was a Christian.

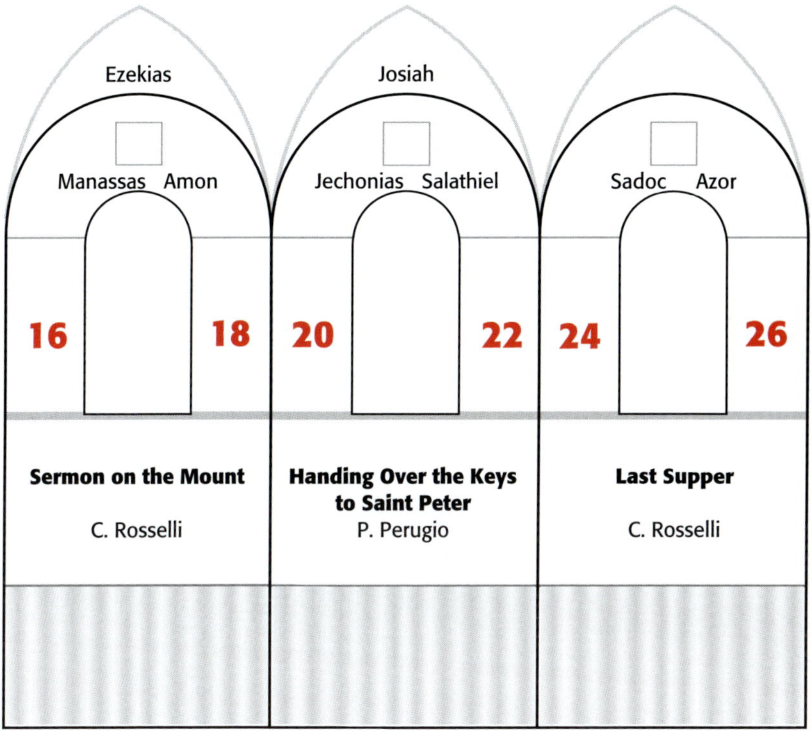

16. St. Callistus I (217 – 222)
He is the first Pope after Saint Peter who is commemmorated as a martyr in the Depositio Martyrum.

18. St. Pontian (7.21.230 – 9.28.235)
One of only 3 Popes to abdicate the Pontificate. He was the first to do so. He abdicated because he had been deported by the anti-Christian Emperor Maximinus. He was sent to a labor camp on Sardinia. He died after only 1 month in the camp.

20. St. Fabian (1.10.236 – 1.20.250)
When the Roman Clergy were considering a successor to Pope Pontian a dove landed on Fabian's head. Until then he was not considered as a possible successor. But the dove was taken as a sign from God and he won the Pontificate.

22. St. Lucius (6.25.253 – 3.5.254)
Immediately after his election he was banished from Rome by Emperor Gallus to Civita Vecchia. Due to his exile he is a confessor. That is one who suffers for faith short of death.

24. St. Sixtus II (8.30.257 – 8.6.258)
He is a highly venerated martyr. Elected just as Emperor Valarian abandoned the policy of toleration toward Christians. The Emperor ordered an edict of execution on bishops, priests, and deacons. On August 6, 258 Pope Sixtus II was seated in an Episcopal Chair addressing a congregation at a private ceremony. Imperial forces rushed in and beheaded the Pope and four other deacons. Two more deacons were put to death that day and four days later Saint Lawrence was martyred on the grill. The bloodstained chair where Saint Sixtus II was executed is behind the alter in his crypt.

26. St. Felix I (1.5.269 – 12.30.274)
Little is known of Pope Felix I.

Sistine Chapel ▪ South Wall ▪ Stories of Moses

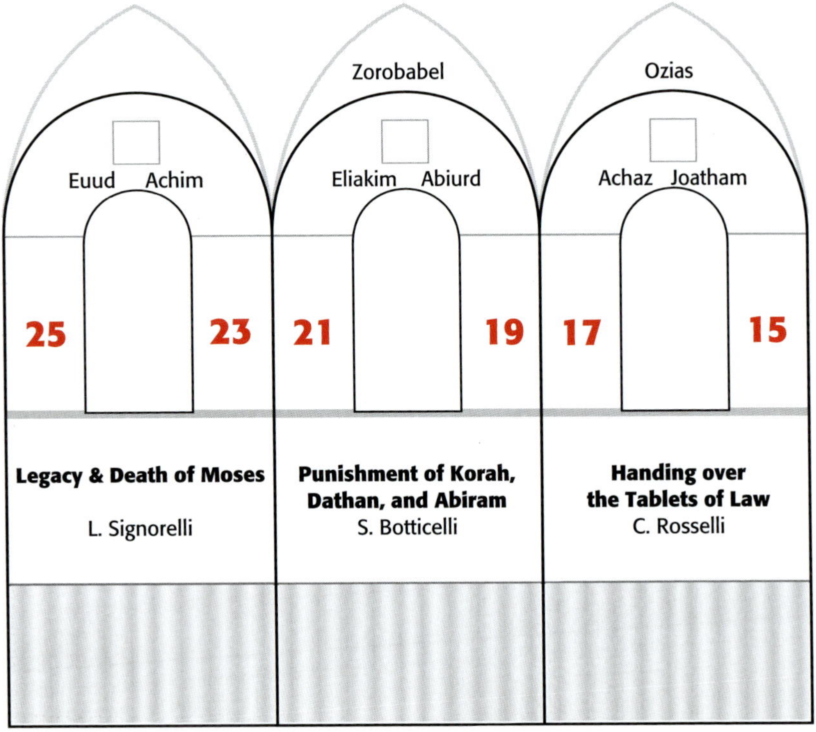

25. St. Dioynsius (7.22.260 – 12.26.268)

One of the most important Popes of the 3rd century because of his organizational and charitable activities. He was also important to the church because of his clarification of the doctrine of the Holy Trinity. His election to the pontificate was delayed due to Emperor Valarians severe Christian persecution.

23. St. Stephen (5.12.254 – 8.2.257)

Best known for his theological dispute with Saint Cyprian over those baptized by heretics and/or schismatics having to be rebaptized upon entrance or return to the Catholic Church.

21. St. Cornelius (March 251 – June 253)

A gap between pontiffs occurred prior to his pontificate due to severe Christian persecution under Emperor Decius. Many leaders of the church were imprisoned. In the spring, the emperor left Rome to fight the Goths. In his absence the persecution subsided allowing for the election of Pope Cornelius.

19. St. Anterus (11.21.235 – 1.3.236)

The first Pope to be buried in the new Papal crypt on the Appian Way.

17. St. Urban (220 – 230)

His was a peaceful Pontificate during the reign of Emperor Alexander Severus with no Christian persecution.

15. St. Zephirinus (199 – 217)

He was accused by the church of not being tough enough on dissidents.

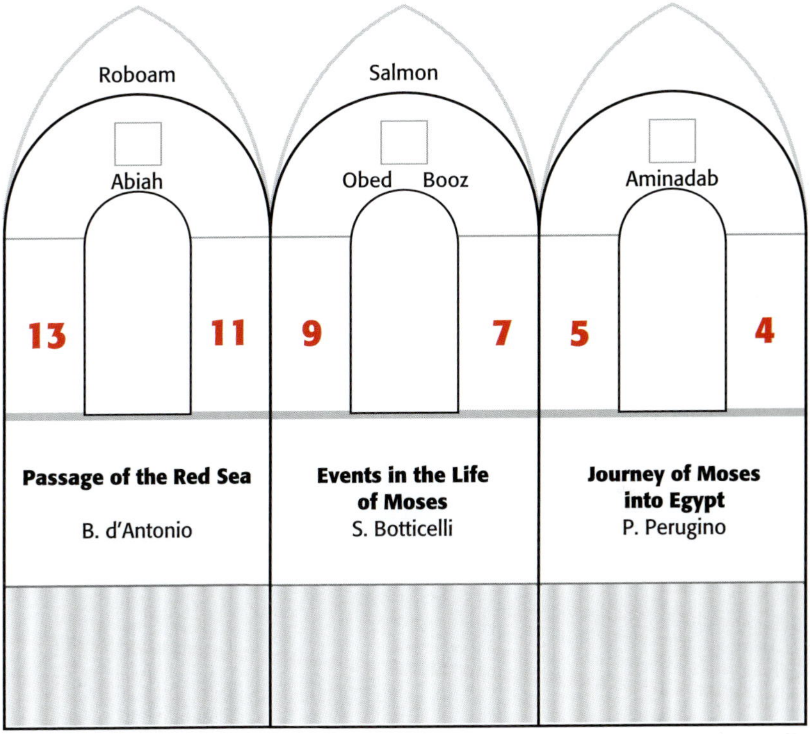

13. St. Eleutherus (175 – 189)

Attributed with the Christian belief that no food is naturally unclean.

11. St. Anicetus (155 – 166)

Forbade clerics to wear long hair. Best known for his serious, but amicable talks with Saint Polycarp (bishop of Smyrna/Turkey). Saint Polycarp was a disciple of Saint John the Evangelist.

9. St. Hyginus (136 – 140)

He was a philospher and Apologist (defender of the faith).

7. St. Sixtus I (115 – 125)

The 6th successor of Peter. Sixtus is sixth in Latin. His decree that sacred vessels only be touched by clergy and another decree that people should chant, "holy, holy, holy" at the beginning of the Eucharistic prayer at mass.

5. St. Evaristus (97 – 105)

Very little information available.

4. St. Clement I (88 – 97)

Known for Clement I which is considered part of the New Testament. In 96 AD he went from Rome to Corinth to reinstate the elders who had been improperly deposed. He exiled the people who instigated the rebellion.

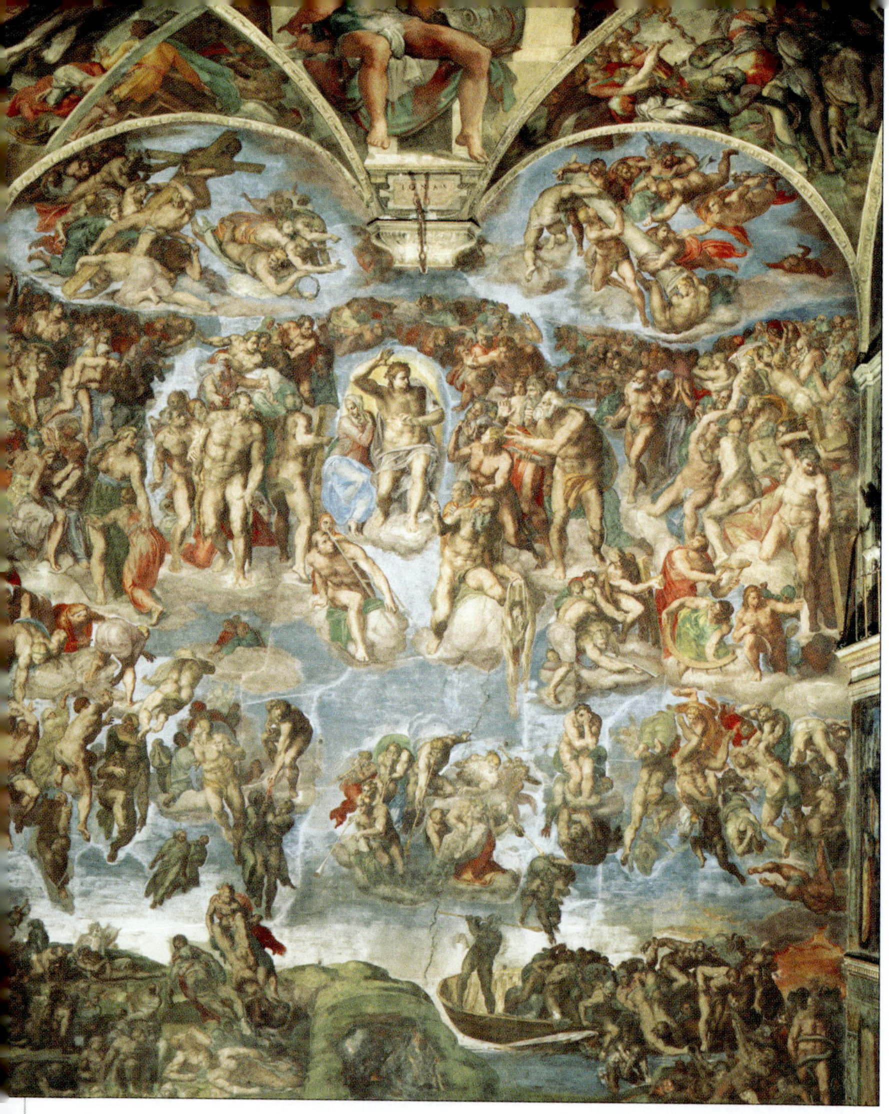

He (Michelangelo) passed most of his life in the midst of tragic disasters...In his most creative years he found himselft alone, perhaps the greatest but, alas, also the last of the giants born so plentifully during the fifteenth century.

Bernard Berenson

Michelangelo was an excellent man; a pity that he did not know how to paint.

El Greco

Without having seen the Sistine Chapel one can form no appreciable idea of what one man is capable of achieving.

Johann Wolfgang Goethe

27 ▪ Michelangelo

The Last Judgement — The Alter Wall

The last Judgement is the depiction of the righteous being escorted into Heaven and the damned being dragged into hell. The Terribilita of Michelangelo is delivered throughout the work. Once again he utilizes what he did best, the human nude, to capture the emotion of the glory and agony of the scene.

The Last Judgment is on the wall of the Sistine Chapel on the Altar side.

Last Judgement scenes were typically placed on West walls of chapels to utilize the setting sun as symbolism of the setting sun on life and that one must earn the right to enter Heaven before it is too late. The Sistine Chapel's Altar being located in the West meant that mass goers viewed the scene at the Pope's back during Mass.

Traditionally, Last Judgement scenes were painted on the wall one saw as they exited the Church and not behind the altar. The scenes were to serve as a final reminder to behave or face the fate of the damned.

The work is organized into four bands. Band one - resurrecting of the dead, the gaping mouth of hell, and the damned being swatted by Charon's oar plus Minos. Band two - ascending elect, trumpeting angels, and descending vices. Band three - John the Baptist, Jesus, Mary, Saint Peter, and other Martyred Saints. Band four - the lunettes showing angels with the instruments of the Passion.

In order to provide the right "canvas" to create the fresco Michelangelo sealed two windows on the wall and removed the Coat of Arms of Pope Julius II from just under Jonah on the Ceiling. Then he removed a fresco from Pietro Perugino(Raphael's Master) from the wall.

In addition to sealing the windows and removing the previous work, Michelangelo changed the slope of the wall. Originally, the wall sloped backward 5 1/2 inches more at the top than from the bottom. He wanted the wall to slope outwards at the top and slightly inward at the bottom so he replastered the wall to slope 11 3/4 inches in at the bottom and loom outward at the top. This would provide the "canvas" necessary to bring to life the dramatic effect needed to produce the Judgement of Christ. This sloping effect "pulled" the viewer into hell while pushing Jesus outward.

Michelangelo was sixty-six when he completed the Last Judgment. He unveiled his Judgement twenty-nine years later on the same day as he unveiled his completed ceiling

The bands of the scene are slightly higher on the left and lower on the right to illustrate the tipping of the scales with the righteous lifted to Heaven, and the damned pulled to hell. Saint Michael is usually shown in Last Judgement scenes holding the scales of judgment, but Michelangelo chose to omit Saint Michael and use the scene itself as the scales. It is also Michelangelo's way to illustrate man's tendency towards vice and sin, versus goodness.

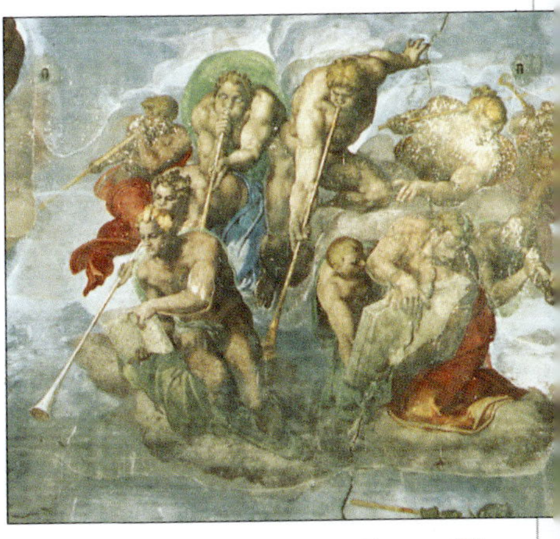

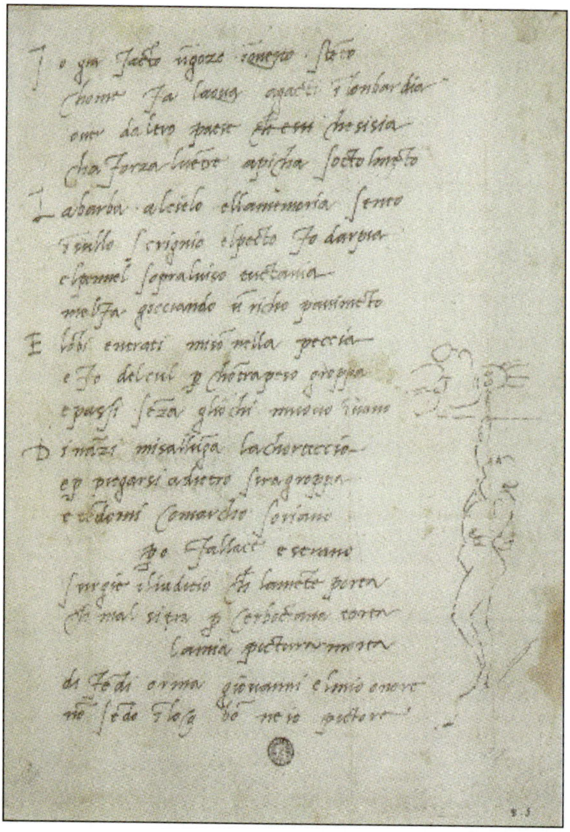

A letter written by Michelangelo to his friend John of Pistoia on his painting the ceiling of the Sistine Chapel.

The above version is in Italian. The version below has been translated to English. Note that Michelangelo closes the letter with the phrase, " I am no painter."

I've got myself a goiter from this strain,
As water gives the cats in Lombardy
Or maybe it is in some other country;
My belly's pushed by force beneath my chin.

My beard toward Heaven, I feel the back of my brain
Upon my neck, I grow the breast of a Harpy;
My brush, above my face continually,
Makes it a splendid floor by dripping down,

My loins have penetrated to my paunch,
My rump's a crupper, as a counterweight,
And pointless the unseeing steps I go.

In front of me my skin is being stretched
While it folds up behind and forms a knot,
And I am bending like a Syrian bow.

And judgement, hence, must grow,
Borne in the mind, peculiar and untrue;
You cannot shoot well when the gun's askew.

John, come to the rescue
Of my dead painting now, and of my honor;
I'm not in a good place, and I'm no painter

Map Of Saint Peter's Basilica

1. Giotto Mosaics
2. Charlamagne
3. Manzu Door
4. Central Door
5. Holy Door
6. Emperor Constantine
7. Michelangelo's Pieta
8. Christina of Sweden
9. Chapel of Holy Sacrament
10. Gregorian Chapel
11. Entrance to Cupula
12. S. Longinus
13. S. Peter
14. Baldacchino
15. S. Helen
16. Clement XIII
17. Throne of S. Peter
18. Tomb of Urban VIII
19. Tomb of Paul III
20. S. Veronica
21. Tomb of S. Leo
22. Tomb of Alexander VII
23. Pius V Monument
24. S. Andrew
25. Clementine Chapel
26. Chapel of the Choir
27. Tomb of Innocent VIII
28. John XXIII Monument
29. Clementina Sobieski

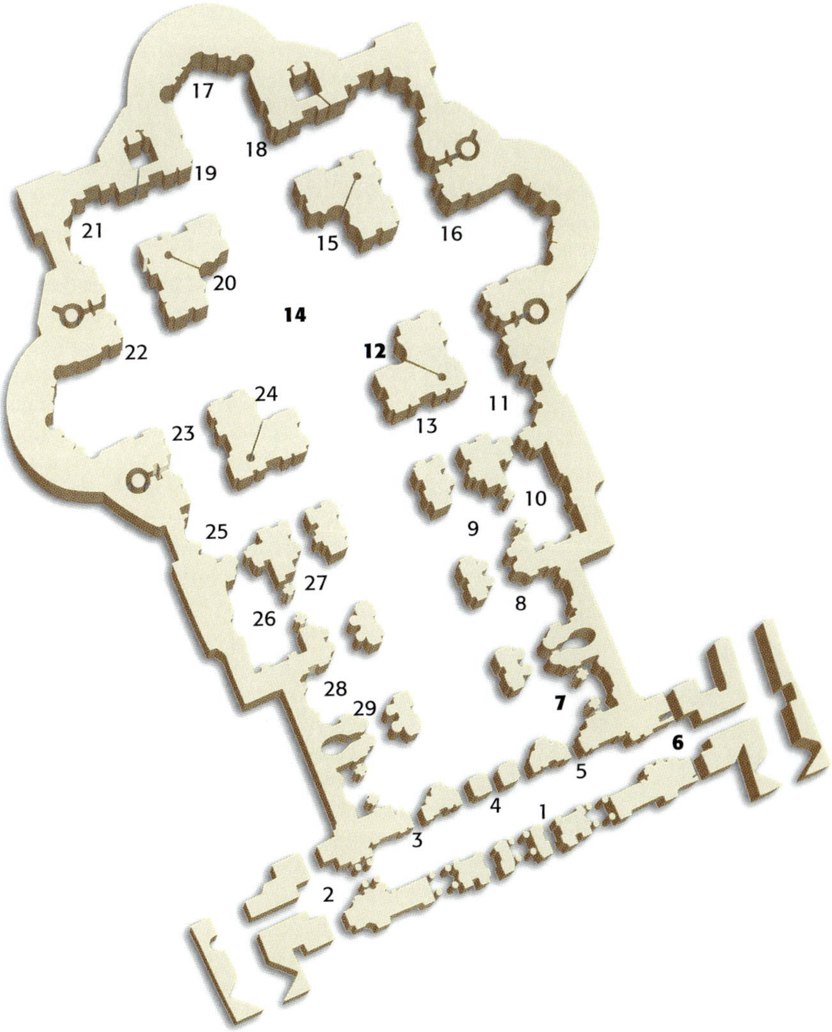

28 ▪ Gian Lorenzo Bernini

Constantine Saint Peter's Basilica

Bernini is the master of sculpting motion. His works are often delivered to the viewer at the time of the Saint's moment of truth. His David is caught just before releasing the stone from his sling. Blessed Ludovica at the moment she truly felt the touch of God. Saint Ludovica is shown as she is pierced by the arrow of God and driven into Divine Ecstasy.

View the Blessed Ludovica at San Francesco a Ripa in Trestavere and the Ecstasy of Saint Theresa at Santa Maria della Vittoria. Both are excellent examples of the Master Gian Lorenzo Bernini's use of motion and drapery to capture a moment of truth.

As the Savior of the Catholic Church Constantine is often honored in the art of the renaissance and Baroque. At the Milvian Bridge in Rome Constantine defeated Maxentius to become the single emperor of the Roman Empire. He Defeated Maxentius under the sign of the Cross delivered to him on the eve of the Battle in a dream. He marked the shields of his Divisions with the Cross and marched to Victory. His army was outnumbered and inexperienced compared to the army of Maxentius. In 313 AD, Contstantine, under the Edict of Milan made Christianity legal and gave back the land and property confiscated by the empire to the Chrisitians. It was still a long road to equality for the Christians, but Constantine in a single edict made the Christian faith honorable and legal in the Roman world.

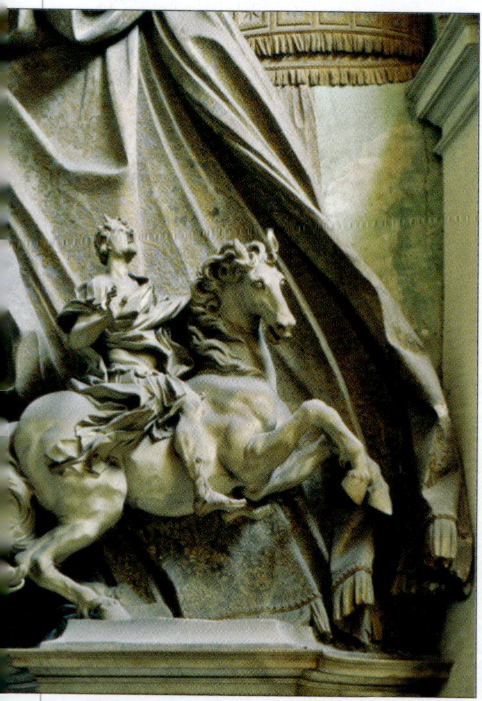

Pope Innocent X asked Bernini to carve a sculpture of Constantine. It was originally meant to be placed in a niche inside Saint Peter's. But the sculpture was too large and had to be placedin the Piano Reale at the base of the newly designed scala Regia. As Bernini sculpted, he quickly uncovered that the statue would be too large, but he continued carving under his original plan claiming that the block prevented him from making any size adjustments.

The statue itself wasn't large enough to completely fill the niche at the base of the Scala Reale so he carved the beautiful flowing drapery behind Constantine. The glorious drapery fills the niche and beocomes part of the sculpture.

Gian Lorenzo Bernini was a master. His statues take on a life all their own. But even the great Bernini had his critics. When the statue was unveiled the critics felt that Constantine couldn't possibly maintain himself on the horse's back without stirrups and reigns. They also felt that Constantine was too small for the horse, that he had the beard of a satyr, and had the look of Saint Francis receiving the stigmata.

29 ▪ Michelangelo

Pieta Saint Peter's • Vatican City

The Pieta was commissioned to Michelangelo by the French Ambassador to Rome named Cardinal Jean de Bilheres Lagaulas. It took two years to complete. At the time of its completion, the Cardinal was seventy years old, he died without seeing it completed. The incredible statue was installed in his funerary chapel in Santa Petronilla attached to the south transept of Old Saints Peter's.

The contract was for Michelangelo to create a clothed Virgin Mary with the dead Christ in her arms. The contract read that Michelangelo would complete the work within one year and that it would be the most beautiful work of marble that exists in Rome. The work was and is so successful that the theme of the Pieta has become synonymous with Michelangelo's Pieta. It is made from one piece of marble.

Completed when Michelangelo was 21, the Pieta is Michelangelo's only signed work. It is signed as:

MICHEL.AGELVS.BVONAROTVS. FLORENT.FACIEBA

This translates to, "Michelangelo, the Florentine, was making." The use of the imperfect tense implies that the work is

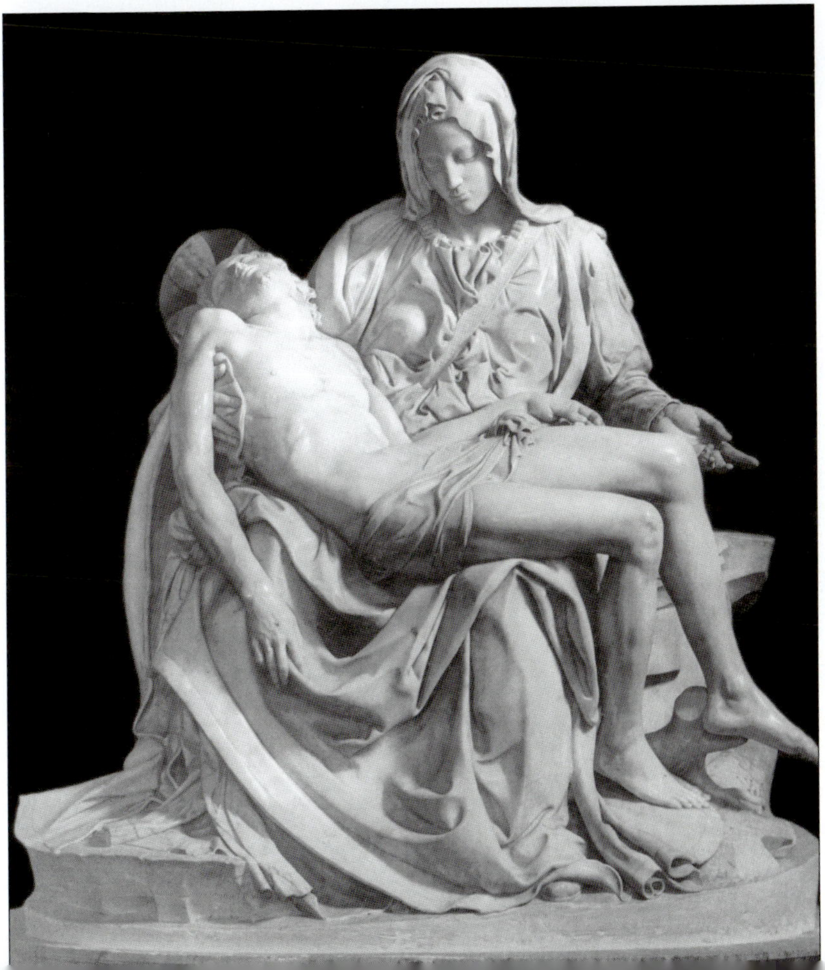

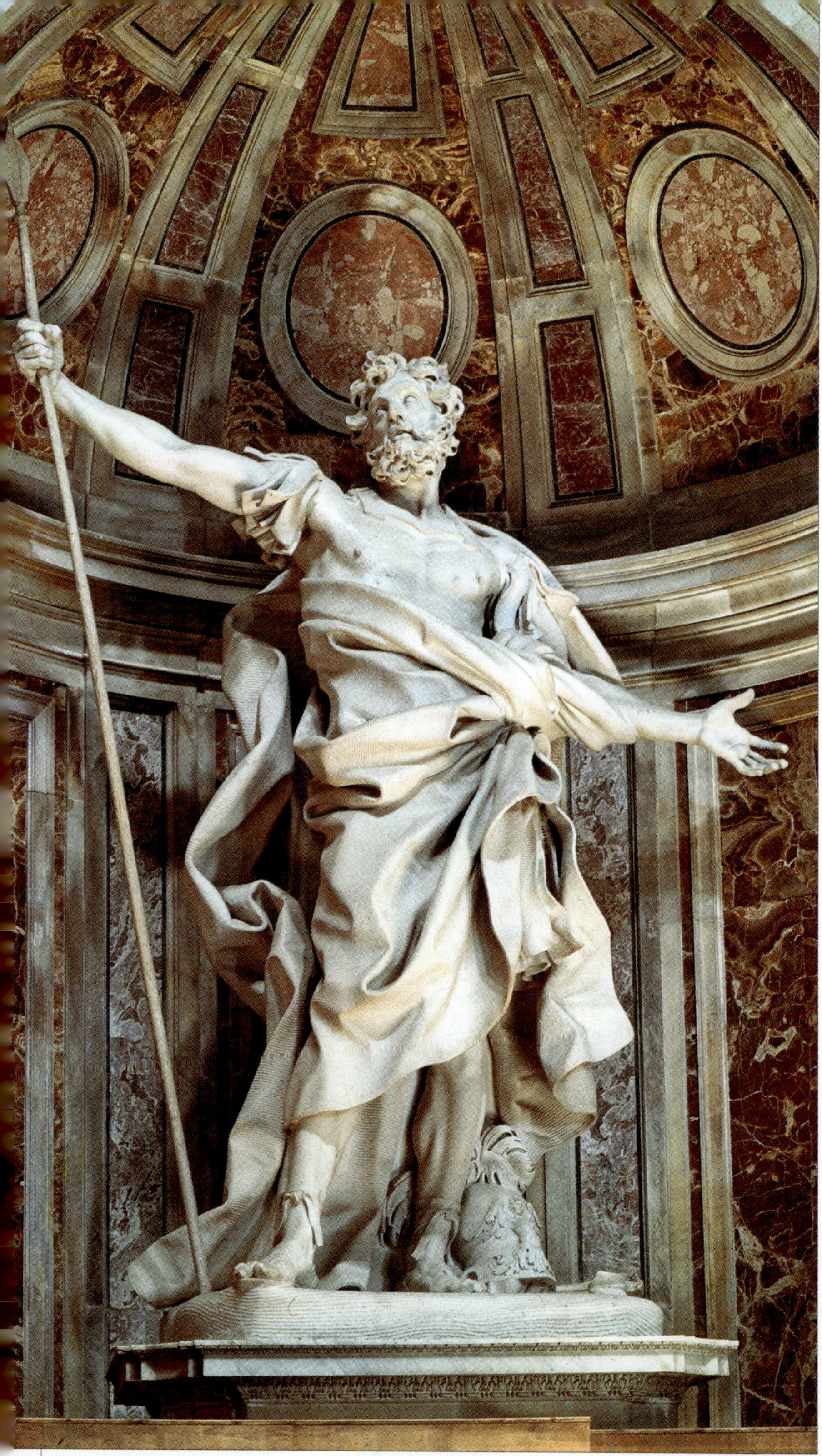

Saint Longinus

not yet complete and serves two functions. One, no mortal could ever complete a work that was to properly represent the Virgin Mary and Jesus Christ... additional work could always be done. Two, the incompleteness implied by the imperfect allows the creator to avoid the critics by claiming modestly that the work is unfinished and therefore any flaws are defensible. Michelangelo's use of the word FACIEBA is a written pun. The word itself is incomplete on the strap across the Virgin Mary. The complete word should be FACIEBAT.

During the Renaissance, it was believed that a master's work should be identifiable by the work itself and not a signature. It was considered an expression of insecurity to sign your work. But, with Michelangelo even a simple signature is a great story. One day Michelangelo went to view the Pieta shortly after it was installed in the chapel. While he was examining the work he overheard some Lombardian visitors praising the work. One of them asked who it was that created such beauty. The answer came, "Our Gobbo from Milan." Gobbo is referring to Christoforo Solari an artist from Lombardy. Michelangelo stood silently. He was angry that all his work would credit another artist. So, one night he shut himself in the chapel as it closed for the evening with his hammer and chisel. And overnight he carved his name across the strap on Mary's chest. A sidebar story is that Michelangelo was discovered by a nun. After she identified him as Michelangelo and was assured of his purpose made him a frittata.

Even the great Michelangelo wasn't without critics. He often heard from viewers that the Virgin was represented too young to have given birth to such an old Christ. Michelangelo told one of his biographers, Ascanio Condivi, that because Mary was chaste and lived a wholesome life she aged more slowly than her years might suggest. Christ, on the other hand aged more rapidly because he was bearing the weight of the sins of mankind so he could deliver us to the gates of Paradise.

30 ▪ Gian Lorenzo Bernini

Saint Longinus Saint Peter's Basilica • Inside

Longinus was a centurion in Rome's army. Like many of his works Bernini chose to repressent Longinus at the crucial test of his life. The statue of Longinus is carved at the moment of his conversion to Christianity when he exclaimed, as he looked up at Jesus on the Cross, "Truly this Man was the Son of God." Saint Longinus is the person who pierced the side of Jesus Christ while he was on the cross to see if he was truly dead. The scar you see on Jesus comes from Saint Longinus.

In Bernini's work Loginus is divested of his helmut and sword, which lay now at his feet. He is represented holding his spear and looking toward Heaven with his arms outstretched in devotion.

31 ▪ Gian Lorenzo Bernini

Baldacchino (Canopy) Saint Peter's • Interior

Long before the planning of the piazza outside Saint Peter's, Gian Lorenzo Bernini had been at work decorating the interior of the Basilica. His first commission was the design and creation of the gigantic bronze Baldacchino.

The canopy marks the tomb of Saint Peter. It is almost one hundred feet high...about eight stories.

The Baldacchino harmonizes the incredible proportions of the Basilica and the new Church of the Counter-Reformation. Partially fluted and wreathed with vines, the columns seem to deny the mass and weight of the tons of bronze resting on them. The metal was stripped from the Pantheon's portico. At the top of the columns are four colossal angels standing guard. Notice the Baldacchino has bees throughout. The bee is the symbol of the Barberini family.

The Pope that commissioned the Baldacchino was a Barberini.

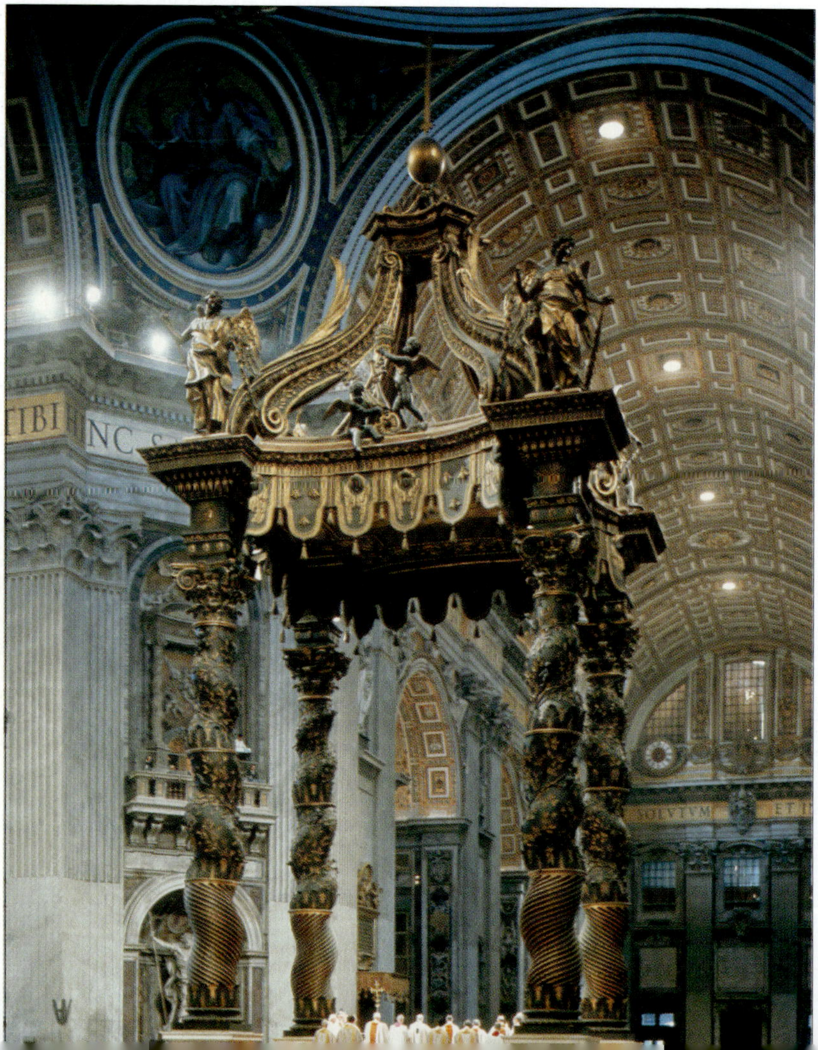

The glorious epicenter of Catholicism is Saint Peter's Basilica. Gian Lorenzo Bernini was called on to bring the church to the foreground and perfect its heavenly appeal. Bernini's largest and most impressive single work was the project to design Saint Peter's monumental piazza. Bernini had to work within the boundaries of the pre-existing design. Four rows of huge Tuscan columns make up the two colonnades which terminate in severly Classical temple fronts. The colonnades deliver a dramatic gesture of embrace as the viewer enters the piazza symbolizing the welcome of the Roman Catholic Church during the Counter-Reformation. By it's sheer scale and theatricality, the completed Saint Peter's Square fulfilled the Church's need in the 17th century by presenting an awe inspiring and authoritative view of the Church.

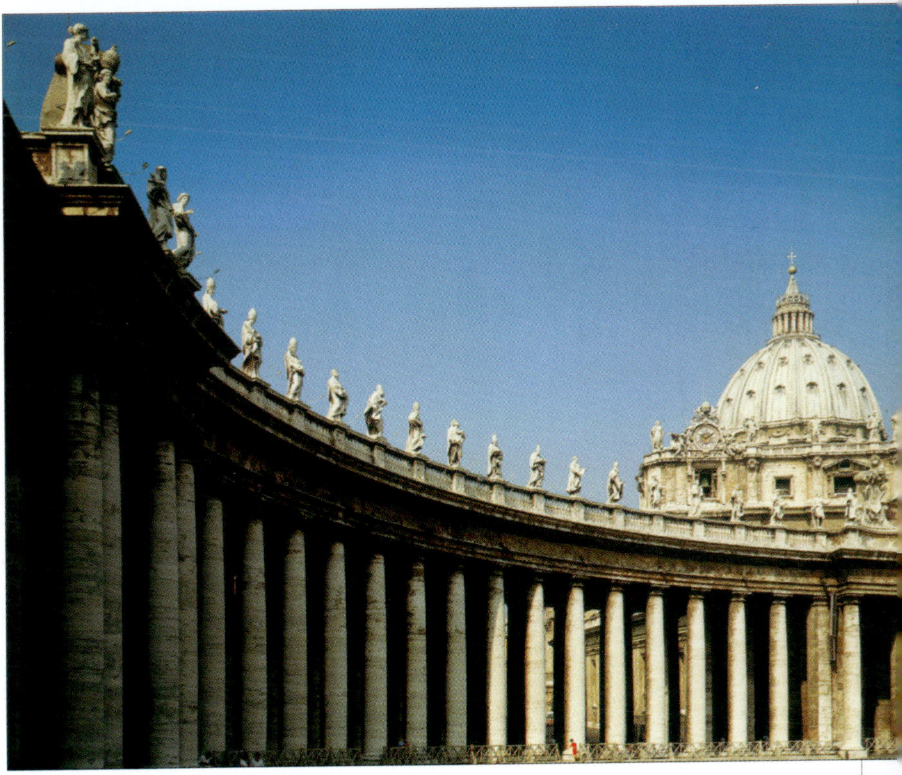

33 ■ Castel Saint Angelo

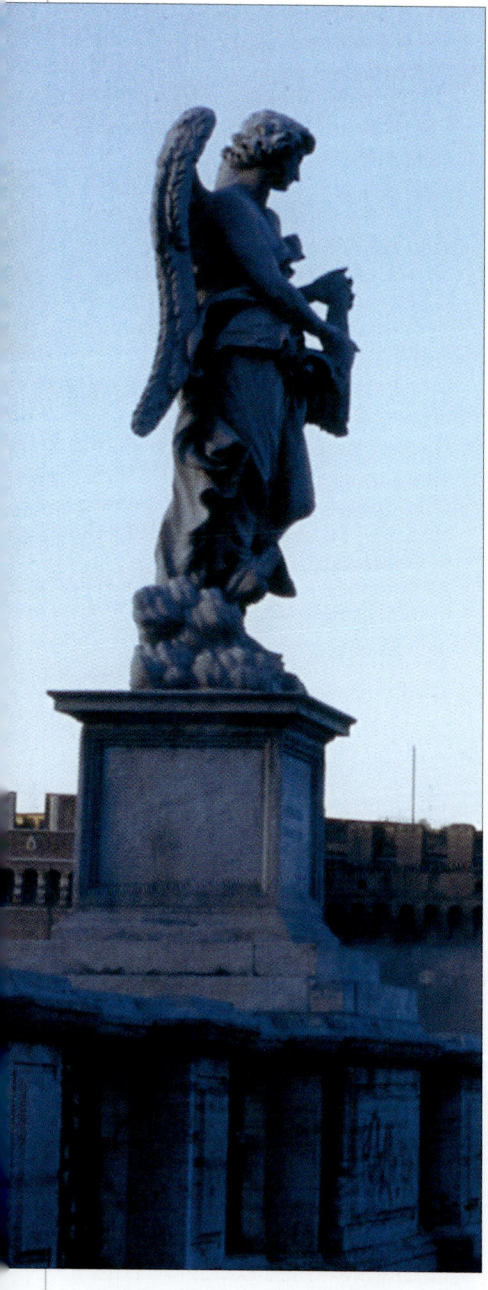

Bernini's Angels of the Passion. These statues are covered in detail on the page dedicated to Ponte Saint Angelo (The Bridge of Saint Angelo).

Originally built as a mausoleum to honor the remains of the Emperor Hadrian Castel Sant Angelo has a long and rich history. In 130 AD its creation was started by Hadrian himself and completed a year after his death in 139 AD.

The castle has played an important role throughout history by protecting Emperors and Popes from mauraudING barbarians or domestic enemies. It is a well fortified, defensible military stronghold. A fortified passage exists between the Vatican and Castel Saint Angelo for safe passage of the Pope during times of crisis. The passage way is called il Passetto.

Castel Saint Angelo has also been used a prison. Two of it's more famous prisoners are Benvenuto Cellini, a 16th century Florentine goldsmith. One of Cellini's more famous sculptures is in the Loggia of Florence of Perseus holding up the head of Medusa. It is a beautiful bronze. The other famous prisoner is Giordano Bruno, the heretical monk that was burned at the stake in Campo di Fiori. You can see a bronze memorial statue of Giordano at the very spot he was martyred (more on Bruno in the Navona Pantheon itinerary.)

Pope Gregory the Great named named it Castel Saint Angelo. He held a procession to end the plague in Rome. As the procession crossed Ponte Saint Angelo he saw the Archangel Micheal sheathing his sword at the top of the Castle. Taking this as a sign from God he built a chapel in Castel Saint Angelo and had a statue placed on the exact spot the he saw him.

34 ▪ Ponte Saint Angelo

Pope Paul III, in 1536, commissioned eight stucco figures to be crafted and placed on Ponte Sant Angelo for the reception of the emperor Charles V. The bridge crossed the Tiber river directly toward Castel Saint Angelo, but more importantly it crossed to Saint Peter's Basilica.

One hundred thirty one years later Pope Clement IX assumed the Papacy. He wished to have the bridge permanently decorated with ten marbles (originally eight) meditating over the instruments of the Passion of Christ. The instruments of the Passion are the Cross, Sponge, Scourge, dice, garment, sudarium, column, nails, crown of thorns, and superscription.

Gian Lorenzo Bernini directed the creation of the statuary. In total, nine artists (including Bernini) contributed to the work.

Twelve statues were created; ten for the bridge and when Pope Clement IX saw how extraordinarily beautiful Bernini's two statues were he insisted they be removed from the bridge and replaced by replicas. The two statues created by Bernini were of angels holding the crown of thorns and the superscription INRI from the Cross. INRI translates to Jesus of Nazareth, King of the Jews.

Each of the statues looks away from the instrument of the Passion they hold.

In 1729 Bernini's grandson offered the two statues completed by Bernini to the Church Sant Andrea della Fratte where they can be seen today.

The names of the other sculptors are Naldini, Francelli, Ferrata, Giorgetti, Lucenti, Guidi Raggi and Marelli.

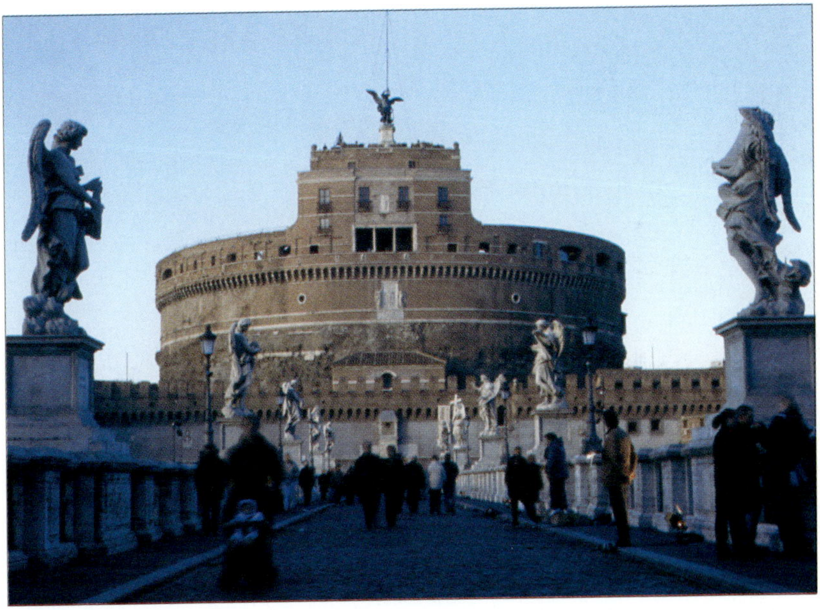

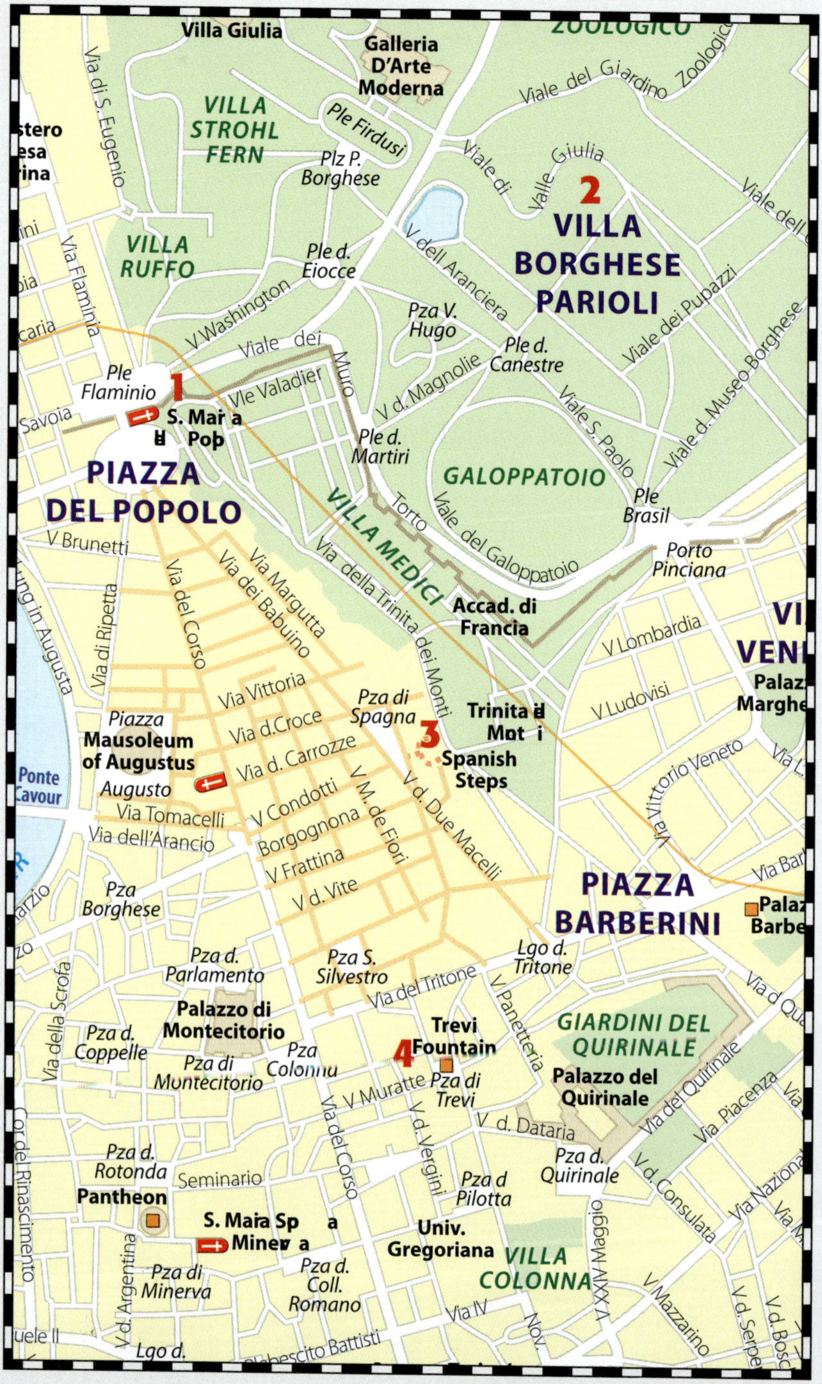

1. Santa Maria del Popolo
2. Borghese Palace
3. Fontana della Barcaccia & the Spanish Steps
4. Trevi Fountain

BORGHESE

Site Hours, Daily Schedule, Address, Phone Numbers and other important information

Site		Mon	Tue	Wed	Thur	Fri	Sat	Sun
Santa Maria del Popolo Piazza del Popolo 12 *close to Porta Pinciana	AM	7:00 to 12:00	7:00 to 12:00	7:00 to 12:00	7:00 to 12:00	7:00 to 12:00	7:00 to 12:00	7:00 to 12:00
	PM	4:00 to 7:00	4:00 to 7:00	4:00 to 7:00	4:00 to 7:00	4:00 to 7:00	4:00 to 7:00	4:00 to 7:00
Borghese Palace Piazzale del Museo Borghese 5 www.galleriaborghese.it (click to English Version at top of page) Buy tickets on-line at www.galleriaborghese.it website Reservations Mandatory You must pick up your tickets 30 minutes prior to scheduled visit Only 360 guests every 2 hours & you must leave at the end of your visit. Ticket office closes at 6:30 Closed December 25 & January 1 Adult Tickets are 10.50 Euro (8.50 Euro + 2.00 Euro reservation fee)	AM PM	X	8:30 to 7:00	8:30 to 7:00	8:30 to 7:00	8:30 to 7:00	8:30 to 7:00	8:30 to 7:00

Spanish Steps Piazza di Spagna At the corners of Via Condotti, Via Due Macelli, & Via del Babuino No tickets necessary Outdoor, 24 x 7 viewing	AM PM	24 x 7
Fontana della Barcaccia At the corners of Via Condotti, Via Due Macelli, & Via del Babuino At the bottom of the Spanish Steps No tickets necessary Outdoor, 24 x 7 viewing	AM PM	24 x 7
Fontana di Trevi Piazza di Trevi No tickets necessary Outdoor, 24 x 7 viewing	AM PM	24 x 7

X = Closed

Map of Santa Maria del Popolo

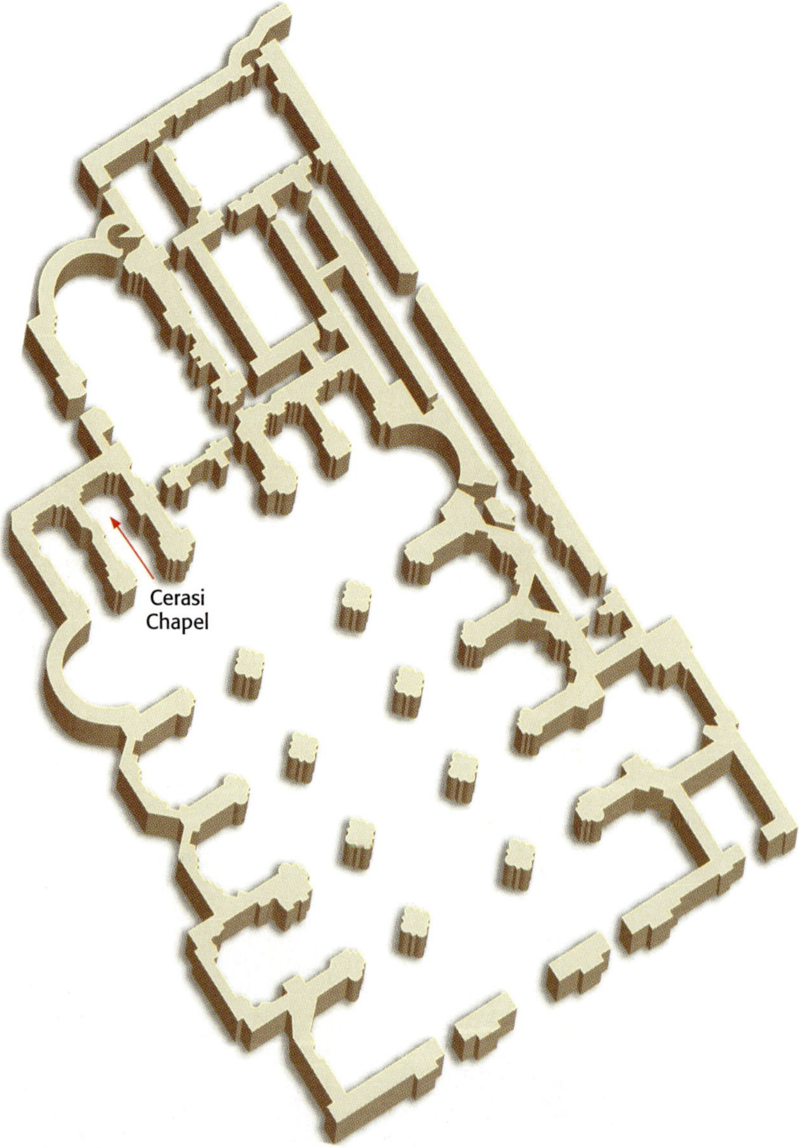

35 ▪ Michelangelo Merisi Caravaggio

Crucifixion of Saint Peter

Santa Maria del Popolo • Cerasi Chapel

Martyred in Rome during the persecution of Nero around 64 A.D. Saint Peter was condemned to the cross. He asked his executioners to set the cross inverted so not to die like Christ. He felt unworthy to share exactly the same fate of the son of God.

You don't see the faces of the executioners in the scene. Saint Peter is bathed in God's light while his killers are covered in shadow. The image is gruesome in its detail. The blood stained spikes through Saint Peter's feet, the mud on the bottom of the man's feet giving leverage to the mounting of the cross. This particular work was criticised because it seemed less of a work about the Crucifixion than a study in mounting a cross. The beauty of the image is the careful examination of the entire scene. The "it's just my job" attitude of the executioners plays into the use of light and dark. Saint Peter, while struggling, is being canonized by God's light.

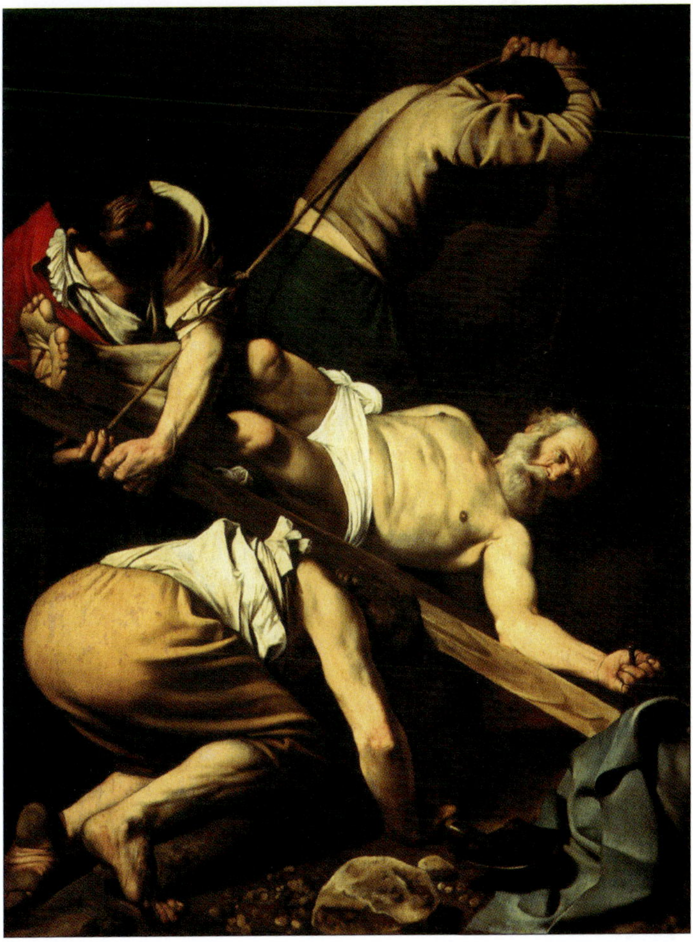

36 ▪ Michelangelo Merisi Caravaggio

Conversion of Saint Paul

Santa Maria del Popolo • Cerasi Chapel

Saul of Tarsus was converted to Saint Paul on a journey from Jerusalem to Damascus, "suddenly there shined round him a light from heaven: and he fell to the earth and heard a voice saying unto him, 'Saul, Saul, Why persecutest me?' And he was three days without sight before scales fell from his eyes" (Acts 9:3 - 9).

The theme of blindness ties the two paintings together. The three days of blindness of Saint Paul and the symbolic blindness of the three executioners harmonize the two masterpieces.

Saint Paul is cast into darkness to experience his calling to God on his own terms. The three men in Saint Peter's canonization are symbolically blind through a lack of accepting God into their lives as they murder the first pope, the keeper of the kingdom, he who holds the keys to heaven.

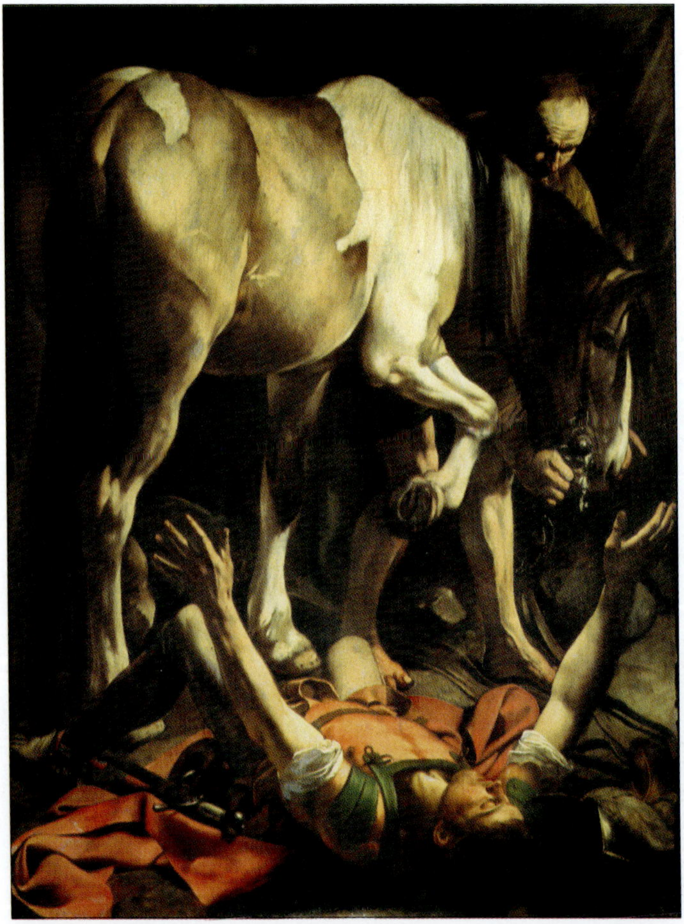

Galleria Borghese • Ground Floor

Piazzale del Museo Borghese, 5
00197 Roma
In a taxi ask for Galleria Borghese - enter from Via Pinciana, Via dell'Uccelliera

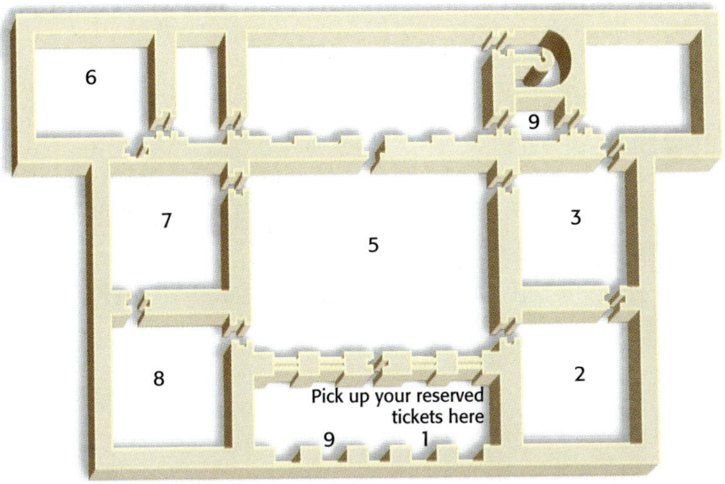

1. Tickets
2. Bookshop
3. Cloak Room
4. Exhibition Hall
5. Lecture Hall
6. Educational Area
7. Bar and Restaurant
8. Toilets
9. Lift and Stairs

You MUST buy your tickets and make reservation ahead of time.
You are limited to a two hour visit.
Daily Hours: Tuesday - Sunday 9:00 am to 7:00 pm
CLOSED ON MONDAYS, December 25, & January 1
Ticket price 8,50 Euro + 2.00 Euro Reservation Fee
Telephone: 39 06 841 39 79
Prepurchase tickets at: http://www.ticketeria.it/
http://www.galleriaborghese.it
Ticket office closes at 6:30

Galleria Borghese • First Floor • Statuary & Caravaggio

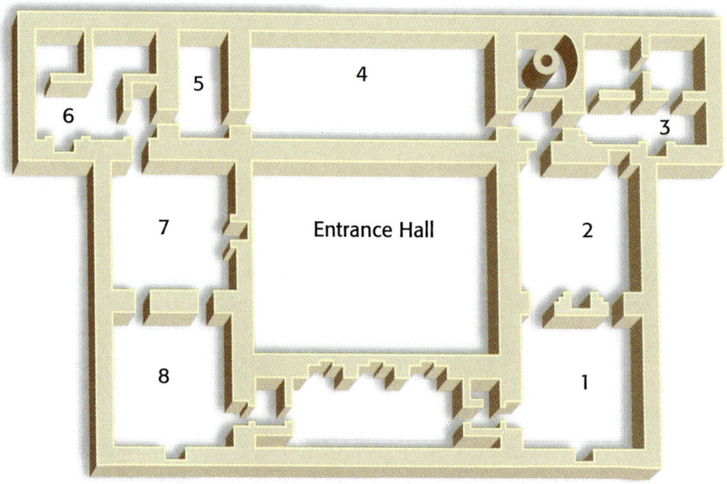

1. Pauline Bonaparte as Venus
2. David
3. Apollo and Daphne
4. Rape of Proserpine
5. Hermaphrodite
6. Aeneas, Anchises, and Ascanius
7. Egyptian - No write-up included
8. Caravaggio Paintings

Galleria Borghese • Second Floor • Pinacoteca

* After the tour of the first floor exit and go back to the ground floor where you picked-up your tickets and follow the signs to the Pinacoteca up the stairs to the second floor

9. Deposition; aka Entombment by Raphael
10. Danae by Correggio – No write-up included
20. Sacred and Profane Love by Titian

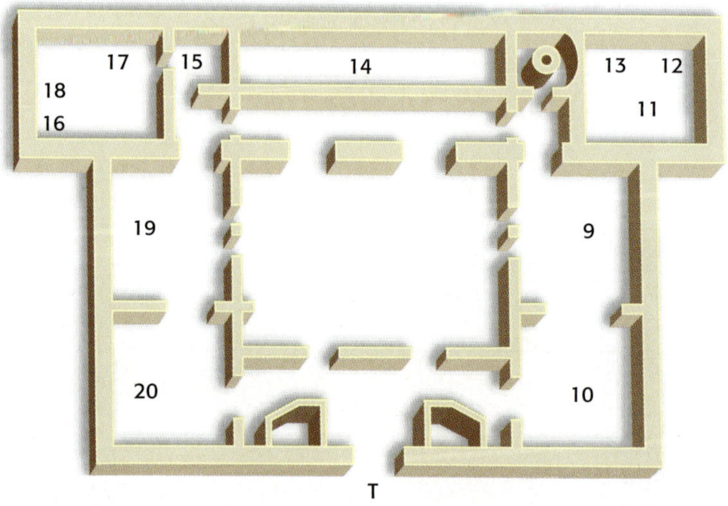

37 ▪ Antonio Canova

Pauline Bonaparte as Venus Victrix

Borghese Gallery

This neoclassical sculpture steps out of bounds for such an important woman. She is the sister of Napolean Bonaparte and posed nude for an artist to sculpt her as Venus Victrix with the victory apple gifted to her by Paris in the Judgement of Paris which was the start of the Trojan War.

Pauline is the perfect figure of classical tranquility and nobility. She clearly believes she is a Goddes

The story of the Judgement of Paris takes place at the wedding of Peleus and Thetis. Thetis is the immortal mother of the Greek hero Achilles. The God Eris (strife) arrived at the wedding angry and uninvited. Who wants strife invited to a wedding? To stir up a little trouble between the hubristic Goddesses Hera, Athena, and Venus in attendance, he rolled a golden apple across the floor announcing, "may the most beautiful take it." All three claimed the apple as their own. Since only one could rightfully own the apple, and the title of most beautiful, a mortal was asked to choose the victor. The mortal was named Paris. He was the son of King Priam of Troy and brother to the feared Trojan warrior Hector. One by one the goddesses undressed for judgement and began to bribe Paris. Hera offered dominion over the world. Athena promised a glorious military career. Venus promised the most beautiful girl in the world would love him. Paris chose Venus. Venus made Helen of Troy who was the daughter of Zeus and Leta and the most beautiful woman in the world fall madly in love with Paris. Paris made away with Helen to Troy, the Greeks followed to fulfill the oath of Tyndareus.

The oath of Tyndareus is the oath the men of Greece took to protect the winner of Helen's choice as a husband. They all agreed that if anything bad should happen to the chosen man all of the other men of Greece would rally to protect him to prevent any "accidents" to Helen's new husband. When Paris made off with Helen, the Oath was invoked and Troy fell to the Greeks over the love of a woman and the honor of the Greeks.

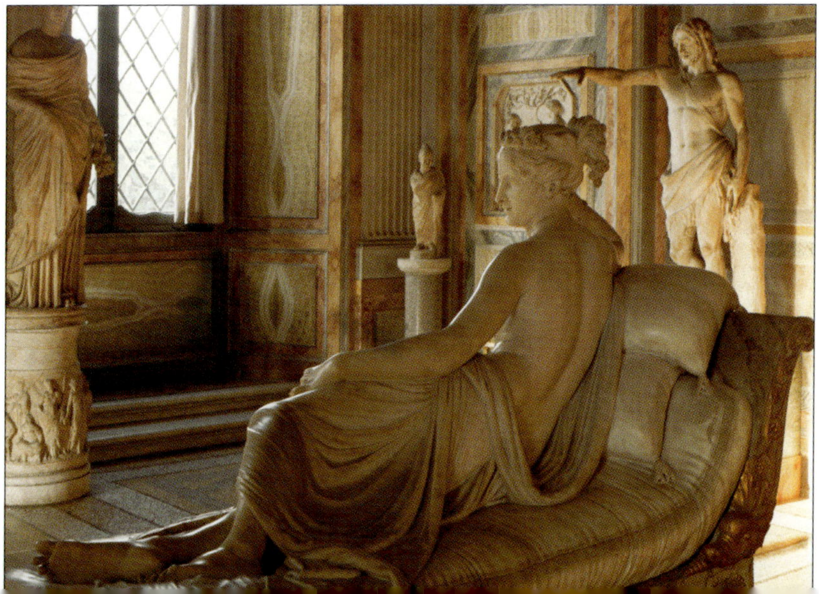

38 ▪ Gian Lorenzo Bernini

David Borghese Gallery

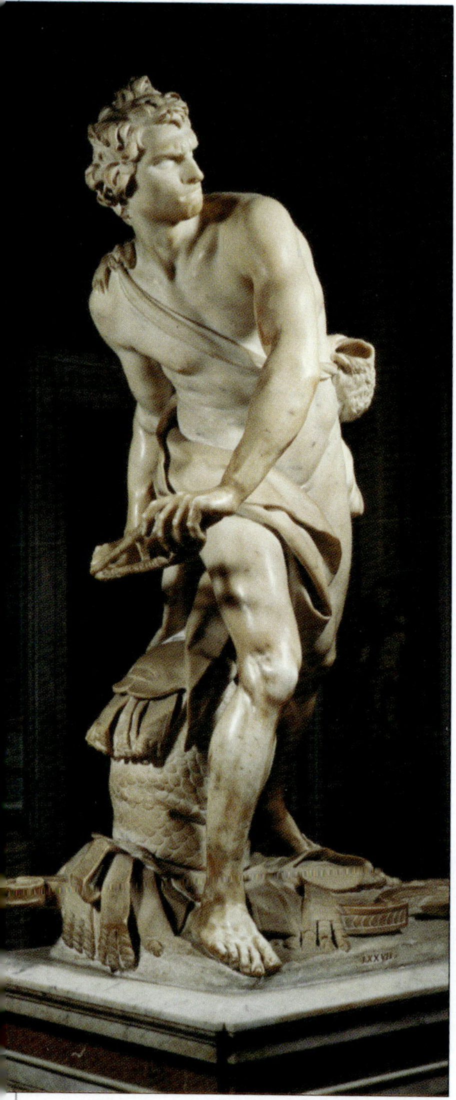

Gian Lorenzo Bernini was the master at capturing a moment in time in stone. He carves his moments with the grace of an angel, and the uncanny ability to freeze the action at the exact moment the subject of his work transcends life as they knew it. Midway through the turn of his body Bernini's David takes aim at Goliath and with the grit of his teeth fulfills his destiny. Conquering a superior foe, David steps away from life as he knew it and becomes symbolic of determination, of mind over matter, of faith.

Compare Bernini's David with that of Michelangelo's David. The two are of the exact same subject, yet completely different in the delivery. Action versus Potential. Explosiveness versus welling up to action.

Bernini carved his David with the traits of himself in David's face. Cardinal Scipione Borghese held up a mirror as Bernini carved so he could capture his own face as David's. The face of David is actually Bernini struggling with his hammer and chisel, concentrating with a Master's determination. He scowls under the strain and pressure of his work... his perfection.

Under David's feet is his armor, his harp decorated with the head of an eagle. The eagle is a symbolic reference to the Borghese family.

4 famous Davids in Italy:

Donatello - after the victory
Verrochio - after the victory
Michelangelo - before the fight
Bernini - during the fight

39 ■ Gian Lorenzo Bernini

Apollo and Daphne   Palazzo Borghese

Apollo, the God of prophecy, healing, poetry, and the arts, had a difficult time finding and keeping love. Apollo has many myths where his love interest changes into flowers or trees.

Daphne was a nymph and daughter of the river god Peneus in Thessaly. Apollo pursued her as a lover, but she rejected him. He chased her into the mountains and to escape, she prayed to her father, who changed her into a laurel tree. The laurel tree is the sacred plant of Apollo.

Gian Lorenzo Bernini sculpted this incredible piece for Cardinal Scipione Borghese. It is hard to believe that Bernini could create the exact moment that Daphne morphs into a laurel tree so perfectly. Daphne's fingers and toes are masterfully done. Her horror stricken face perfectly captures her fear. Apollo looks shocked as he is witness to yet another morphing love interest. Bernini was very proud of this work and spoke of how beautiful and light the hair of Daphne turned out. It is an amazing piece.

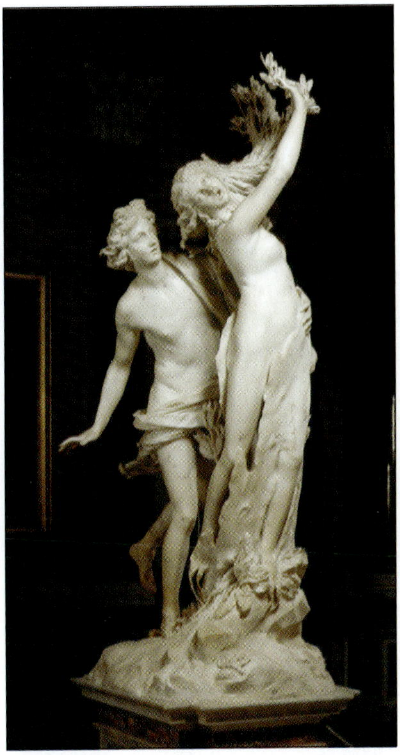

In his book, Metamorphoses, Ovid writes of Apollo's other unsuccessful love affairs.

Apollo loved the young boy Hyacinth. While Hyacinth was practicing the discus throw a gust of wind caught the discus, it swerved and hit Hyancinth in the head killing him. Apollo grew the Hyacinth flower from his blood.

Cyparissus was another love of Apollo. Cyparissus had a pet deer that he accidentally killed. He was so grief stricken that he asked Apollo to force him to mourn forever. Apollo consented turning him into the Cypress tree which grows throughout Italy and Greece in Cemetaries as a symbol of mourning.

Priam, the king of Troy, and his wife Hecuba had twin daughters - Helenus and Cassandra. Cassandra grew into a beautiful woman and Apollo wanted her as a lover. She preteded to accept Apollo as a lover on the condition that he make her a prophetess. He agreed. Cassandra, after being made a prophetess refused Apollo's affections. He then added a condition that Cassandra would always speak the truth and see the future, but no one would believe her prophecy. She foresaw the downfall of Troy a number of times, but none of the Trojans believed a word she spoke.

Apollo is also famous for his Oracle at Delphi. Raphael places Apollo at the center of his work Parnassus in the Signature room in the Raphael Rooms of the Vatican. The Parassus is adjacent to the more famous School of Athens.

40 ▪ Gian Lorenzo Bernini

Pluto and Proserpina Borghese Palace

The abduction of Proserpina by Pluto is a famous story.

Prosperpina is the Roman name for Persephone and Pluto is the Roman name for Hades.

Prosperpina was picking flowers in a little town in Sicily named Enna. Pluto abducts her to be his wife and brings her to the underworld.

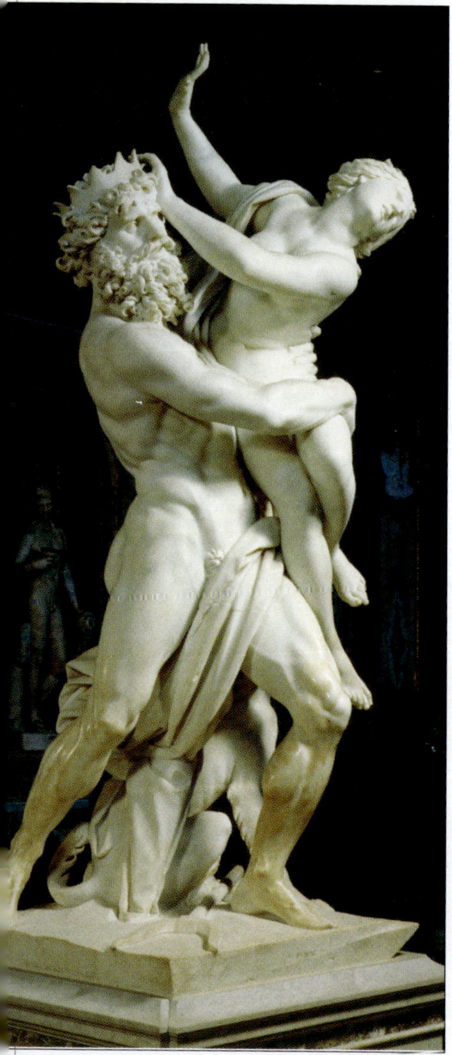

Demeter, Prosperpina's mother, is enraged and goes to Zeus to beg for his assistance. Zeus agrees to help and has Hermes steal her back from the underworld. While in the underworld Prosperpina ate three seeds of a Pomegranite and as a result is forced to spend 3 months of the year in the underworld as Pluto's wife.

Demeter is the Goddess of Agriculture and as punishment for her daughter having to spend time in the underworld won't allow any crops to grow while she is away. The months away are the winter months.

Dante Gabriel Rossetti was a Pre-Raphaelite painter and poet. In his beautiful Proserpina Holding the Pomegranite painting he includes in the background of the painting this sonnet:

how far away that light, shining above the wall!

It scarcely flashes through. Then, in a moment,

it will lead me from this gloom, to the gate above.

How far away those flowers on Enna's hills from this fruit of your gloomy shades. O Tartarus! that brought me my bitter future. And O! how far that open sky from this eternal gloom that must cover me - forever.

And O! how far the nights still to be passed, from days that once have been.

How far am I removed from my old self! In aimless search I listen for the word one pitying heart might breathe to another's soul. Its broken voice will someday murmur condolence in my ear,

O poor Proserpina, even we lament your fate.

41 ▪ Gian Lorenzo Bernini

Goat Amalthea Nursing Zeus

Borghese Gallery

A mythological scene capturing the Goat Amalthea nurturing Zeus to life along with a satyr. This is one of Bernini's first works. It was commissioned of him by the Borghese family. The first four sculptures created by Gian Lorenzo were classical or mythological in their subjects. The works created in order are: Goat Amalthea, (Bust of Pope Paul V), Aeneas, Rape of Proserpina, and Apollo chasing Daphne.

The story of Zeus and the Goat Amalthea is one of the Titans being replaced by the Olympians. Rhea, Zeus's mother, bore six children with the Titan Cronos. The children were Hestia, Hera, Demeter, Hades, Posieden, and Zeus.

In order to avoid a prophecy which stated that he would be replaced by his own children, Cronos devoured each of his children at birth. Rhea traveled to the island of Crete to give birth to her last child Zeus and hide him from Cronos. In order to fool Cronos, Rhea wrapped a stone in a blanket and gave it to Cronos to eat. He did, and thought he avoided the prophecy of his own downfall.

Rhea hid Zeus in a mountain cave to be nursed and raised by the Goat Amalthea. Zeus grew to manhood killing his father and freeing his siblings from the Cronos. This changed the gods from the Titans to the Olympians.

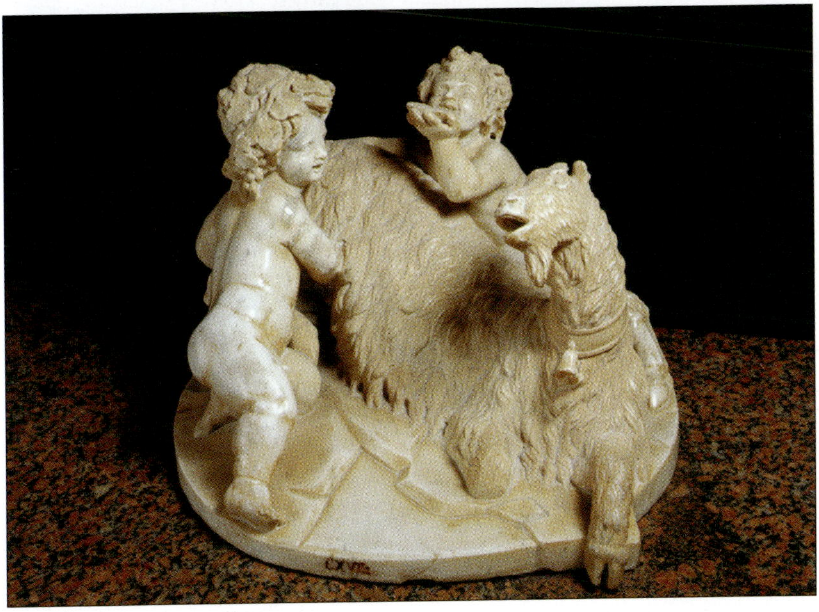

- A famous image of Cronos devouring his children is painted by Goya. It is kept at the Prado Museum in Madrid.
- Our Zodiac has the sign of the Capricorn. The Capricorn is the son of the Goat Amalthea. In order to thank Amalthea for his life he raised her son Capricorn to the heavens and placed him among the stars to rest eternally

42 ▪ Gian Lorenzo Bernini
Aeneas, Anchises, and Ascanius
Borghese Palace

This is one of Gian Lorenzo Bernini's first works for Cardinal Scipione Borghese. It is made from one of the largest blocks of marble ever used by Bernini.

Aeneas is the son of Anchises and Aphrodite. Aeneas, the legendary founder of Rome escapes from Troy with his father Anchises on his shoulders carrying the gods of Troy. His son Ascanius carries the eternal flame that will light the sacred hearth of the Goddess Vesta in their circular temple in the Roman Forum. The eternal flame is tended to and protected by the Vestal Virgins of Rome.

The Romans had no explanation for their origins. When Augustus became Emperor of Rome after his Uncle Julius Ceasar bequeathed him the empire Augustus had a Roman Mythology created with the assistance of Virgil.

The journey of Aeneas often mirrored that of Odysseus. Both have to overcome trials and tribulations until they are allowed to make it home. Aeneas lands in Carthage, Sicily, faces the blinded Cyclops Polyphemus, visits the Sybil at Cumae on the Amalfi Coast of Italy near Naples, travels to the underworld, and is granted passage on the boat of Charon across the river Styx. And, finally, Aeneas goes on to found Rome.

Virgil's Aenead was unfinished at the time of his death. He had instructed his assistants to burn the unfinished work, but Augustus stepped in to save the epic poem.

By saving the work, the Romans have a mythology of their origin, Augustus is immortalized, we learn the details of the Trojan Horse and the fall of Troy, come to know the basis of the hatred between Carthage and Rome, and Bernini is given the story with which to carve this magnificent statue.

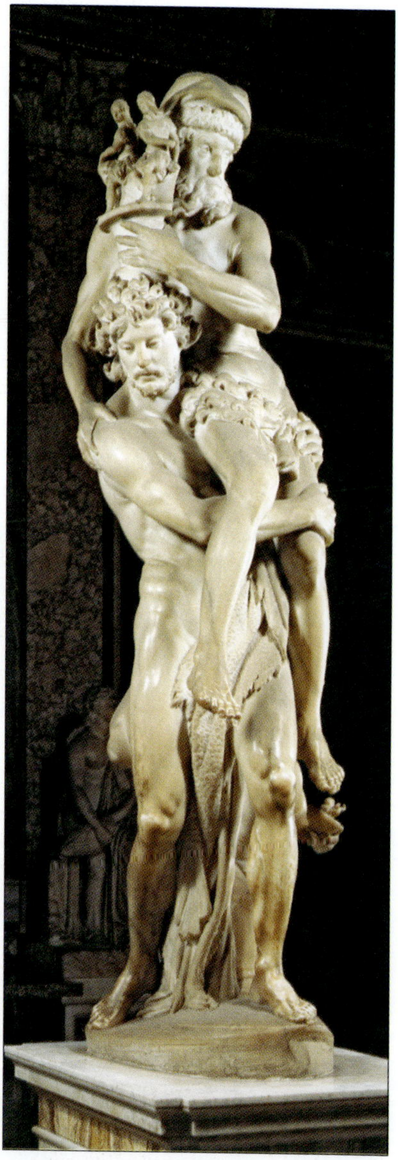

Other details of the Aeneas and the Vestal Virgins are contained in the page on the Capitoline Wolf in this packet.

Michelangelo Merisi Caravaggio

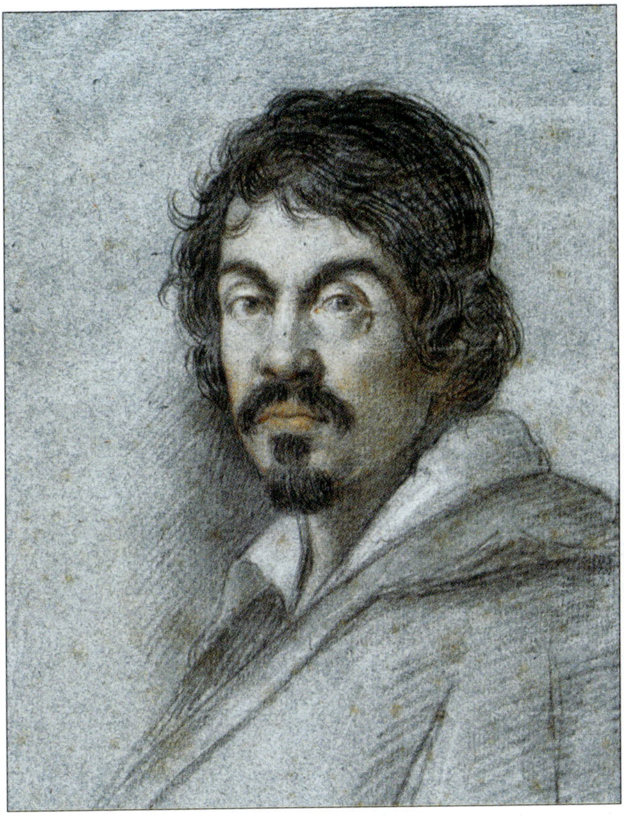

He was born less than 10 years after Michelangelo Buonarroti died & he was Shakespeare's younger by seven years

Born in Caravaggio near Milan in 1571 Michelangelo Merisi di Caravaggio was not readily accepted by his peers or the art community of the seventeenth century. Critics of his day remarked that his paintings fell somewhere between "the sacred and the profane."

Michelangelo Merisi departed from the normal depiction of religious or mythological scenes. His use of light and dark delivered an emotion and drama never before seen in painting. He used his contemporary Rome and Romans to depict Biblical scenes and bring scripture to life in the present tense.

Caravaggio deliverd his soul, his desires, and his fears through his paintings. He lived an unsavory life by frequenting brothels, gambling, and drinking. He killed a man in a sword fight. He lived with a cardinal. He had a bounty on his head. He fled Italy and lived in Malta to avoid capture. He died an untimely death in 1597 on his return from Naples to Rome seeking a pardon by the Pope for the murder of Ranuccio Tomassoni.

Caravaggio was in Rome on February 17, 1600 when Giordano Bruno was burned at the stake in Campo di Fiori during the Inquisition.

His use of light is called tenebrism from the Italian word for shadow – tenebroso.

43 ▪ Michelangelo Merisi Caravaggio

Saint John the Baptist

San Giovannino • Borghese Gallery

Saint John is portrayed in his animal skins as a hermit. The lamb is shown with him from John 1:24, "behold the lamb of God." Besides the lamb Saint John is often shown with a cross made of sticks or a scroll. The vines the lamb is eating are symbols of the Eucharistic wine.

The Gospels name John as the son of Zechariah and Elizabeth. He was born six months before Jesus. His mother Elizabeth was the Virgin Mary's older cousin.

Saint John left his parents for a life of atonement in the desert. He preached conversion and baptized people in the Jordan River. Christ himself, came to be bapitized by Saint John.

Shortly after Saint John baptized Jesus he was imprisoned by Herod because Saint John reproached him for living with Herodias, Herod's brother's wife.

During a banquet, Herod promised Salome anything she wanted because she danced so well. Salome was the daughter of Herodias. Herodias encouraged her daughter to ask for the head of Saint John on a silver platter. Not wanting to appear foolish by not granting the request Herod had Saint John decapitated immediately and delivered his head on a platter.

This work was purchased by Cardinal Scipione Borghese after the artist's death.

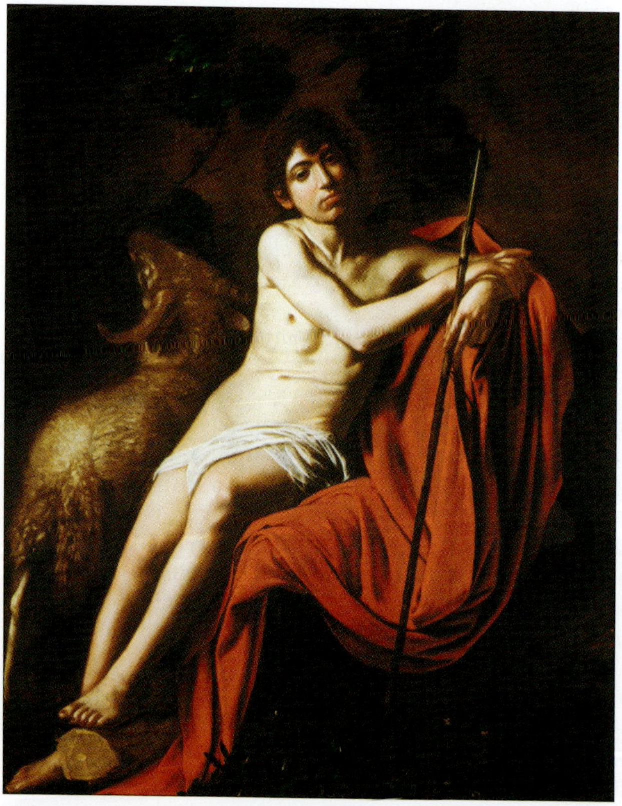

44 ▪ Michelangelo Merisi Caravaggio

Sick Bacchus

Il Bacchino Malato • Borghese Gallery

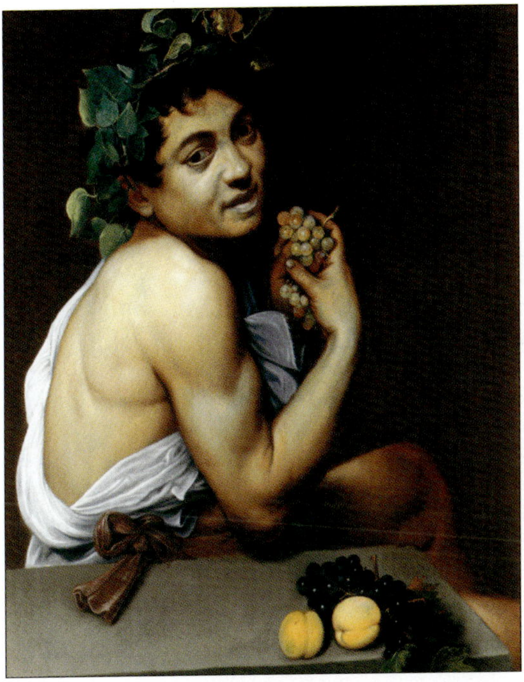

Il Bacchino Malato is closely tied to another great Caravaggio painting named Boy with a Basket of Fruit. Both paintings were completed within eight months of one another in 1593.

The god Bacchus is a lively, vibrant god that allowed his followers to lose their inhibitions through drink. He was the god of luxuriant fertility and the god of wine. The other name for Bacchus is Dionysus. The annual festival attributed to him is called the Bacchanalia. The classical symbols of Bacchus are grape leaves and grapes.

Another attribute of Bacchus is creativity stirred by drink. It was thought that when a person drank it aroused their creative spirit. They became happy and this happiness drove them to be artistically inspired. The Romans had a saying, "In vino veritas." This means, "in wine there is truth." The ancients understood clearly that the more one drank the looser their tongue seemed to become.

Caravaggio painted his self-portrait as a sick Bacchus (Il Bacchino Malato). He has given himself a pale and jaundiced look with yellowing grape leaves as his crown. He tucks his right elbow in close to his body almost as if he was shy or fearful. The painting delivers saddness and sickliness to the viewer through a god that typically depicts the loss of inhibition.

Some believe that this painting is Caravaggio's commentary on the effects of wine on his soul. He may have felt that that wine was a bad influence on him. Other critics believe that this was a homoerotic image created by Caravaggio. It is thought to be homoerotic due to the shape of the peaches on the table. Do they look like buttocks to you?

45 ▪ Michelangelo Merisi Caravaggio

Saint Jerome Writing

San Girolamo • Borghese Gallery

This work was commissioned directly from Caravaggio by Cardinal Scipione Borghese. Scipione was the nephew of Pope Paul V.

The red cloak is one of Saint Jerome's symbols. He is often shown scantily clad to depict him as a hermit. He went into seclusion in the desert of Chalsis to become a monk. His other emblems are the book, the skull, a lion, and a Cardinal's hat. The hat is a misinterpretation. During his lifetime, Cardinals did not wear hats (in fact they didn't until 1252). Artists in the middle-ages began to depict him as a Cardinal. This was also a mistake.

Saint Jerome's most famous legend comes from him removing a thorn from the foot of a lion. This helped the lion recover from its wound and bound the lion to him. This is symbolic of compassion conquering brute force. In many depictions of Saint Jerome you will find the lion underfoot or in the background.

In addition to being a hermit, Saint Jerome struck himself in the chest with a rock. This was to help him conquer the temptation of the flesh. He thought his pain brought him closer to God and further from sin.

Caravaggio's light bathes Saint Jerome in the image. His pen is the division between God's light and redemtion and immortality portrayed by the skull. The skull is often a symbol of vanity and death. It is the illustration of our mortality.

He was also known for revising a translation of the Bible.

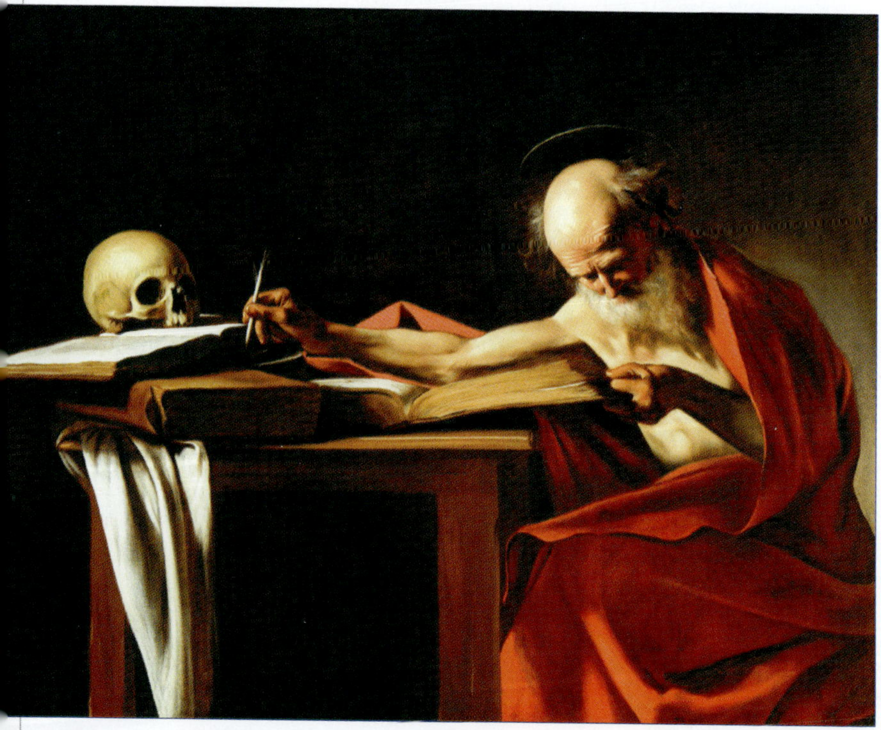

46 ▪ Michelangelo Merisi Caravaggio

Madonna dei Palafrenieri Borghese Gallery

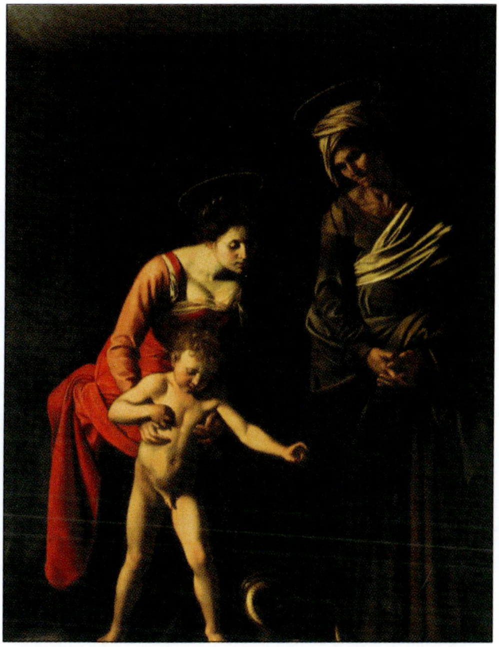

In 1605, Pope Paul V authorized the demolition of Old Saint Peter's. The decoration of the new basilica would keep the next five Pontificates busy. The work was managed by Gian Lorenzo Bernini and through him Caravaggio would earn his first alterpiece.

The Confraternity of the Palafrenieri had one of the seven privileged alters at Old Saint Peter's. The rights to those seven alters was transferred to the new transept designed by Michelangelo Buonarroti.

The Patron Saint of the Order of the Palafrenieri is Saint Anne (the Virgin Mary's Mother). Saint Anne, Jesus, and Mary enact a symbolic event. Together Jesus and His Mother crush the head of the serpent which represents original sin. During the Counter-Reformation, Rome decided that Jesus and Mary would crush the serpent together to conflict with the Protestant view that Jesus alone would vanquish sin and redeem humanity.

When the work was complete, the Confraternity deemed it unacceptable. This may have been due to Christ's nudity or the minor role of their Patron Saint Anne in the scene. After the Council of Trent, the Church was hypersensative to the claims of Martin Luther and the Protestant Reformation that lascivious nudity in art was perilous to the flock.

The Virgin Mary wears the clothing of a young Roman woman. She and Jesus are bathed in the light of God. Saint Anne is only partially covered in the light. Jesus reaches into the darkness to touch Saint Anne. She appears old and in a funeral dress.

After the Confraternity declined the work, Cardinal Scipione Borghese bought it.

47 ▪ Michelangelo Merisi Caravaggio

Boy with a Basket of Fruit

Giovane con la canestra di frutta • Borghese Gallery

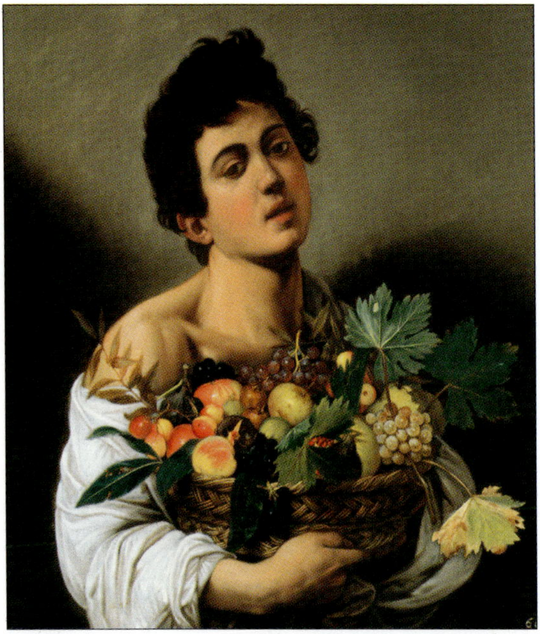

The Boy with a Basket of Fruit is considered one of his more straight forward paintings. The boy seems to be looking directly at the viewer in a provocative stare. The viewer gets pulled into the scene. His shoulder is exposed, mouth slightly open, his eyes holding your eyes, and head slightly tilted. It seems as if the boy is about to speak as you anxiously await his words.

This painting is tied to Caravaggio's self portrait as Il Bacchino Malato. Boy with a Basket of Fruit was painted within eight months of Il Bacchino. Both paintings were painted for Cavaliere d' Arpino. Here Caravaggio begins to utilize light and shadow. He does so in Il Bacchino, but to a slightly lesser extent.

Caravaggio delivered his model and fruit for the painting exactly as he saw them. The model is thought to be Mario Minniti; a young Sicilian. Caravaggio's relationship with the model seems real and emotionally charged. The grape leaf hanging down is wilted and browned. The over-ripe figs pop open. Both the fruit and the model represent life. They are not perfect representations of either.

- The Borghese family was one of Caravaggio's biggest patrons.
- Michelangelo Merisi Caravaggio takes the name Caravaggio from the town he was born. His namesake city is 25 miles east of Milan.

48 ▪ Michelangelo Merisi Caravaggio

David with the head of Goliath

Davide con la testa di Golia • Borghese Gallery

David holds the head of the slain Goliath. He stands symbolically like justice with a sword in his right hand, but rather than the scales of justice in his left, he bears the trophy of his Biblical enemy. The bruised forehead, dripping blood, lifeless eyes, partly darkened in the shadows with his mouth hanging open is Caravaggio himself. He painted himself as the slain Goliath in one of his last images.

Caravaggio was a wanted man for slaying a fellow Roman. On Via Pallacorda Caravaggio fought with Ranuccio Tomassoni over 10 scudi he owed Tomassoni from a gambling debt. Swordplay ensued resulting in Caravaggio cutting his enemy in the inner thigh. The cut was meant to be insulting, but it was a deep wound and Tomassoni bled to death.

Caravaggio fled Rome to avoid conviction and death himself. The Tomassoni family was well connected politically and declined an offer to settle financially. Due to his flight, Caravaggio was pronounced guilty and condemned to death. The sentence was Bando Capitale which means that anyone encountering him had a right to kill him and claim a reward by severing his head as proof.

David with the Head of Goliath was Caravaggio's way of artistically rendereing his plight. He portrayed an agile young man with his head in order to claim a bounty. He lived out his final days in exhile hiding from his actions. He spent time on Malta and in Naples. On Caravaggio's way back to Rome to meet with Cardinal Borghese regarding the bounty on his head, he was murdered.

The letter HOCS on the sword mean, "Humilitas Occidat Superbiam." That is 'humanity kills pride' in Latin.

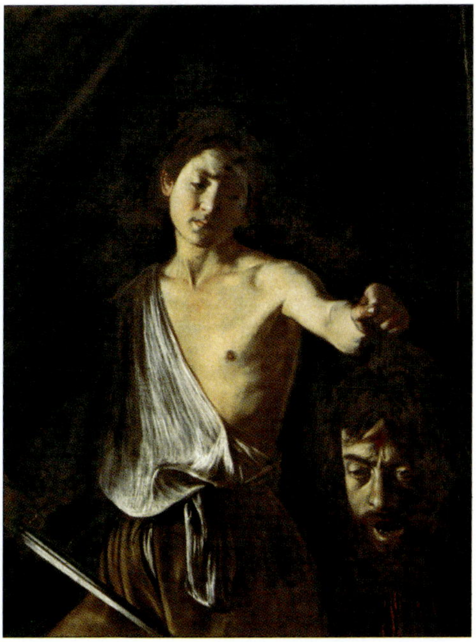

49 ▪ Raphael Sanzio

Entombment – a.k.a. Deposition

Borghese Gallery

Raphael signed the work on the rock below the bearer of Christ's upper body. The beautiful work was destined for San Francesco al Prato in Perugia.

It was commissioned by Atalanta Baglioni. Her son Grifonetto was murdered by a blood relative at her doorstep to gain control of Perugia. Her son's killer was murdered a short time later. The painting represents the pain of a bereaved mother at the loss of a child. In this case, Atalanta Baglioni likens her loss to that of the Virgin Mary. In the righthand corner Mary has fainted, imitating Christ's Passion on the Cross as Christ himself is carried to His tomb.

This work was highly sought after. It was secretly purchased from Perugia by Pope Paul V. In 1608, the Pope gifted it to his nephew Cardinal Scipione Borghese.

The men carrying Christ strain under His weight. While Mary Magdalene moves toward Christ and the Virgin Mary faints in the background. In the distant right corner the Cross is still standing. This work was one of the first to step away from the concept that a painting had to have a single focus.

Some art historians feel that this painting is forced with the individuals that make up the scene all operating independently without cohesiveness. Do you feel the figures are stifly posed? Are they unnatural?

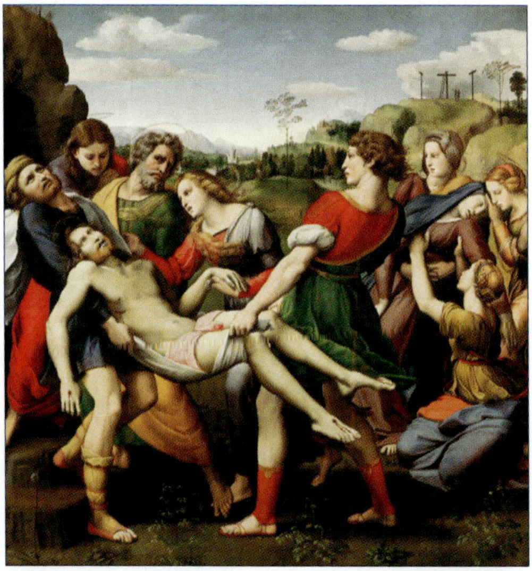

Giorgio Vasari in his Lives of the Artists writes:

"How generous and kind Heaven sometimes proves to be when it brings together in a single person the boundless riches of its treasures and all those graces and rare gifts that over a period of time are usually divided among many individuals can clearly be seen in the no less excellent than gracious Raphael Sanzio of Urbino."

50 ▪ Titian – a.ka. Tiziano Vecellio

Sacred and Profane Love Borghese Gallery

This painting was created to celebrate the marriage of Nicolo Aurelio and Laura Bagarotto. Aurelio's coat of arms can be found on the sarcophagus. The crest of Ms. Bagarotto can be found in the silver bowl resting on the sarcophagus.

The seductive scene places two loves in the same frame. One love is dressed representing celestial love, profane love. The clothing represents a fleeting life on earth appealling to our human senses. The love on the right with no clothing represents sacred love. The love of the heavens. She bears the eternal flame of God's love.

The floral wreath in the hair and on the lap of the dressed celestial love is symbolic of fertility. She is surrounded by emblems of fecundity. The stallion on the sarcophagus and the rabbit on the left side of the painting come together to express the purpose of marriage, of earthly love.

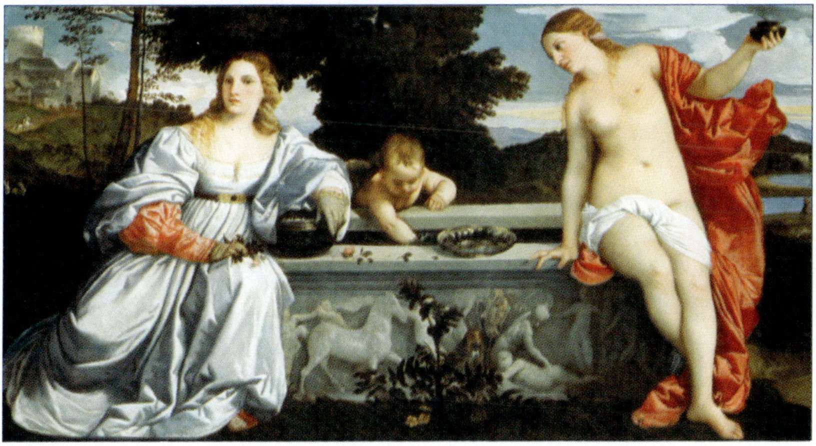

51 ▪ Gian Lorenzo Bernini
Fontana della Barcaccia & the Spanish Steps

Fontana Barcaccia

In 1626 Pietro Bernini designed a new fountain for Piazza di Spagna. Pietro was the father of the famous Roman Baroque sculptor Gian Lorenzo Bernini. On the day the last payment for the fountain was received Pietro Bernini passed away. In his stead, Gian Lorenzo carried the family name and honor by continuing his father's work as engineer, architect, and sculptor. Using his father's design Gian Lorenzo crafted the beautiful fountain at the base of the most famous steps in the world. The fountain's design is that of ship. It's prow and poop are identical. The ship is slightly lower than the pavement. It was designed in this way to accomodate the low water pressure in this area of Rome.

The bees on the fountain are the symbols of the Barberini family. At the time of the fountains creation Pope Urban VIII was the Vicor of Christ.

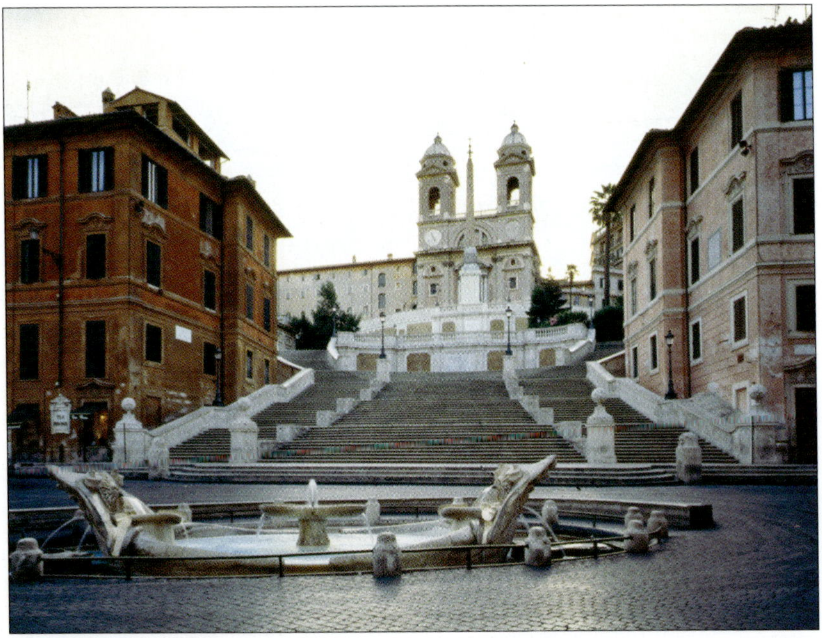

Spanish Steps

The Spanish Steps are so named bacause of their proximity to the Spanish Embassy to the Vatican located near the piazza. The stairs are a beautiful Baroque. France's King Louis XV financed the project. The steps are beautiful when the Azaleas bloom. They are also a great place to relax and let the evening pass you by while you enjoy the throngs of tourists and locals who make a night of relaxing on the steps.

52 ▪ Trevi Fountain *Fontana di Trevi*

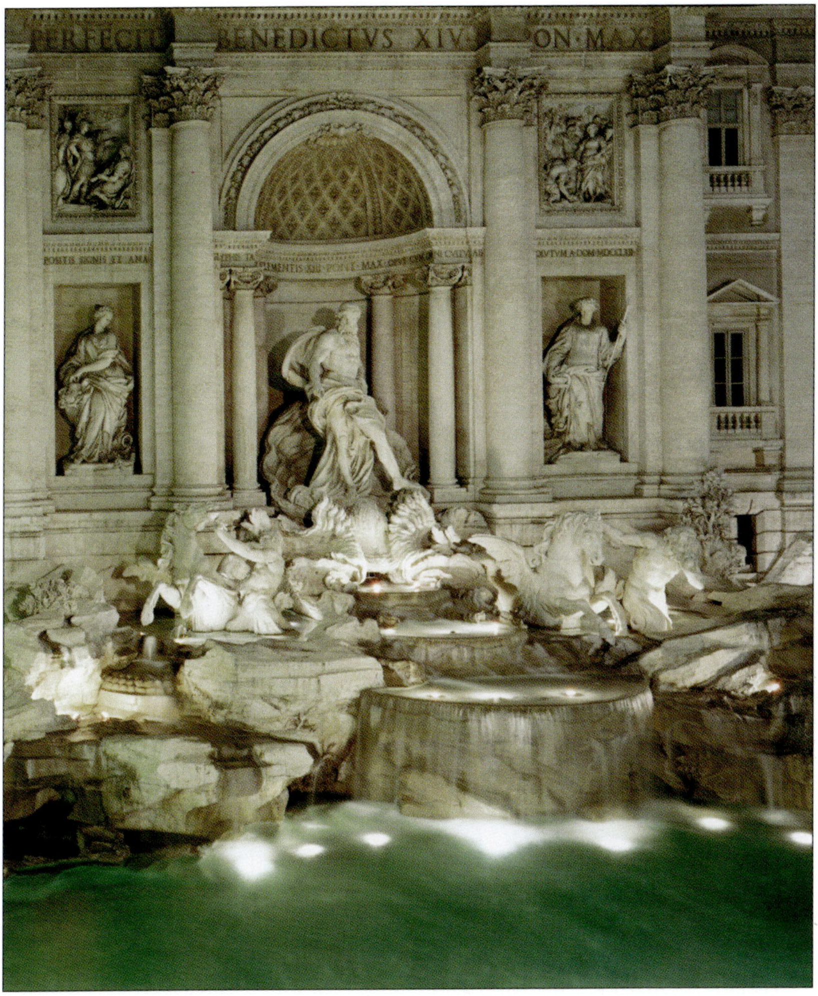

The Trevi Fountain is one of the most beautiful fountains in the world. The sculpture in the basin is Ocean riding a shell-shaped carriage drawn by sea horses. The sea horses are ridden by Tritons. The interpretation of the scene is how the Gods tamed the ocean and gave it to man. At the top of the fountain in the niches are two scenes. On the right, the virgin Salubrity indicating to the Roman soldiers the spring that feeds the fountain. On the left is Abundance, surmounted by Agrippa approving the design of the aqueduct to take water from the spring that feeds the fountain.

Trevi Fountain earned its name through slang Italian. The word for three streets is tre vie. The fountain takes its name from the intersection of the three streets that come together where the fountain was built.

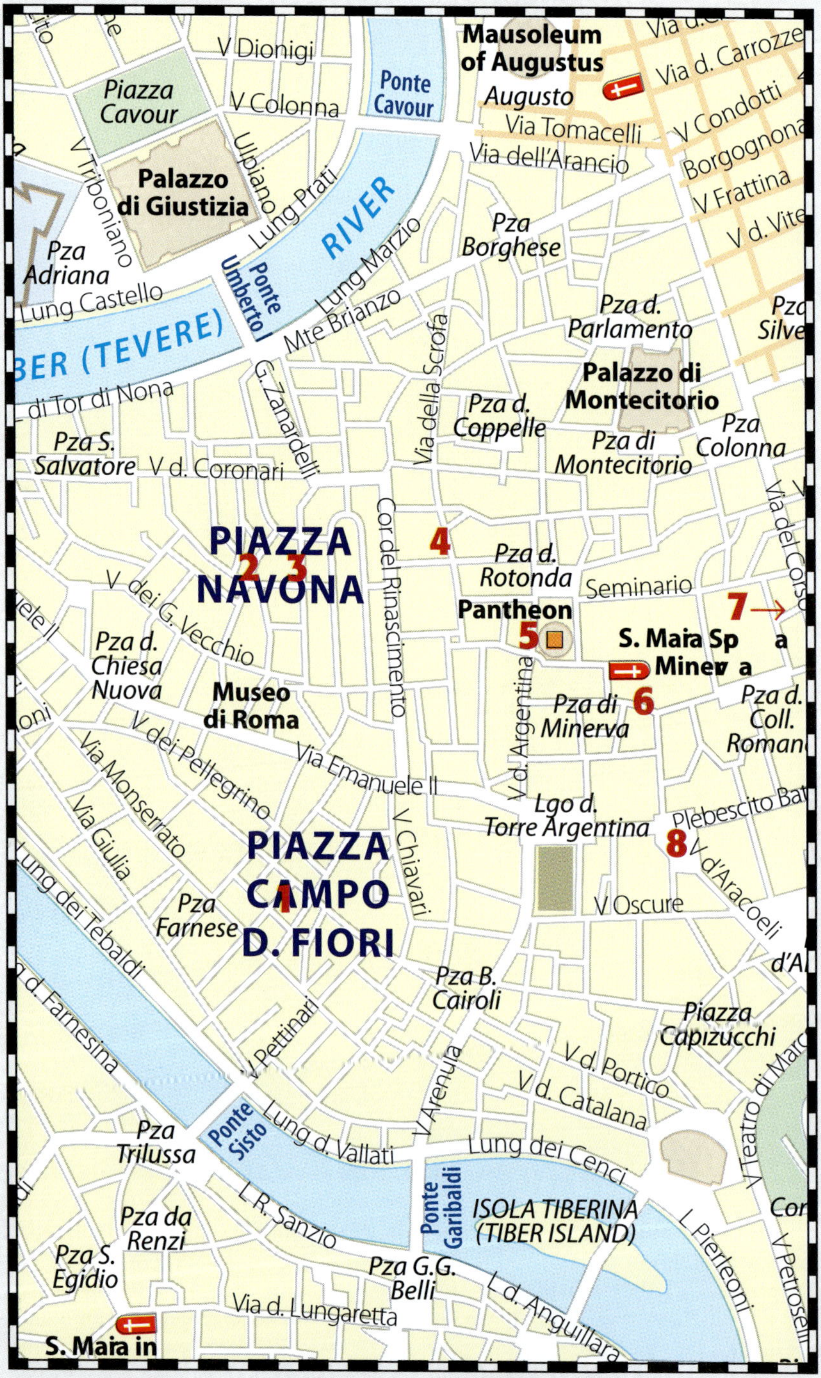

1. Giordano Bruno in Campo di Fiori
2. Piazza Navona: Rome
3. Fountain of Four Rivers
4. San Luigi dei Francesi
5. Pantheon
6. Santa Maria Over Minerva
7. Saint Ignazio
8. Il Gesu

NAVONA PANTHEON

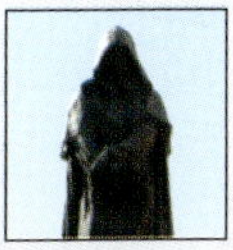

Site		Mon	Tue	Wed	Thur	Fri	Sat	Sun
Palazzo Farnese Servizio Culturale French Embassy Piazza Farnese 67, 00186 Rome Now the French Embassy you must write for entry permission to view the inside. Then call to receive your scheduled visit time at 06 / 686011	AM PM	By appointment only to view inside ceiling 24 x 7 to view exterior						
Campo dei Fiori Square where Via del Pellegrino, Via Giubbonari, Vei dei Baullari, and Piazza della Cancellaria. No tickets necessrary. Outdoor, 24 x 7 viewing	AM PM	Market open Monday through Saturday from 8:00 to 1:00 The piazza is busy throughout the day and night						
Giordano Bruno Square where Via del Pellegrino, Via Giubbonari, Vei dei Baullari, and Piaaza della Cancellaria. Statue in Campo dei Fiori No tickets necessary. Outdoor, 24 x 7 viewing	AM PM	24 x 7						
San Luigi dei Francesi Piazza San Luigi dei Francesi No tickets necessary Free Admission	AM	8:30 to 12:30	8:30 to 12:30	8:30 to 12:30	8:30 to 12:30	8:30 to 12:30	8:30 to 12:30	8:30 to 12:30
	PM	3:30 to 5:00	3:30 to 5:00	3:30 to 5:00	X	3:30 to 5:00	3:30 to 5:00	3:30 to 5:00

Site		Mon	Tue	Wed	Thur	Fri	Sat	Sun
Pantheon Piazza della Rotonda No tickets necessary. Free Admission	AM / PM	8:30 to 7:30	8:30 to 7:30	8:30 to 7:30	8:30 to 7:30	8:30 to 7:30	8:30 to 7:30	9:00 to 6:00
Santa Maria Sopra Minerva Piazza della Minerva No tickets necessary. Free Admission	AM / PM	7:30 to 7:00	7:30 to 7:00	7:30 to 7:00	7:30 to 7:00	7:30 to 7:00	7:30 to 7:00	7:30 to 7:00
Sant'Ignazio Piazza Sant'Ignazio No tickets necessary Free Admission	AM	7:30 to 12:30	7:30 to 12:30	7:30 to 12:30	7:30 to 12:30	7:30 to 12:30	7:30 to 12:30	7:30 to 12:30
	PM	4:00 to 7:15	4:00 to 7:15	4:00 to 7:15	4:00 to 7:15	4:00 to 7:15	4:00 to 7:15	4:00 to 7:15
il Gesu Piazza del Gesu No tickets necessary Free Admission	AM	7:00 to 12:00	7:00 to 12:00	7:00 to 12:00	7:00 to 12:00	7:00 to 12:00	7:00 to 12:00	7:00 to 12:00
	PM	4:00 to 7:00	4:00 to 7:00	4:00 to 7:00	4:00 to 7:00	4:00 to 7:00	4:00 to 7:00	4:00 to 7:00

X = Closed

53 ▪ Giordano Bruno in Campo di Fiori

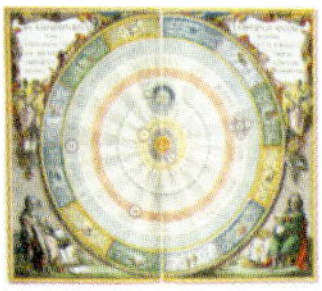

Giordano Bruno was burned at the stake on Feberuary 17, 1600 in Campo dei Fiori for denying the Holy Trinity (Father, Son, and Holy Spirit).

He was born in Naples and went to school at the Monestary of Saint Domenicas. This was the same school where Saint Thomas Acquinas taught. He joined the Domenican Order then, without explanation, broke his vow and fled Italy.

Giordano Bruno wrote 20 books and traveled throughout Europe, preaching. He supported the Copernican theory of a heliocentric universe. Bruno preached a philosphy that made the mysteries of the Virgin Mary, the crucifixion, and the church meaningless. He believed the Bible was a book only the naive could take literally. This was a very serious position in 1600. He coined the phrase, "Libertes Philosphica." (The right to think freely) Throughout his travels, Bruno held audiences with Queen Elizabeth of England and King Henry III of France. He worked to make known his position and gave little thought of appeasing the powers of the Church or any Royal House.

After years of travel, he came back to Italy hoping to take the position as the chair of mathmatics at the University of Padua. He was not given the position. While he was in Venice he was arrested and extradited back to Rome. In Rome, he was imprisoned for seven years but refused to recant his heretical religious position regarding the Holy Trinity.

He was ultimately sentenced and charged by the Grand Inquisitor in Rome. Bruno answered the sentence of death by fire with, "perhaps you, my judges, pronounce this sentence against me with greater fear than I receive it."

As he burned at the stake he was offered a crucifix. He scornfully pushed it away.

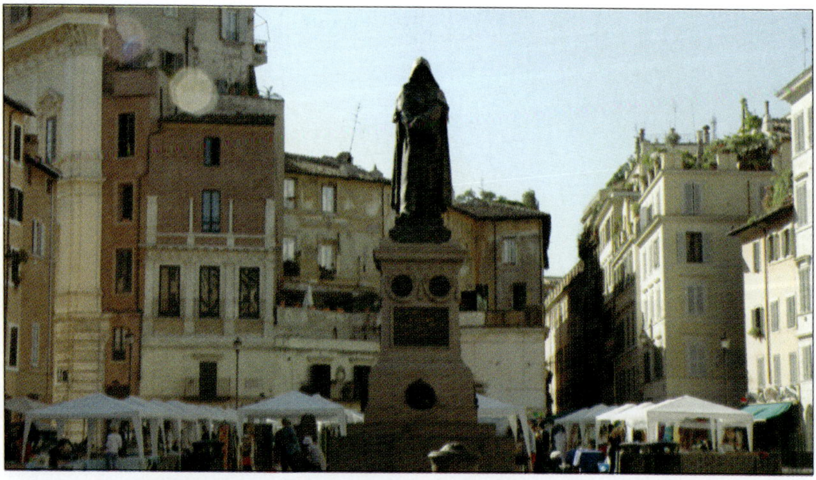

- He was born five years after Copernicus died.
- Galileo was given the position as the chair of mathmatics at the University of Padua in 1592

54 ▪ Piazza Navona

This is one of the most beautiful Piazzas in all of Italy. It brings forth all that we hope to see in Bell'Italia. You will find cafes, street vendors, beautiful buildings, wonderful restaurants, and three incredible fountains.

As you stand in the Piazza you will notice that the buildings on the perimeter create an oval. Piazza Navona stands over the ruins of Domitian's circus. Domitian was an emperor of the Roman Empire. The ancient Romans would come to Domitian's circus to watch chariot races and other forms of entertainment. You are literally standing in the center of the facility where the athletes and horses would run during a race. The fountains on the end of either side of the piazza mark the spot where the charioteers would turn to continue down the other side of the track.

The fountain you see in the center of Piazza Navona was created by Gian Lorenzo Bernini and is called Fontana dei Quattro Fiumi. In English that means the fountain of the four rivers. The church on the piazza is called Sant'Agnese in Agone.

The piazza is as lively in the evening as during the day. After your dinner bring a bottle of wine and enjoy the show. Or grab a gelato and enjoy a bella passegiatta.

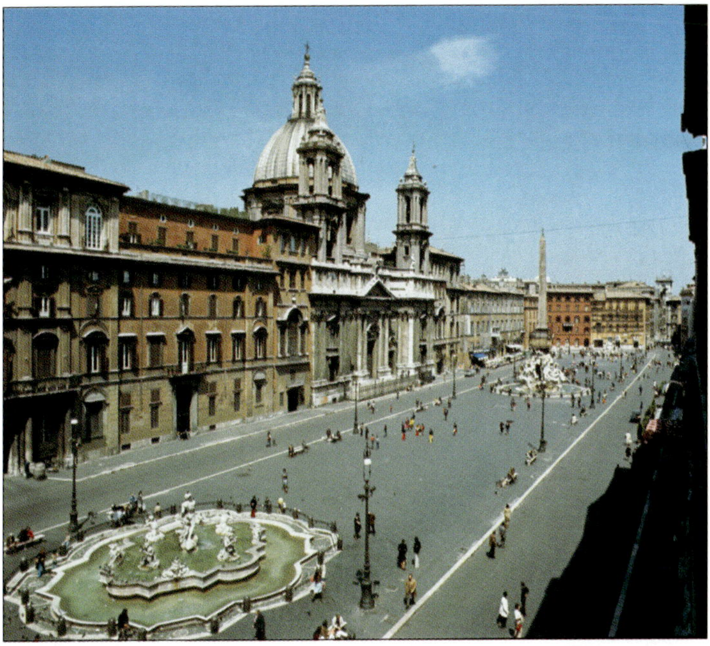

▪ The two fountains at either end of Piazza Navona are named Fontana di Nettuno and Fontana del Moro. Fontana de Nettuno is the fountain with Neptune striking down with his trident. The Fontana del Moro is the one with the figure blowing into the shell.

55 ▪ Fountain of Four Rivers

Fontana dei Quattro Fiumi: Roma

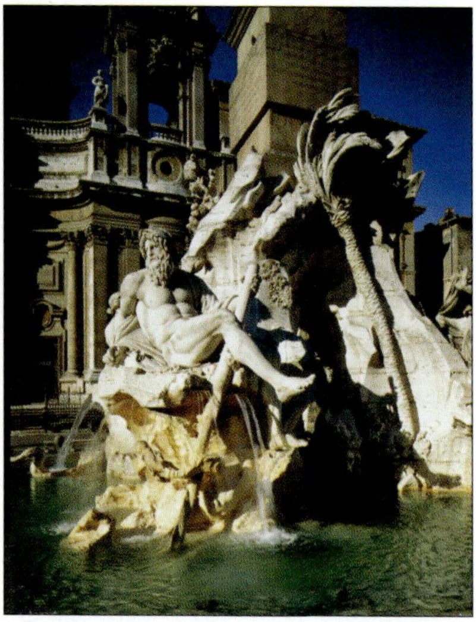

La Fontana dei Quattro Fiumi was created by Gian Lorenzo Bernini for Pope Innocent X. The fountain was unveiled to Rome in 1651. The Pope's coat of arms, the dove and olive branch, decorate the pyramid rock formation supporting the ancient Egyption Obelisk. The obelisk once stood in the Circus Maxentius on the Appian Way.

The fountain represents the four great rivers of the world - the Ganges (India), the Danube (Germany-Romania), the Nile (Egypt), and the Plate (Argentina - Uraguay).

The figure representing the Nile River is veiled to indicate that the river's source was unknown. The Plate river is represented by the figure leaning back with his hand in the air. One of Bernini's rivals designed the Church Saint Agnese in Agone and Bernini illustrates for all to see his dislike of the design and his rival through the fear and repulsion in the figure representing the river Plate. It is also thought to represent Bernini's fear of the Catholic Church collapsing. You decide which theory is plausible. The Danube is represented by the figure holding the shaft. Finally, the remaining figure represents the Ganges.

Rome is a city of beautiful fountains. Bernini is largely responsible for this. Water plays a large role in the history of Rome as far back as the Ancient Empire and her Emperors. The Emperors and Popes all thought water symbolized their ability to harness nature, and in so doing bring, life and better living to Rome's citizens. Each fountain represents the patrons ability to successfully harness nature thus illustrating his power. While water was fundamental to the development of Rome, the city has a two-sided relationship with the element. Through Rome's aqueducts and fountains nature was harnessed and her citizens cleaned and quenched. But, water proved to be her Achilles heel. When the barbarians from the North stormed Rome all they did was knock out sections of her aqueducts and Rome was shortly conquered. The ancients referred to Rome as Regina Aquarum which means Queen of Waters.

56 ▪ Michelangelo Merisi Caravaggio

Calling of Saint Matthew

San Luigi dei Francesi • Contarelli chapel

These two beautiful paintings depicting the images of the Calling of Saint Matthew and his Martydom were created by Caravaggio for the Jubillee of 1600 under Pope Clement VIII. The Jubilee would draw over one million holy pilgrims to the new Jerusalem. These works would be Caravaggio's first public commission. The content of the work was decided by the late French Cardinal Matthieu Cointrel (Contarelli in Italian). The Cardinal left a large financial gift to the church with clear instruction that Saint Matthew, his patron saint, was to decorate the walls of his new chapel in the National French church in Rome. Cardinal Contarelli wished the works to be done in fresco for its durability, but Caravaggio would have been unable to utilize his stylistic use of contrasting light and dark so he was given license to choose the medium. He chose oil on canvas.

Caravaggio capitalized on the low light of the chapel. Viewers were plunged into the scene being pulled into the darkness. The vibrant light illuminating Matthew in both scenes seems to select the viewer as well.

The scenes illustrate Saint Matthew's passage from mortality to immortality.

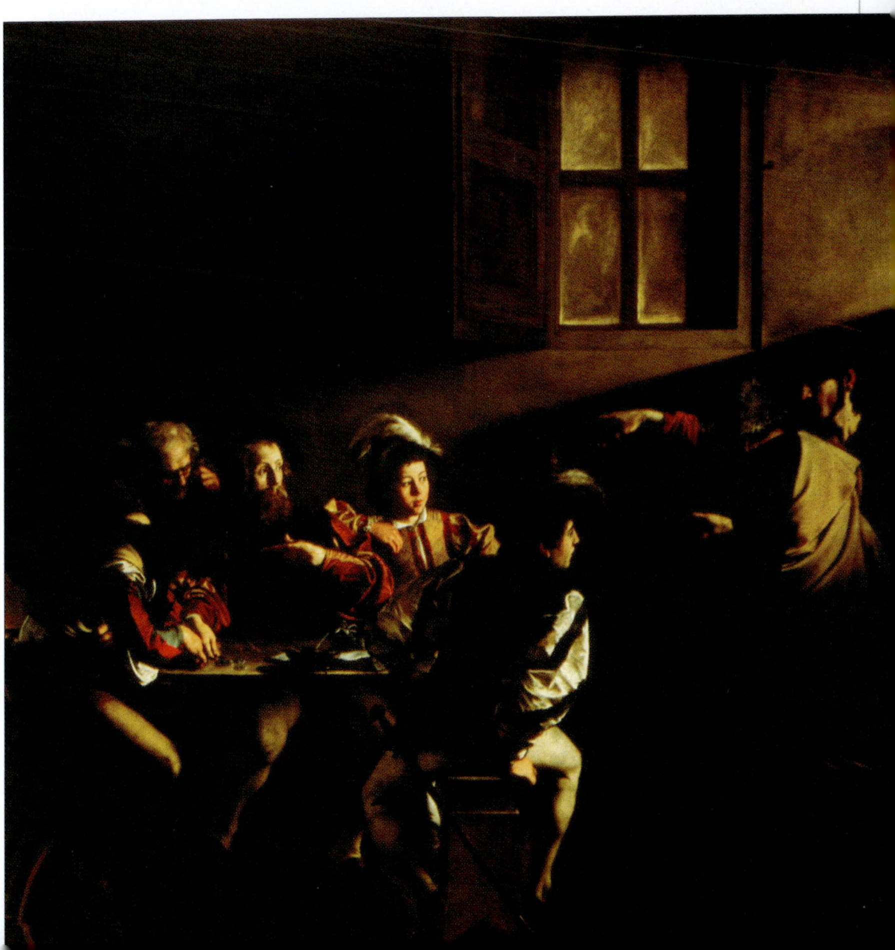

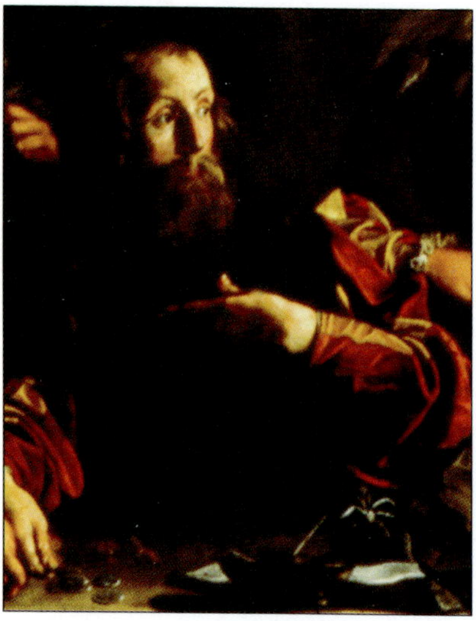

The Calling of Saint Matthew

The Calling is a peaceful scene; calm in its delivery. Levi (Saint Matthew's name before being called by Jesus) points to himself, seemingly confused by the calling.

Jesus points to Levi from the extreme right of the scene. The hand of Jesus takes the form of the hand of Adam in Michelangelo's Creation of Adam in the Sistine Chapel. Jesus has a slight halo.

His hand is just under the window and the heavenly light. The light is the connection between Jesus, Levi, and the duty that Jesus asks of him.

The confusion of Levi must come from the fact that he is a wealthy tax collector and sinner. Jesus finds him at a table counting the collected money for the day and with a simple "follow me" all for Levi was left behind as he becomes Saint Matthew.

This is a typical drama examined by Caravaggio - who would be chosen by God and why? How will one know when they are being called or tested? Who is worthy of selection?

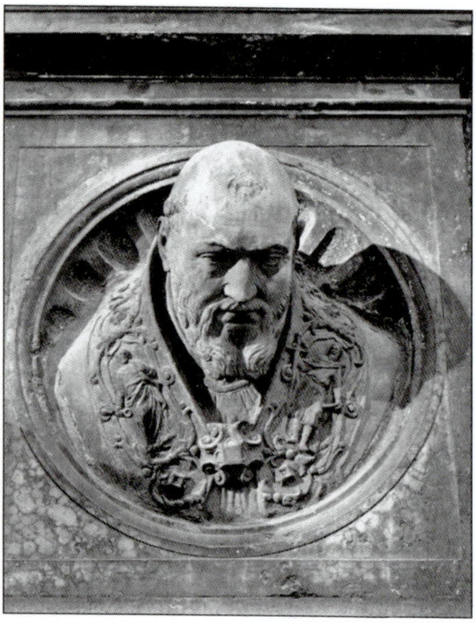

Clement VIII, 1536-1605

Pope during the Jubilee year of 1600 that initiated the work to be done on the Contarelli Chapel of San Luigi dei Francesi. Pope Clement VIII was the fourth Pope elected within the space of one year and four months. The three previous popes died due to illness.

He was an austere Pope. Though he suffered from the gout. Every month he traveled on foot to the seven pilgrimage churches of Rome. However, he was big on conspicous consumption and was extraordinarily nepotonistic. He named three of his nephews to the College of Cardinals and turned the affairs of the church over to them almost exclusively. One of his appointed nephews was only 14.

Pope Clement was a staunch supporter of the Council of Trent, revised many liturgical books, added many books to the Index of Forbidden Books banning all Jewish texts. He increased the severity of the Inquisition. During his pontificate, he sent more than 30 people to burn at the stake. His most famous victom is the immortalized Dominican Philosopher Giordano Bruno who was burned at the stake in Campo dei Fiori. A statue still stands on the spot he was executed in 1600.

57 ▪ Michelangelo Merisi Caravaggio

Martydom of Saint Matthew

San Luigi dei Francesi • Contarelli chapel

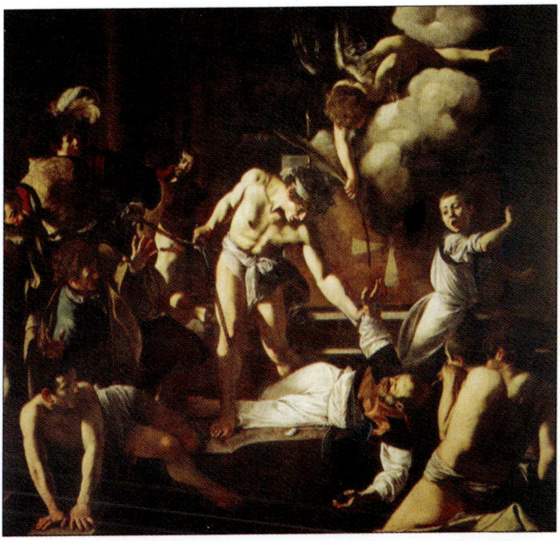

The Martydom of Saint Matthew is chaotic. Saint Matthew seems to be the only calm person in the entire scene while he is bathed in God's light. It is shattered over the others in the scene. They almost seem to run from it.

Saint Matthew was martyred while celebrating mass in a church in Ethiopia. King Hirtacus, incensed at the Apostle, because the King was to wed the virgin Ephigenia, sent a swordsman to stab him in the back. The swordsman stabbed him at the alter while Saint Matthew was performing a baptism. The stabbing taking place at a baptism however was the choice of the artist. The Bible does not have the event taking place during a baptism. Baptism of the old church was full immersion, explaining the lightly clad assembly. The dressed assembly in the scene wear contemporary Roman garb of Caravaggio's day. The contemporary clothing of Rome is also worn in the Calling of Saint Matthew.

In the center of the scene is the assassin holding onto Saint Matthew's wrist to finish off his work. Already stabbed and bleeding, Saint Matthew glances towards the angel passing the Martyr's Palm of Victory to the Saint. Saint Matthew's hand, as it is pulled by the assassin, reaches for the palm and simultaneously makes spiritual contact with the Cross on the altar. Saint Matthew also takes the form of Christ on the Cross. These are all signs of salvation.

- A Jubilee Year is once every 50 years. The holy door in each of the 4 major basilicas in Rome are opened. The Pope uses a silver hammer and hits each door three times. It falls open and the pilgrims walk through the door of redemption. The four basilicas are: St. Peter's, St. Paul's, St. John Lateran, and Santa Maria Maggiore.Holy Pilgrims are required to visit each of the four basilicas during Jubilee years.

Map of San Luigi dei Francesi showing Contarelli Chapel

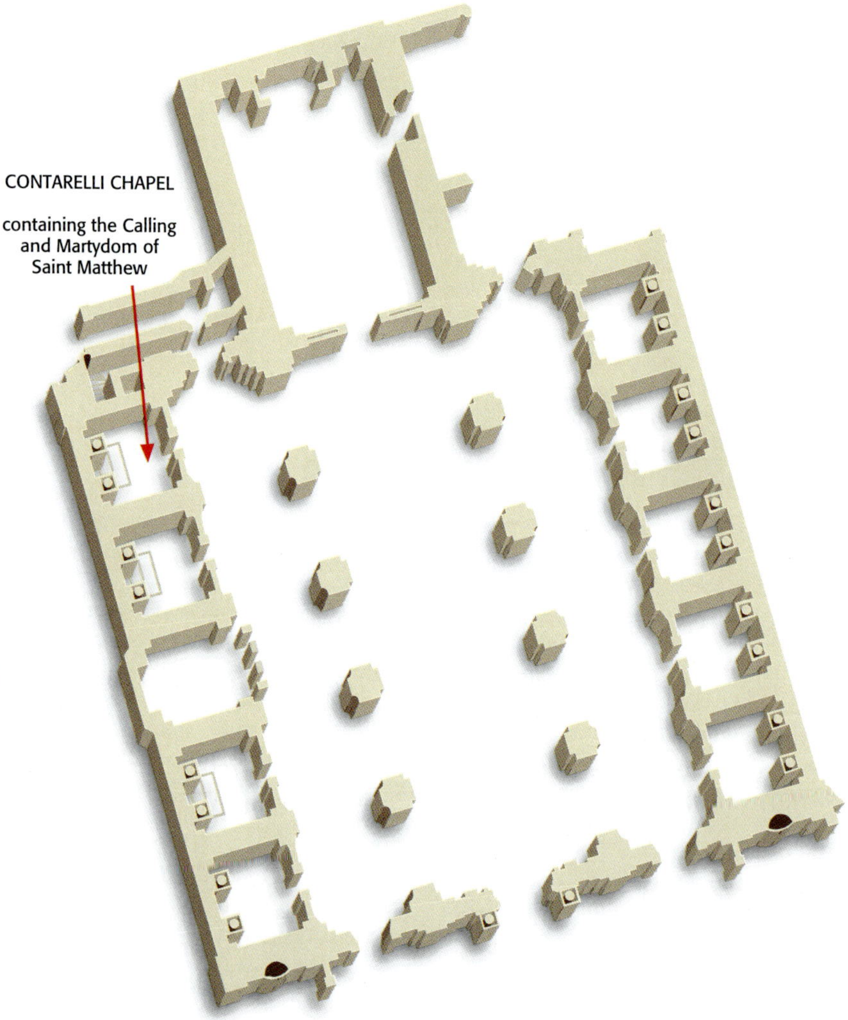

58 ■ Pantheon

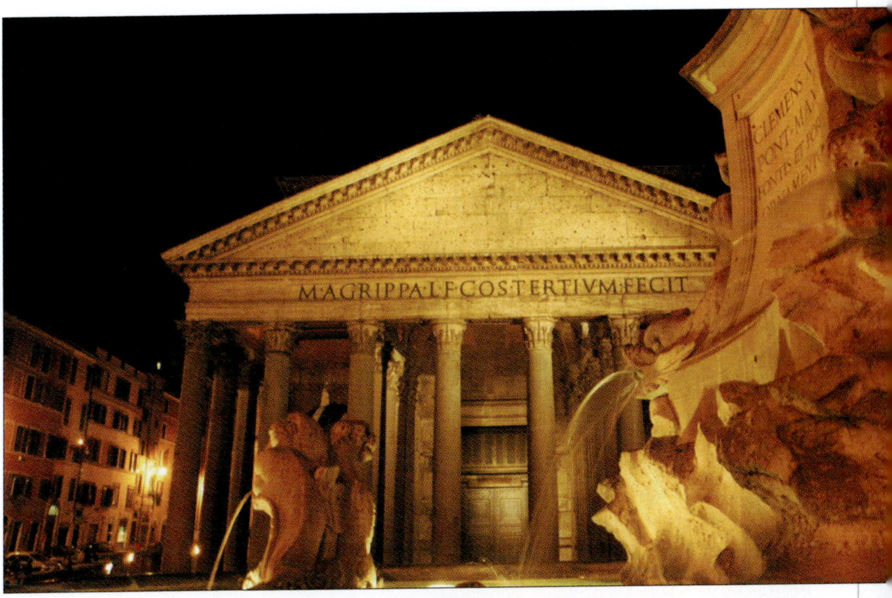

M·AGRIPPA·L·F·COS·TERTIVM·FECIT

Marcus • Agrippa • Luci • Filius • Consul • Tertrium • Fecit
Marcus • Agrippa • Son Of Lucius • In His Third Consulate • Made It

This onetime pagan temple is the best preserved monument of imperial Rome.

The reason for the Pantheon remaining intact is that it was consecrated as a church in AD 608. The building did, however, receive its share of plundering. In 655 AD, the gilded bronze covering the dome was stripped. Then in the 17th century, Pope Urban VIII removed the bronze beams of the portico using the bronze to produce the Baldacchino that covers the high altar in Saint Peter's Basilica.

Raphael Santi of Urbino is buried here. Raphael was one of the most beloved artists the Renaissance had ever known. He decorated the walls of Pope Julius II's library in the Vatican with some of his most famous works named, The School of Athens and The Disputa. The rooms now bear his name. Over his tomb it reads, "Here lies Raphael. While he lived, Mother Nature feared to be outdone; and when he died, she feared to die with him."

The columns in the front are carved from single slabs and were shipped by barge to Rome from Egypt. Each column was cut to measure at different times and each column takes four or more people to hold hands to touch at the base. The marble decorations inside are built by cutting a marble slab in half to create a mirror image, it is then polished and placed on the floor, or wall, as decoration. Think of the engineering and architectrual accomplishment of the ancients.

The oculus at the top is 30 feet across and is the only light source. The dome is 142 in diameter and 142 feet from the floor. The domes weight is lessened by its coffered ceiling.

The dome of the Pantheon was the largest ever built until 1960. The diameter of the dome is exactly equal to its height.

59 ▪ Santa Maria Sopra Minerva *Santa Maria Over Minerva*

Risen Christ

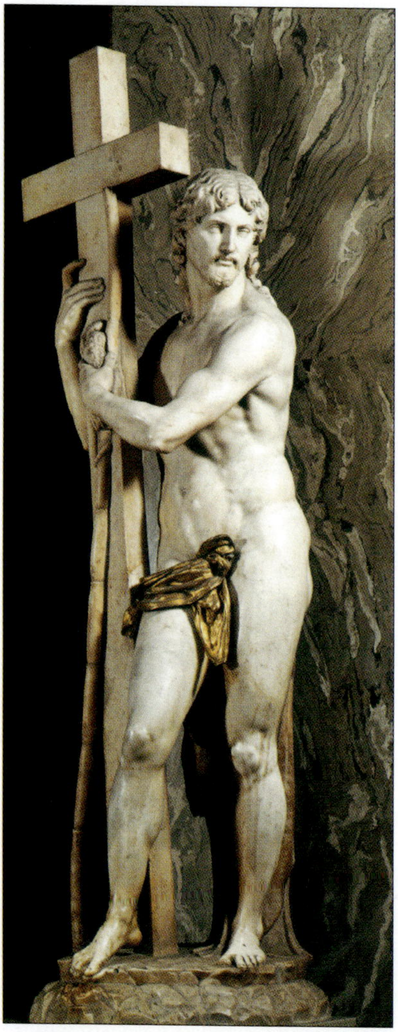

Two of the best sculptors the world has ever known have graced this church with their art.

The obelisk in front comes from the Roman artist Gian Lorenzo Bernini. Bernini is the artist who created the fountain in the center of Piazza Navona, and countless other masterpeices throughout Rome. The obelisk is set atop an elephant in the Piazza in front of the church. The obelisk comes from ancient Egypt and is inscribed with original hieroglyphics.

Michelangelo sculpted the Risen Christ set at the alter. The church is worth a visit to see a Michelangelo many people don't even know exists. It is only a few steps away from the Pantheon and will provide you with a look at the work of Michelangelo without the throngs of people you would encounter in front of his other, more famous, creations.

The church takes its name, Santa Maria Sopra Minerva, from the fact that the church is literally built over a pagan temple to Minerva. Minerva to the Romans was Athena to the Greeks. She was the patron Goddess of intelligence, meditation, defensive war, and inventiveness.

The church is one of the few Gothic churches in Rome. It was erected by the Dominican Order in 1280.

The church is also the burial site of the priest and artist Fra Angelico.

60 Fra Andrea Pozzo

Glorification of Saint Ignatius Saint Ignazio

One of the most beautiful ceilings in Rome, Fra Andrea Pozzo created his masterpiece in Sant Ignazio from 1691 - 1694. It is one of the finest illustrations on the use of perspective in the world. As you gaze at the work you feel as if you are being lifted into Heaven.

Like the ceiling at Gesu the work is created using the architecture of the church. Where the wall and ceiling meet, so begins the painting. It appears as if God peeled off the roof to give the faithful church-goers a glimpse of Heaven. Saint Ignazio is of the Jesuit order and was decorated during the counter-reformation in the Baroque style.

Fra Andrea Pozzo was so proficient at the use of perspective he wrote a treatise on the subject. Using his expertise he left nothing to chance. He placed a disk in the nave floor to mark the exact spot one should stand to enjoy the entire work and the illusion created through perspective. As you stand on the mark on the floor you are simultaneously on earth and in Heaven. As Paradise mingles with the terrestrial plane, you view Saint Ignatius being carried into Heaven as Christ awaits. The four corners of the world are included: America, Europe, Asia, Africa. Baroque art is meant to touch you visually, spiritually, and emotionally. It is theatrical in its delivery. Combining sculpture, architecture, and painting with the sound of music creates a harmony that provides a sensory overload. Baroque churches were built with acoustics in mind to utilize sound and art in order to bring the faithful that much closer to God.

Take time to view the individuals that combine to make this ceiling beautiful. The Cross, Jesus, the Angels, the Golden shine of Heaven, the amazing colors of the togas, the white of the Angel's wings, the painted columns that look as if they truly continue into Heaven from the church. In its "busyness" you will find a calming effect. In its openess you will feel as if you are being escorted into Heaven by an angel yourself. I have added a track of music to the end of this audio component. It will allow you to hear the music, view the work, and for a moment appreciate the masterpiece as Pozzo intended. Move to the disc on the floor and prepare to be escorted into Heaven.

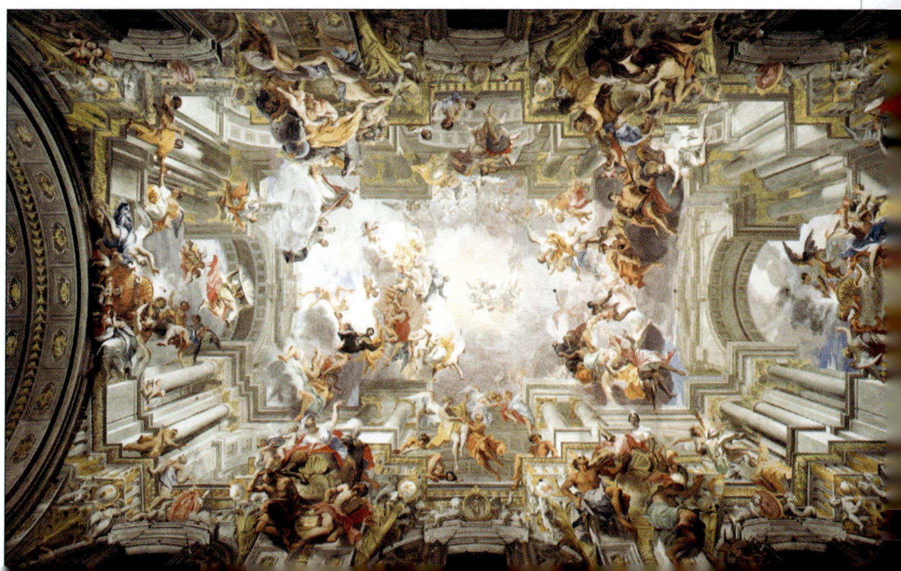

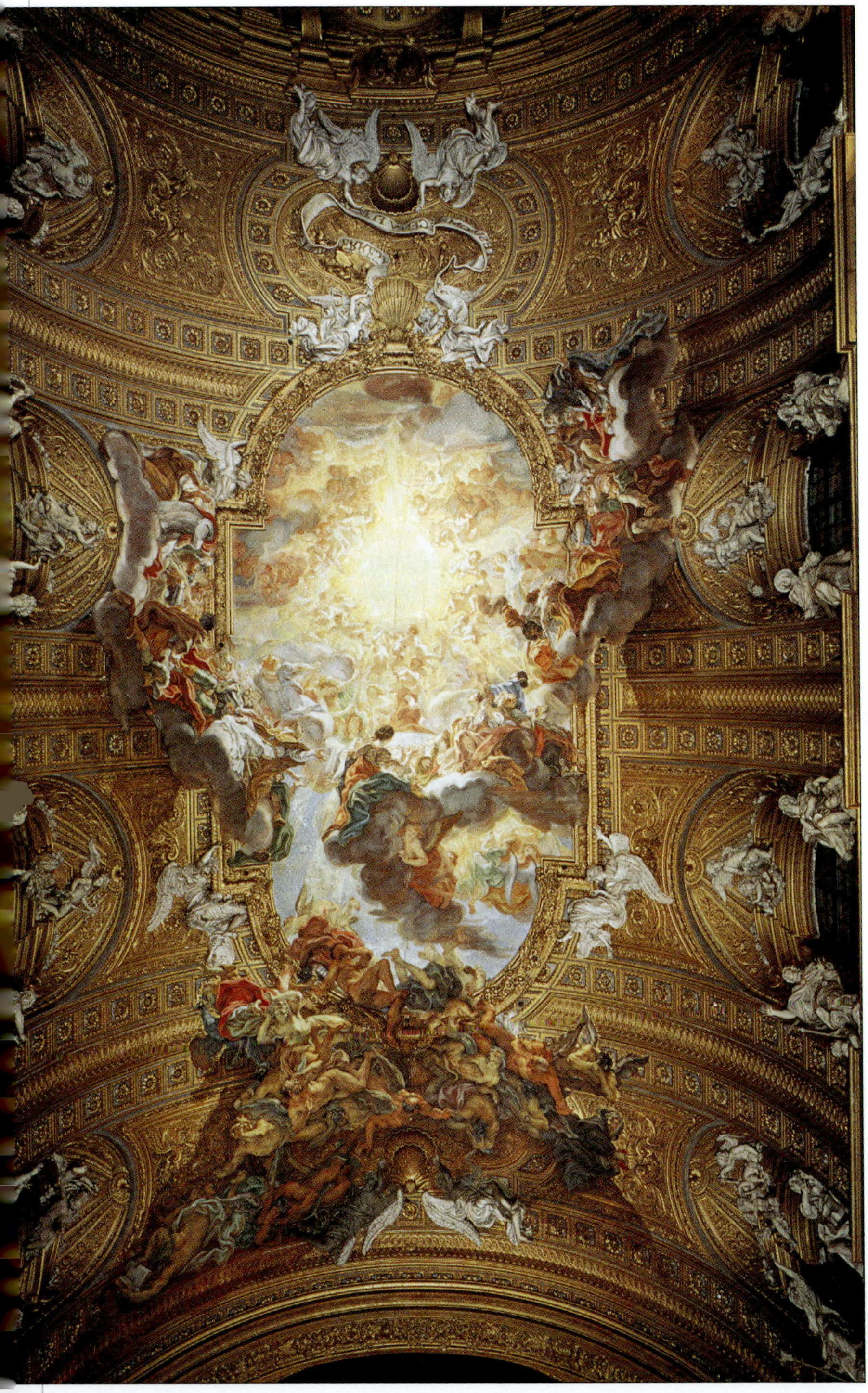

61 ▪ Giovanni Battista Gaulli

Triumph In The Name Of Jesus Il Gesu

The mother of Jesuit churches in Rome, Il Gesu is the prototype of all Counter-Reformation churches. Its architecture influenced ecclasiastical building in Rome for more than a century and was exported by the Jesuits throughout Europe. Though consecrated in 1584 the inside of the church wasn't decorated for 100 years or more. The original intention was that the interior be left plain to the point of austerity, but when it was finally embellished no expense was spared. For sheer unadulterated grandeur no church in Rome, with the exception of Saint Peter's can compare.

The most striking element is the ceiling, covered with frescoes swirling down and merging with the painted stucco figures. The illusion of space in the two-dimensional painting becomes the reality of three-dimensions in the sculpted figures. The painted ceiling is known as the Triumph In The Name Of Jesus. The figures representing evil cast out of heaven are hurtling down onto the observer. The effects of the Baroque Art at Gesu have this concept in mind: Faithful Catholic worshipers will be uplifted into the heavens, while Protestants and heretics will be flung into hell fire. The goal of Baroque Art is to bring Passion and Worship through the eyes in direct conflict with the spartan decor of reformative Protestantism.

Church Authorities realized that such ceiling paintings offered perfect opportunities to impress on the viewers the Catholic Church's glory and power.

The visual effect created by Giovanni Battista Gaulli personifies the high emotion of the Baroque. The Gilded architecture opens up in the center of the ceiling to offer the worshipers a glimpse of Heaven. The artist represented Jesus as a barely visible monogram, IHS, in the blinding radiant light that floats Heavenward. In direct contrast, sinners are violently thrown back down to earth.

Gaulli created the magnificent ceiling from the year 1676 to 1679. The symbol of Jesus is placed in the light and made dificult to see so the viewers would have to seek Jesus, and Heaven, in the work as in life.

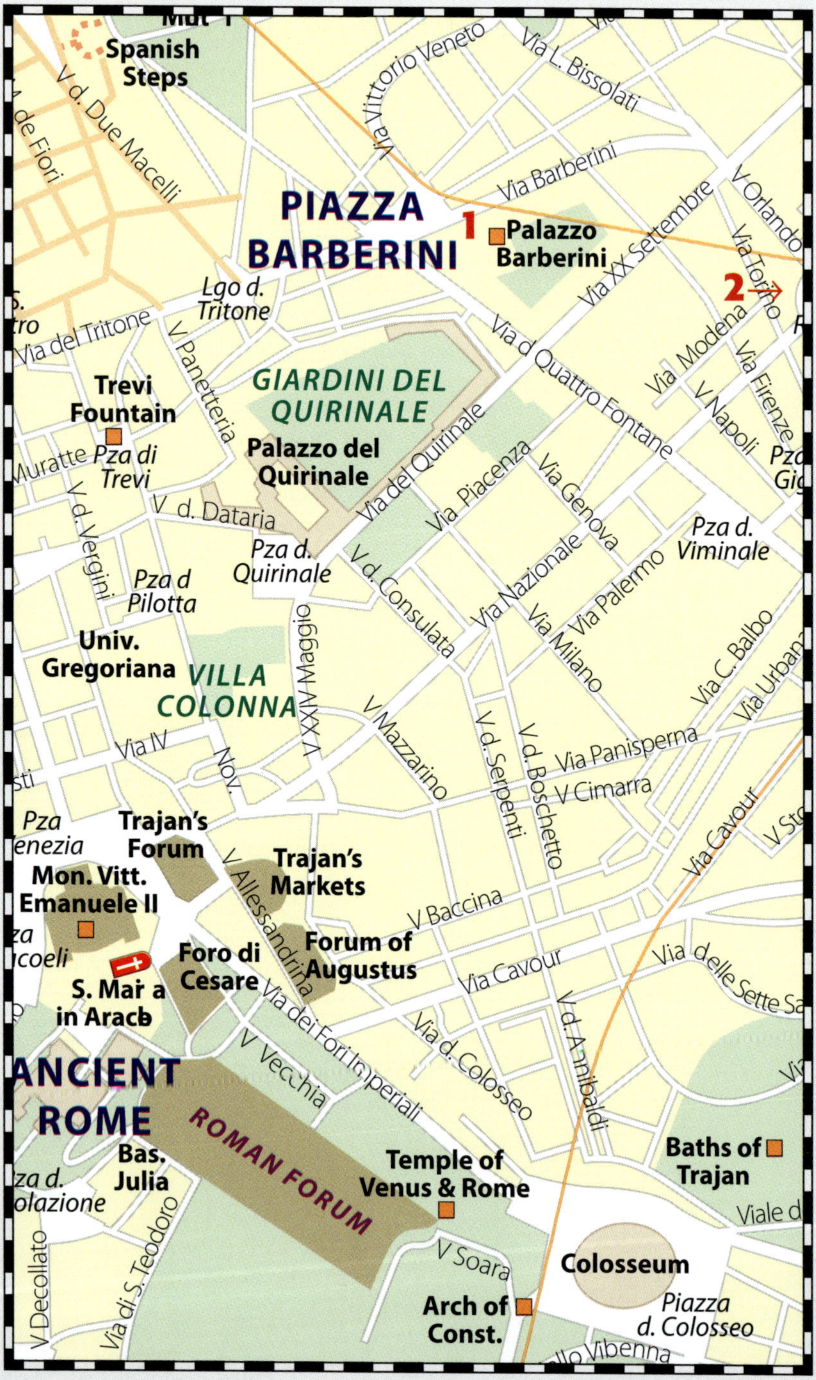

1. Palazzo Barberini
2. Santa Maria del Vittoria

BARBERINI

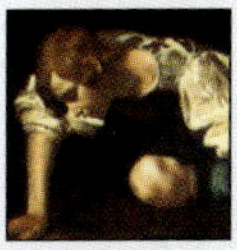

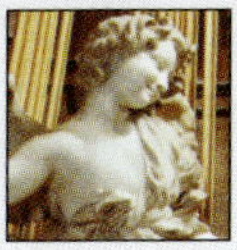

Site Hours, Daily Schedule, Address, Phone Numbers, and other important information

Site		Mon	Tue	Wed	Thur	Fri	Sat	Sun
Palazzo Barberini & Galleria Nazionale d'Arte Antico Via Barberini 18 www.galleriaborghese.it Buy tickets on-line at www.galleriaborghese.it website Ticket office closes thirty minutes before closing Closed December 25 & January 1 Reservations Recommended Adult Tickets are 6.03 Euro	AM PM	X	8:30 to 7:30	8:30 to 7:30	8:30 to 7:30	8:30 to 7:30	8:30 to 7:30	8:30 to 7:30
Santa Maria della Vittoria Via XX Settembre 17 No tickets necessary Free Admission	AM	8:30 to 11:00	8:30 to 11:00	8:30 to 11:00	8:30 to 11:00	8:30 to 11:00	8:30 to 11:00	X
	PM	3:30 to 6:00	3:30 to 6:00	3:30 to 6:00	3:30 to 6:00	3:30 to 6:00	3:30 to 6:00	3:30 to 6:00

X = Closed

62 ▪ Pietro da Cortona

Triumph of the Barbarini Gran Salon Ceiling

Galleria Nazionale d'Arte Antica di Palazzo Barberini

Barberini Gallery

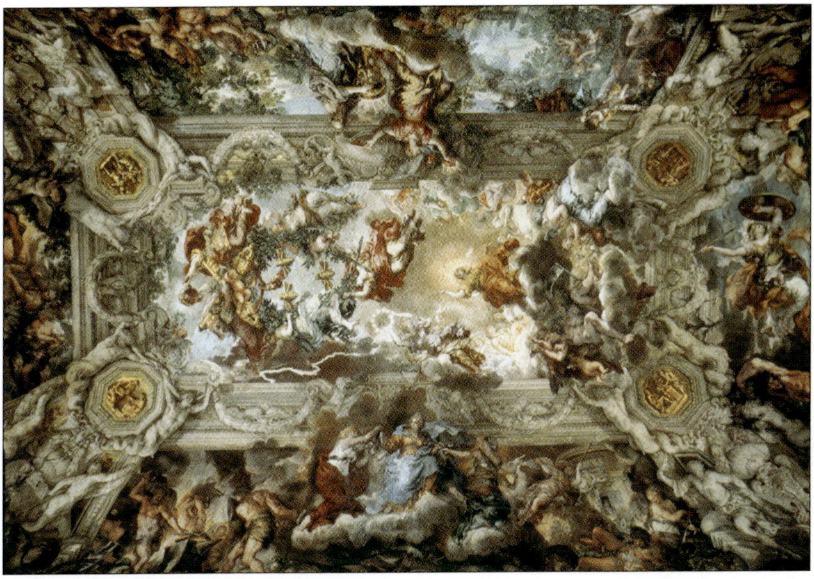

Maffei Barberini became Pope Urban VIII in 1623. In honor of his triumph, he built a beautiful palace for his family. The entire residence is gorgeous, but the Gran Salon is the most decorated. The ceiling is painted by Pietro da Cortona.

The Barberini palace is also home to many 13th - 16th century paintings by many of the world's great masters like El Greco, Filippo Lippi, Caravaggio, and Raphael. The Barberini Palace is also home to the National Gallery of Art.

Pietro da Cortona was a Tuscan painter. The Barberini family also hails from Tuscany. His work on the ceiling is breathtaking. It overwhelms the viewer with both a view of Heaven, and the glory of the Barberini family.

The fresco focuses on the accomplishments of the Barberini family. Divine Providence appears in a halo of light directing immortality with a halo of stars. The halo of stars reinforces the eternal grace of the Barberini family. The laurel wreath (another symbol of immortality) also aims at the legacy eternal of the Barberini. The bees are the symbol of the Barberini. The laurel wreath is supported by the virtues: Faith, Hope, and Charity, and floats around bees. The Papal Tiara and Keys of Saint Peter represent the Pontificate of Pope Urban VIII.

- Where you see bees on fountains or architecture of Rome you can be certain the Barberini family played a role. A perfect example is the fountain at the bottom of the Spanish Steps.
- Four of the most beautiful ceilings in Rome: Sistine Chapel, El Gesu, Saint Ignazio, and Palazzo Barberini.

63 ▪ Raphael Sanzio

La Farnarina

Galleria Nazionale d'Arte Antica di Palazzo Barberini
Barberini Gallery

One of Raphael's most proudly signed works, this exquisite portrait has his name across her left arm signifying his eternal possession of her. The name of the woman in the portait is Margherita Luti. She was a baker's daughter from Siena and was thought to be Raphael's mistress.

Raphael was engaged to the niece of a cardinal. Some historians believe that while Raphael was engaged to the cardinal's niece he was secretly married to Margherita Luti and this secret was taken to the artist's grave.

The evidence of Raphael and Ms. Luti being married come from this portrait. Margherita is sensous, showing her half-naked body with a sultry expression and a covered stomach. She is cupping her left breast.

The nuptial allegories in the painting further suggest marriage versus just an affair. The allegories are the brooch pinned to the silk turban. Women of the age often wore this on their wedding day. The arm band on her arm with his name on it goes beyond an artist's signature of a work. This signature is boldly centered and on the Ms. Luti. In no other work of Raphael will you find so bold, and yet personal, a signature. The foilage in the background is myrtl and quince. They are symbolic of love, fecundity, and fidelity.

The portrait was left unfinished at his death. Assistants from Raphael's workshop added the finishing touches.

Giorgio Vasari writes in his Lives of the Artists of Raphael, "Raphael was a very amorous man who was fond of women, and he was always quick to serve them. This was the reason why, as he continued to pursue his carnal delights, he was treated with too much consideration and acquiescence by his friends. When his dear friend Agostino Chigi commissioned him to paint the first loggia in his palace (Villa Farnesina), Raphael could not really put his mind to his work because of his love for one of his mistresses; Agostino became so desperate over this that, through his own efforts and with the assistance of others, he worked things out in such a way that he finally managed to bring this woman of Raphael's to come and stay with him on a constant basis in the section of the house where Raphael was working, and that was the reason why the work came to be finished."

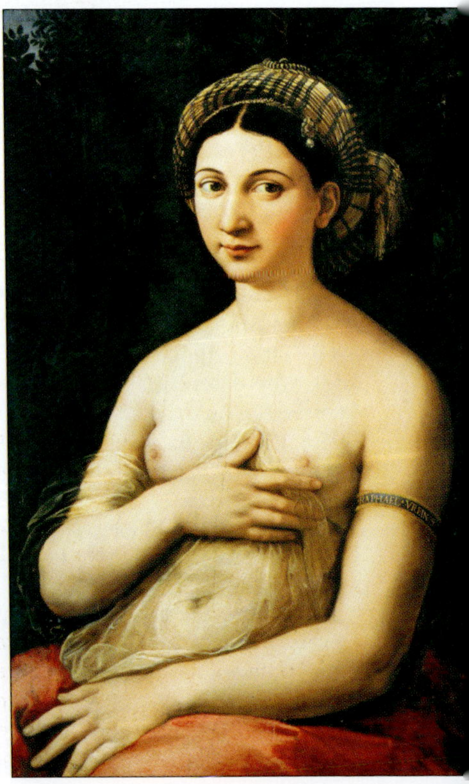

64 ▪ Michelangelo Merisi Caravaggio

Narcissus

Galleria Nazionale d'Arte Antica di Palazzo Barberini

Barberini Gallery

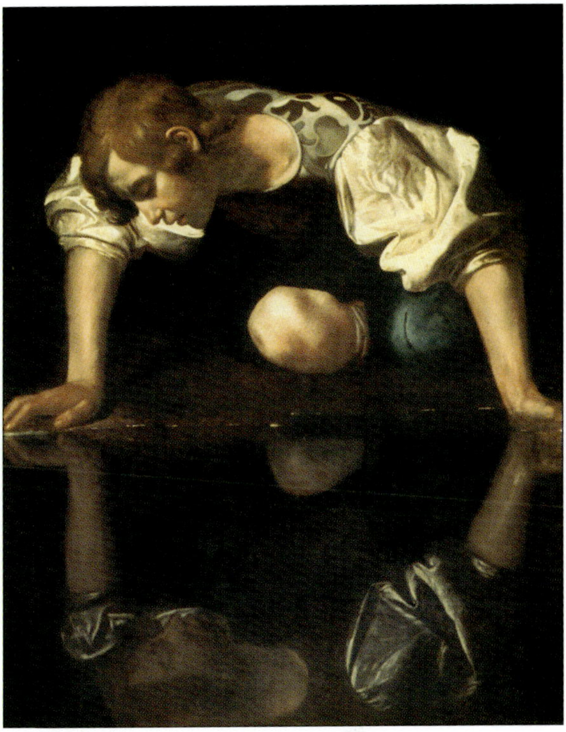

The story of Narcissus is captured perfectly in Caravaggio's image of the event. This is one of his rare mythological paintings.

The image itself holds true to the form of Caravaggio. He used contemporary Roman clothing in the image versus the traditional garb of Ancient Greece.

Narcissus was a proud, beautiful youth who didn't want to give himself to any lover. He felt no lover was worthy of him. One of his spurned potential lovers shouted, "may Narcissus love one day so, and himself not win over the creature whom he loves." Nemesis, the God of Vengeance, heard the wish and judged the plea righteous. After a hunt in the woods, Narcissus came upon a still dark pond and fell in love with his own image reflecting back at him from the dark water.

The water is like a pool of oil with the quiet reflection of Narcissus. The reflection represents the anguish of hubris and pride...of arrogance.

Today a white flower with a yellow center that grows near the edge of water is called the Narcissus flower.

The painting has been questioned by Art History scholars in the past to not come from the hand of Caravaggio. The issue has not been completely settled, but it is now regarded as a true Caravaggio.

65 ▪ Michelangelo Merisi Caravaggio

Judith Beheading Holofernes

Decapitazione di Oloferne Galleria Nazionale d'Arte Antica di Palazzo Barberini • Barberini Gallery

The Biblical story of Judith comes from Judith 13 : 1 - 12. She was a beautiful Hebrew woman who delivered her taken city of Bethulia from the conquering Assyrians. Posing as a deserter, she entered the Assyrian camp of Holofernes. Taken by her beauty, he brought her into his tent for the night. When Holofernes fell asleep she cut off his head with the assistance of her handmaiden.

Virtuous Judith sets free her city from the prideful Holofernes. Although she executes him, she does so at an arm's length and without emotion. It is as if she is fulfulling a prophesy and not acting on her own. Caravaggio's famous light falls upon Judith making her almost angelic in the midst of the horrific act. The handmaiden looks on intently. Caravaggio made her look like an old woman. This is the artist's choice. In the Bible no reference to a handmaiden or her age is made. Caravaggio was fascinated with the gruesome image of decapitation. He painted several images that included heads being cut off or that had been completely removed. This is one of his more famous paintings of decapitation. The scene is taken directly from the Bible. This particular Biblical event can be found in the Sistine Chapel painted by the hand of the other Michelangelo. (look on the map of the Sistine Chapel ceiling. In the corner of the entrance wall near the scene of the drunkeness of Noah is Michelangelo's interpretation). The other famous rendition of this event is painted by a female artist named Artemisia Gentileschi. It is in Florence at the Uffizi Gallery. Her recreation is similar, but even more aggressive in its delivery. Artemisia's version has Judith slicing with purpose.

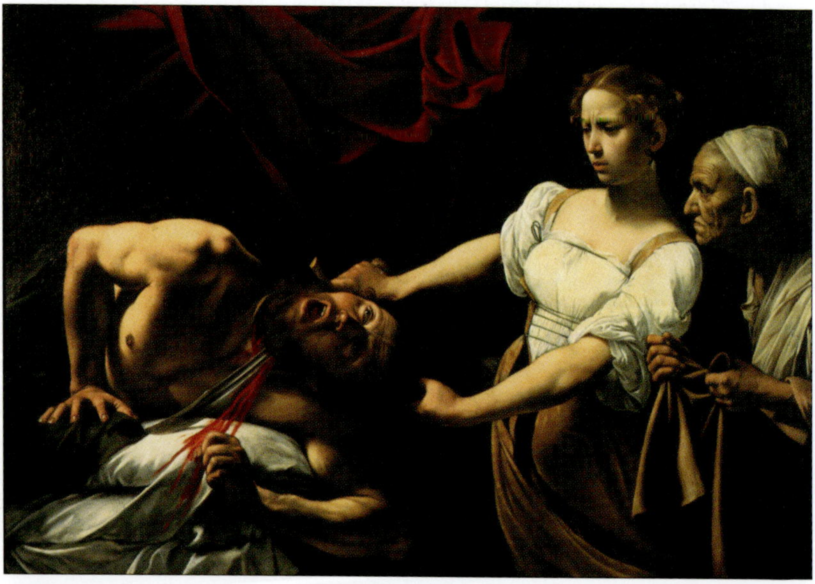

Judith is dressed as a contemporary Roman with her bodice undone and her laces pulled open.

66 ▪ Gian Lorenzo Bernini

The Ecstasy of Saint Teresa

Santa Maria della Vittoria • Cornaro Chapel

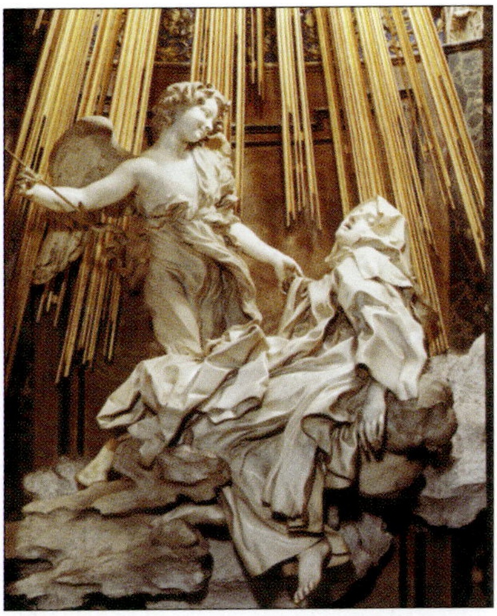

In this piece, one of his masterpieces, Bernini attempts to remove the barrier between the art and the viewer. He wants each viewer to be pulled into the scene. Bernini hopes to give a little of the divine action to the viewer and cause a dreamlike reality. He works to achieve his goal by using all of his skills from sculpture, architecture, painting, and decoration.

The image is of the moment that Saint Teresa was pierced by the angel with the arrow of God. Saint Teresa herself described the event, "with a flaming arrow the angel pierced my heart repeatedly with a flaming, golden arrow, whereupon the pain was so great that I screamed aloud; but simultaneoulsy I felt such infinite sweetness that I wished the pain to last eternal. It was not bodily pain, although, it affected to a certain extent the body. It was the sweetest caressing of the soul by God."

Bernini recreates this image. The seraph, a figure of heavenly beauty, is about to pierce the heart of Saint Teresa with the mystical arrow of God's love. When the arrow pierces Saint Teresa it creates the union of God and the Saint. She swoons in an ecstatic trance. Her arms and legs fall numb, her head sinks back, her eyes are half-shut and her mouth opens in an almost audible moan. The entire moment takes place on a cloud.

This masterpiece is in the Cornaro Chapel and was commissioned by the benefactor Cardinal Federico Cornaro. He and his ancestors sit in the boxes watching the event unfold. In reality, the viewers would not be able to see the action simply due to their positioning. They are discussing the scene as the mystical ecstacy plays out in front of them.

The masterpiece is bathed in natural light and enhanced by the golden sculpted beams added by Bernini. This sculpture is one of the most moving in Rome. The entire image places you at the scene. You can almost hear the chatter of the men in the boxes viewing the scene. You can feel the pain and pleasure of Saint Teresa. The angel has an impish grin on her face as she delivers God's love.

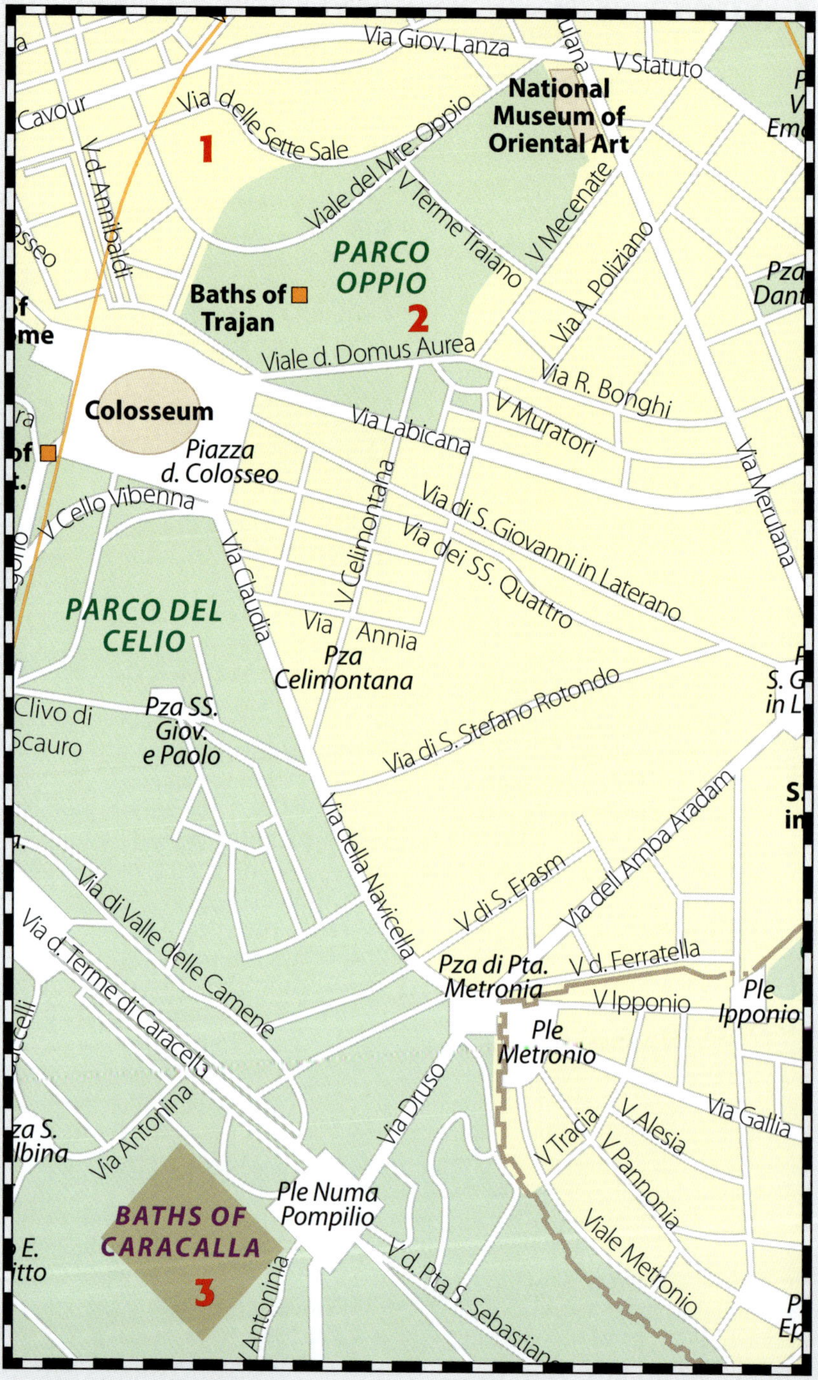

1. San Pietro in Vincoli
2. The Golden House of Nero
3. Baths of Caracalla

VINCOLI

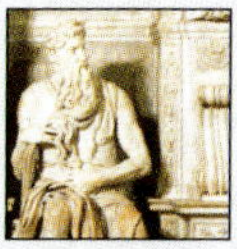

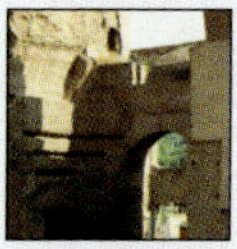

Site Hours, Daily Schedule, Address, Phone Numbers, and other important information

Site		Mon	Tue	Wed	Thur	Fri	Sat	Sun
San Pietro in Vincoli Piazza San Pietro in Vincoli Open until 7:00 from May through September	AM	7:00 to 12:30	7:00 to 12:30	7:00 to 12:30	7:00 to 12:30	7:00 to 12:30	7:00 to 12:30	7:00 to 12:30
	PM	3:30 to 6:00	3:30 to 6:00	3:30 to 6:00	3:30 to 6:00	3:30 to 6:00	3:30 to 6:00	3:30 to 6:00
Domus Aurea Viale della Domus Aurea 1 Buy tickets at http://www.pierreci.it Reservations Mandatory Adult tickets are 5.00 Euro	AM / PM	9:00 to 7:45	X	9:00 to 7:45	9:00 to 7:45	9:00 to 7:45	9:00 to 7:45	9:00 to 7:45
Terme di Caracalla Via delle Terme di Caracalla 52 Buy tickets at http://www.pierreci.it Adult tickets are 6.00 Euro	AM / PM	9:00 to 2:00	9:00 to 4:30	9:00 to 4:30	9:00 to 4:30	9:00 to 4:30	9:00 to 4:30	9:00 to 4:30

X = Closed

67 ▪ Michelangelo Buonarroti

Moses & the Tomb of Julius II

San Pietro in Vincoli

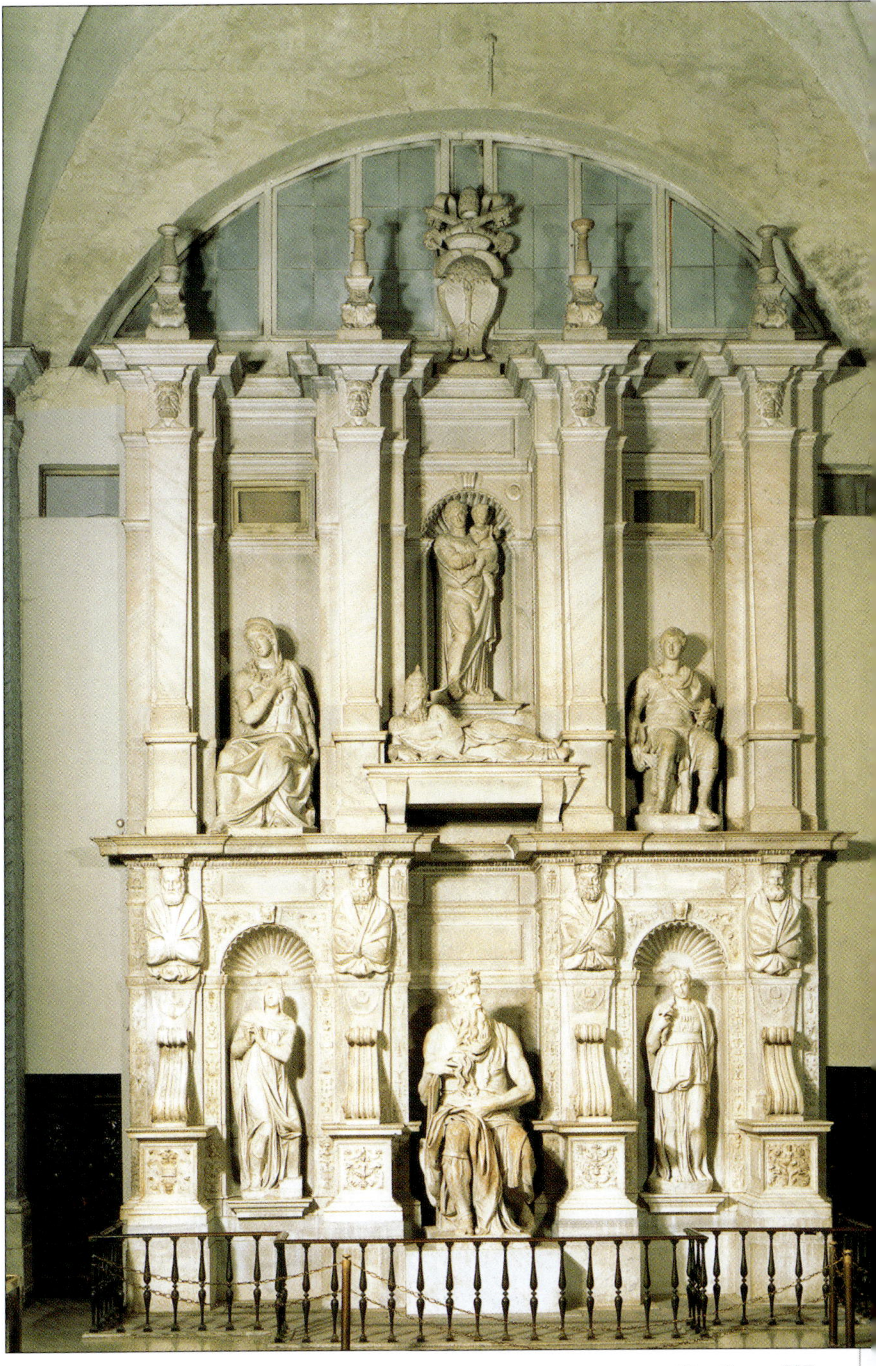

Michelangelo Buonnaroti may very well be the world's finest artist. He was a master sculptor, a master painter, and a master architect.

Pope Julius II requested that Michelangelo create his tomb. The tomb was the first project requested of him by the Papacy and specifically Pope Julius II. Originally, the tomb was to be placed in Saint Peter's Basilica. It was to be the grandest ever crafted in order to speak volumes to all who saw it about the power and majesty of the great Pope Julius.

Michelangelo personally took on the responsibility of harvesting the marble from Carrara to be used on the project. It took him eight months to collect the necessary marble. Literally tons of marble was cut from the mines and dropped off in the the piazza in front of Saint Peter's.

Once the great Michelangelo began the sculpting he was often visited by Pope Julius. The workshop was very near the Vatican. In order to control any courtly jealousy, Pope Julius had a covered passage built to allow him inconspicous entry into Michelangelo's workshop without arousing any unnecessary jeolousy toward the artist. Unfortunately, envy was unavoidable in Rennaissance Italy and tensions built up toward Michelangelo from other artists in the Papal court; namely the Papal architect Bramante.

In the middle of the work, the Pope was urged to stop work on his earthly resting place by Bramante. The pope was told that one shouldn't create his tomb while alive to prevent any early depatures from this realm. Bramante's plan succeeded.

Michelangelo continued his labor unaware of the Pope's change of heart. The remaining marble from Carrara arrived in Rome and Michelangelo paid for the marble, the workers, and the transport from his own pocket. When the artist requested an audience with the Pope to discuss the project and receive repayment from the expense of the marbles, the Pope had an attendant tell Michelangelo he was unavailable. Returning the next morning, Michelangelo was still not granted an

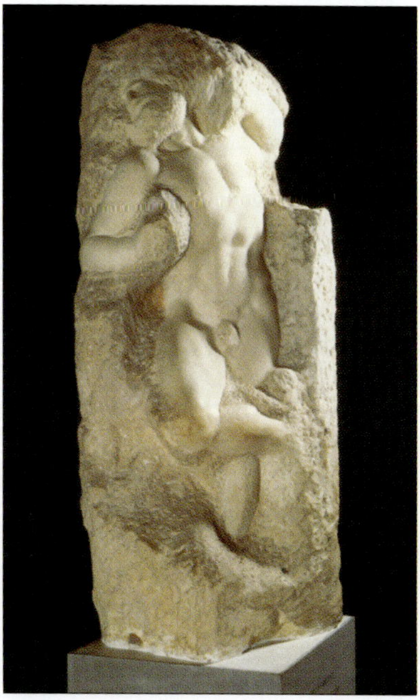

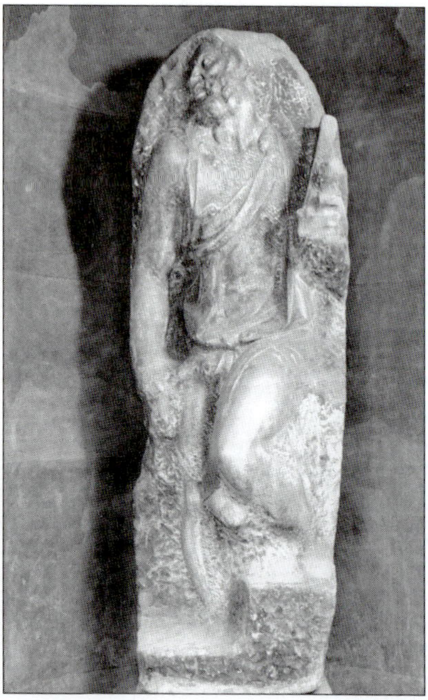

audience. Michelangelo grew annoyed. A bishop was present and came to the artist's aid saying to the servent, "you must not know who this man is." The servent replied, "I must follow the orders of my superiors." At that moment Michelangelo realized that the Pope was avoiding him. Michelangelo was already insecure and always thought the courts were consipiring against him. Michelangelo yelled, "And you may tell the Pope that from now on, if he wants me, he can look for me elsewhere."

The artist raged back to his workshop and told his servents to sell all of his possessions in Rome and send the money to him in Florence. Then he fled Rome for Florence on horseback removing himself from Papal authority as quickly as possible.

Extremely angry, Pope Julius sent letter after letter for Michelangelo's immediate return to Rome. Michelangelo ignored all requests. He even refused to return to Rome when the Pope sent his men to fetch him in person. The henchmen, afraid of returning empty handed, asked the artist to sign a document proving that they tracked him down and it was he who refused to return through no fault of their own. Michelangelo signed the document but did not budge from his home city.

The letters continued and were addressed to Piero Soderini who was the gonfaloniere (ruler) of Florence. The Pope demanded of Soderini that Michelangelo be returned by fair means or foul to Rome immediately. After the third letter Piero went to Michelangelo and said, "you have tried the Pope as a King of France would not have done. However, he is not to be kept waiting any longer. We do not want to go to war with him over you and place our state in jeapardy. Therefore, make ready to return."

Michelangelo prepared to return to Rome. As preparations were being made the Pope marched with his army to Bologna to regain the lost Papal territory. Rather than continue on to Rome Michelangelo went to meet Julius in Bologna. At the first audience since fleeing Rome the Pope said to Michelangelo, "you were supposed to come to us, and

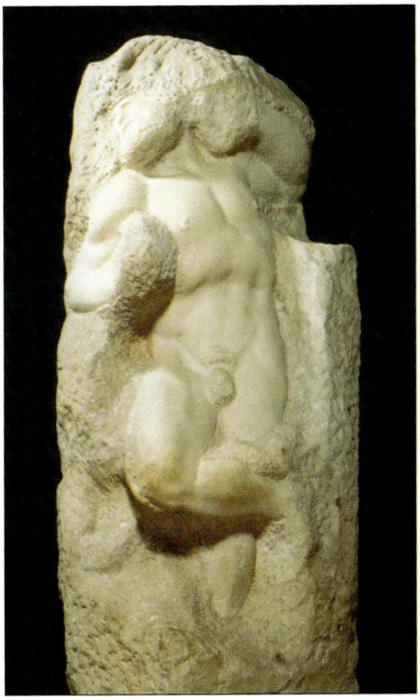

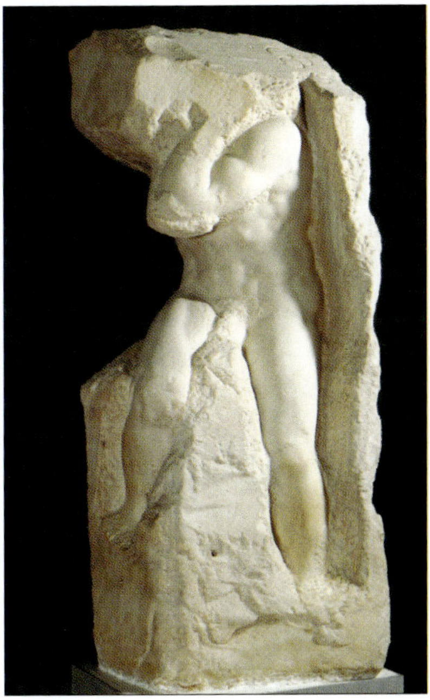

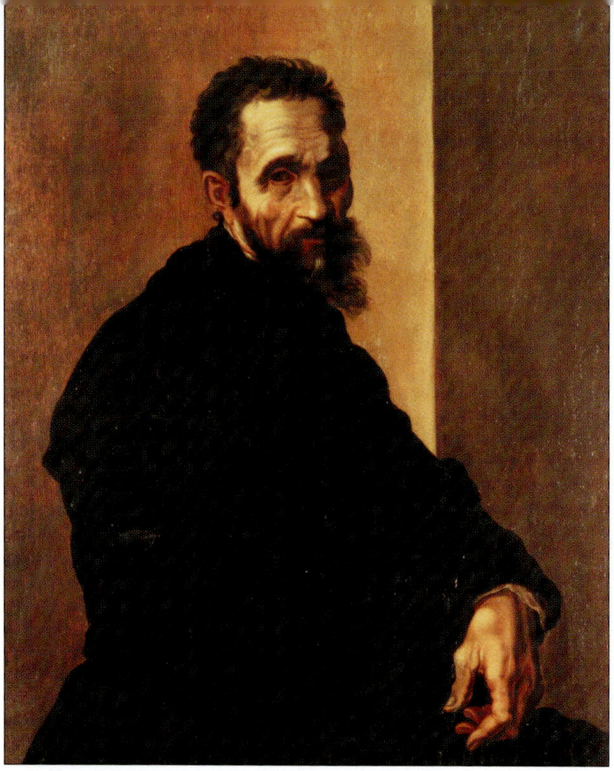

you have waited for me to come to you." (Bologna was closer to Florence than Rome)

Michelangelo knelt before him and begged forgiveness. A cardinal that accomponied the Pope to Bologna interjected on Michelangelo's behalf. Pope Julius took the opportunity to scold the cardinal allowing him to aim his anger at Michelangelo through the outspoken cardinal. This saved face for Julius, delivered the messege to Michelangelo, and allowed the event to put behind them both.

Sixteen months after Michelangelo's audience in Bologna, He completed a bronze statue of Julius at his request. The statue is since lost. It was in fact reduced to molten bronze and reused to make a canon to be used against the army of Rome and the Pope. After the commission was complete Michelangelo returned to Rome.

Julius was still resolved to not complete the tomb. This is the point where Bramante put into the Pope's mind to have Michelangelo paint the ceiling of the chapel. The suggestion from Bramante came with malice. It was his intention to use the ceiling to set Michelangelo up for failure. Bramante's strategy was to have Michelangelo refuse the work thus angering the Pope and placing himself out of favor or accepting the commission, but failing. Failure would dishonor the great Michelangelo and place him behind the graceful Raphael. Bramante knew well that the artist was a sculptor and not a painter.

Michelangelo pushed the Pope to have Raphael do the work. Julius flatly refused the suggestion. After Michelangelo attempted in vain to refuse the commission, citing his being a sculptor and no painter, he ultimately accepted the job. In true Michelangelo fashion after he accepted the job he redesigned the already designed ceiling and shut the doors on the chapel until he was finished with his work.

The tragedy of the tomb continued. Nearing death Julius put his nephew in charge of the completion of his tomb. When Julius died the new Pope (Pope Leo X) pulled Michelangelo off of the project to do work for the new Papacy.

Leo forced the Rovere family to release Michelangelo from his obligation of the tomb in the form of a leave of absence.

After Leo X passed away, the Papacy was in the hands of Pope Paul III. Paul III once again pulled Michelangelo off of work on the tomb. Once again Michelangel was back in the chapel. This time he completed the Last Judgement.

Paul III worked with the Rovere family and Michelangelo to strike a new contract that allowed Michelangelo to complete the tomb, but a much smaller tomb than was originally agreed to with Julius himself. While working out the details Paul III and ten cardinals came to Michelangelo to view his plans for the alter wall and saw the completed Moses.

The Cardinal of Mantua said, "This statue alone is sufficent to do honor to the tomb of Pope Julius."

The new contract that was struck created a much smaller tomb. The new tomb was to have only one side versus the four. It was to have fewer than the originally designed forty statues. In fact the new design was to use the statues already carved by Michelangelo which included the statues that you see today on the tomb. In addition to the statues the Popes remains were to placed inside the tomb. Around the tomb would be narrative scenes in bronze telling the story of the Pope and his accomplishments.

The tomb is believed, even in its greatly reduced design, to be the finest tomb ever created.

Three of the statues are by the hand of Michelangelo. The three done by the great artist are the Moses, the contemplative life to the right, and the active life to the left.

Julius would have been disappointed to see the design of his tomb. Michelangelo was present in 1545 and saw it placed at San Pietro in Vincoli.

The great Moses of Michelangelo is an awesome work. He holds the tablets of law under one arm and his beard in the other. The energy of Moses is pent up and ready to burst. His muscles seem to jump through his light clothing You can almost sense the immanent action of the beautiful Moses as he ponders his words at the very moment before he stands up. On his head are two horns that come from a mistranslation of Hebrew text. Rather than horns they should be rays of light.

The prisoners or slaves carved by Michelangelo that are on display in Florence at the Accademia were to be placed on the tomb to represent the subjugated provinces of the Pontiff Julius. Each slave illustrated the provinces made obedient to the Apostolic church. Other statues were to be created to repressent all of the virtues of the liberal arts and sciences.

The tomb was to be crowned with a statue of Heaven smiling as she bore a coffin and received Julius, and Cybele the goddess of the earth, who was to look unhappy to remain in a world deprived of virtue after the death of the pope.

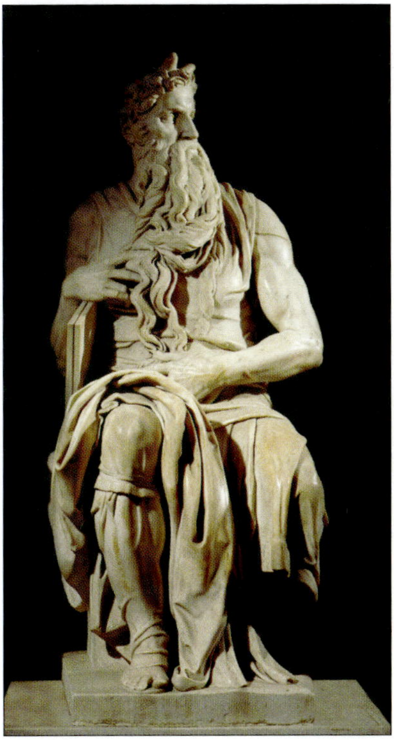

Nero, the fifth emperor of Rome, ruled from 54 - 68 A.D. During his reign, he built an enormous palace the likes of which the world will never see again. It consumed three (Palatine, Esquiline, and Caelian) of the seven hills of Rome. Where the Colosseum stands today, Nero had built a private lake contained within the walls of his private villa.

Originally, Nero built his first palace called Domus Transitoria. Then, in 64 A.D. the great fire of Rome burned much of the city. Many feel that Nero himself set the fire to clear a path for his new and grander palace called Domus Aureo or Golden House. Nero blamed the small Christian population living in Rome for the fire.

The majesty of the Golden House was incredible. In it Nero erected a statue of himself that stood 120 feet tall. It was placed in his Vestibule. The house had a triple colonnade a mile long (consider the colonnade in Saint Peter's square. It is enourmous, but dwarfed by Nero's colonnade).

Also built within the walls of the Golden House were tracks of country, vineyards, fields, pastures, and woods. Nero didn't even have to leave Rome to enjoy the country. He literally created a country villa in the center of Rome. That would be like building a villa that contained the whole of Central Park in New York City today within the walls of the house. Nero brought in domestic and wild animals. The ceiling tiles would open up and drop flower petals and perfume on guests.

Nero imprisoned the most famous decorator in Rome, Fabullus, within the villa in order to paint the walls in fresco.

The emperors that followed Nero knew that in order to win back the Romans, they had to give back the land and hills that Nero's Golden House consumed, so they did. Trajan's bath is now built over Domus Aurea. The majority of the house is underground today, but what remains is impressive.

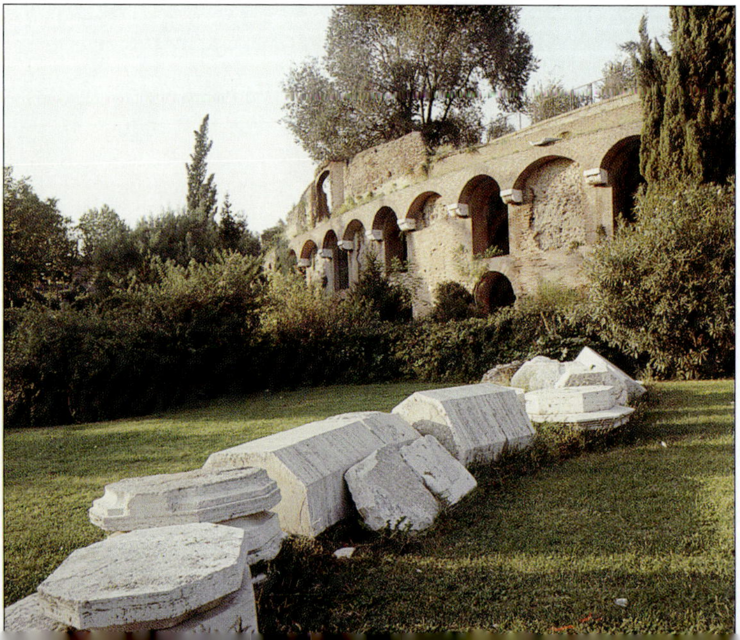

69 ▪ Baths of Caracalla

The ancient Romans took sequential plunges into three distinct baths within the complex. First, in cold water called the frigidarium. Second, in warm water called the tepidarium. And third, in hot water called the caldarium.

The Baths (Terme) of Caracalla were started by Septimius Severus in 206 A.D. Caracalla completed them in 217 A.D. Severus was the father of Caracalla.

Caracalla's bath was the biggest and best bathing and recreational facility in the empire. It was paid for with Imperial funds. It is made of brick and concrete and is used today as a concert hall in the summer for outdoor music and theater. The walls are 140 feet high.

The dome of the bath house was as large as the one on the Pantheon. The complex was lit by sunlight coming through the top of walls where the vaulted ceiling and wall met. Caracalla had the complex richly decorated with stuccoed vaults, mosaic floors, marble faced walls, and enormous statuary. The exterior was a landscaped Roman garden.

In addition to bathing, the Romans would come to enjoy a lecture, the library, the colonnaded excercise court called a palastrae, or the enormous swimming pool called the natatio.

The complex could fit 1600 people at one time.

As a final glorious touch, the floors were heated by way of circulated heat. The Roman engineers and architects would build a space between the floor and the sub-floor to capture air. Under the subfloor a fire burned. The fire would heat the air between the two floors and walls and heat the entire complex.

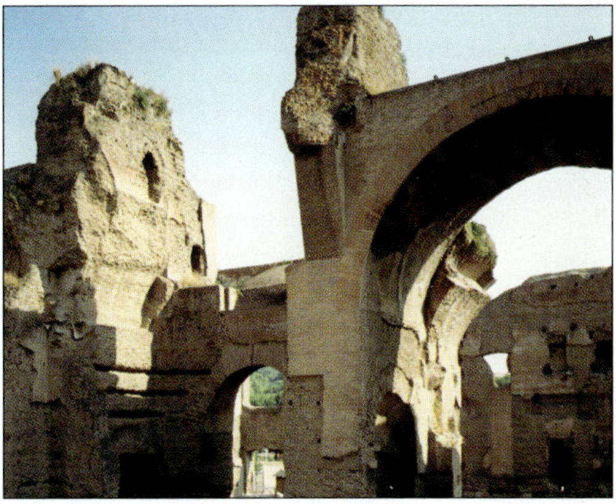

Caracalla was a ruthless emperor. His father Severus ruled for eighteen successful years. Caracalla and his brother Geta were given the title Augustus as teenagers. This would be the first time the empire would be ruled by three emperors. Caracalla and Geta absolutely hated each other and after their father's death (died at 66) didn't speak or see one another until public events. They literally split the palace in two and each had their half guarded by armed soldiers. Then on February 27, 212 AD, Caracalla accorded his mother's pleas to meet with Geta and bring peace among the emperors. In his mother's apartment, under a flag of truce, he had his soldiers rush in and assassinate his brother Geta in their mother's arms. And to insure no retribution for the death of his brother Caracalla killed over 20,000 of Geta's friends, associates, and allies. Then Caracalla promptly left Rome never to return.

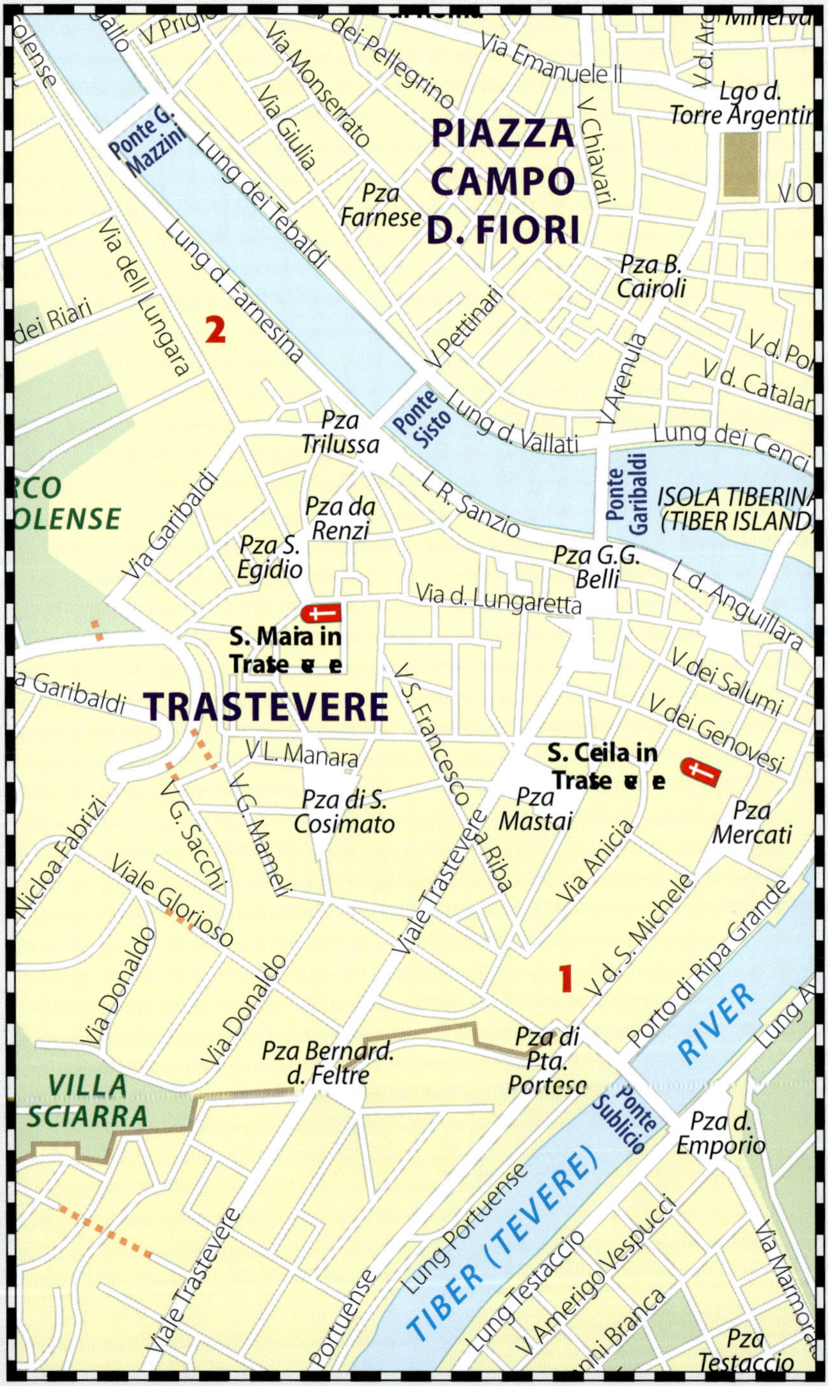

1. San Francesco a Ripa
2. Villa Farnesina

TRASTEVERE

Site Hours, Daily Schedule, Address, Phone Numbers, and other important information

Site		Mon	Tue	Wed	Thur	Fri	Sat	Sun
San Francesco a Ripa Piazza San Francesco d'Assisi 88 in Trastevere No tickets necessary Free Admission	AM	7:00 to 12:00	7:00 to 12:00	7:00 to 12:00	7:00 to 12:00	7:00 to 12:00	7:00 to 12:00	7:00 to 12:00
	PM	4:00 to 7:00	4:00 to 7:00	4:00 to 7:00	4:00 to 7:00	4:00 to 7:00	4:00 to 7:00	4:00 to 7:00
Trastevere The entire neighborhood of Trastevere It is well worth an afternoon of exploring. Try to get lost among Rome's favorite neighborhood.	AM PM				24 x 7			
Villa Farnesina Via della Lungara 230 in Trastevere http://www.lincei.it/informazioni/villafarnesina/index.php email farnesina@lincei.it to make reservations Closed on December 25 and January 1 Adult tickets are 5.00 Euro	AM PM	9:00 to 1:00	9:00 to 1:00	9:00 to 1:00	9:00 to 1:00	9:00 to 1:00	9:00 to 1:00	X

X = Closed

70 ▪ Gian Lorenzo Bernini

The Blessed Lodovica

San Francesco a Ripa • Altieri Chapel

This is one of Bernini's last sculptures, and one of his best. Here Bernini does what he was famous for - capture a moment of transformation. In this glorious statue he captures Blessed Lodovica at the moment of her death. It is divine rapture.

Bernini captured her last moments on earth and as you gaze at her in her chapel it is almost as if you are spying on a very private moment between her and God. With her head thrown back onto the pillow and her hands pressing her body she seems to feel her soul lifting from her corporeal body to enter heaven. She parts her lips emitting her last earthly sigh.

Bernini's handiwork is incredible. He seems to make the marble appear soft and light. I find the work to be one of the finest examples of hammer, chisel, and stone in Italy. It is amazing how Bernini tranformed the stone to life.

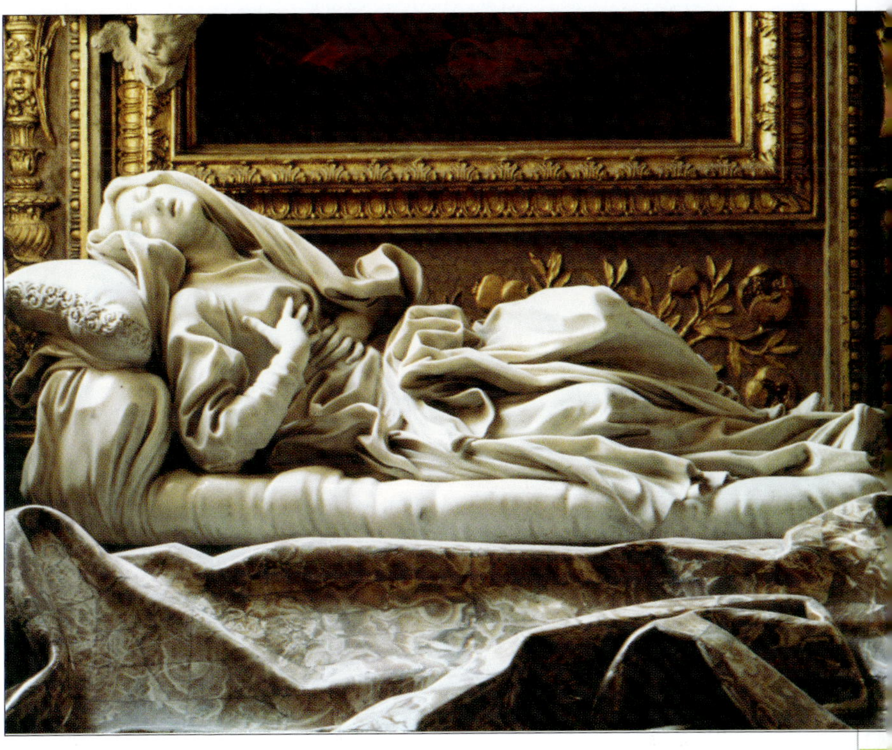

Villa Farnesina

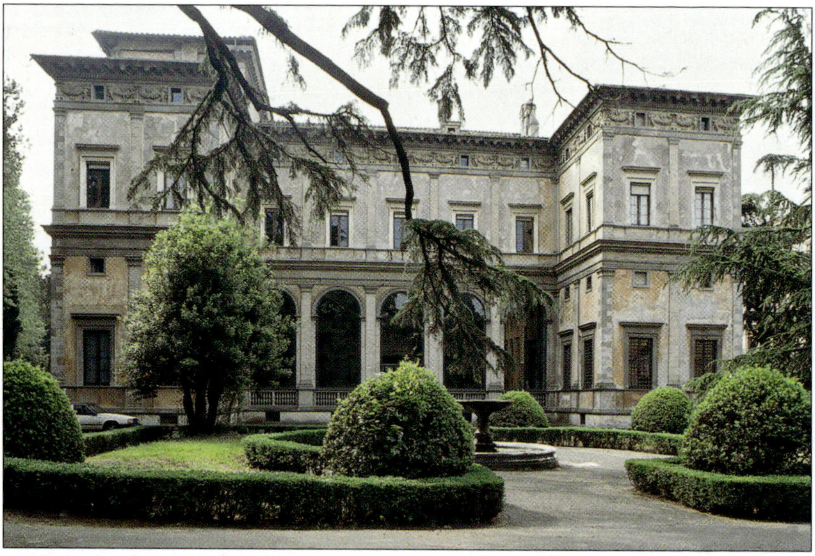

The Sienese banker Agostino Chigi purchased the villa as his Roman residence. He wished to illustrate his success as a businessman as well as his good taste. Agostino Chigi became enourmously wealthy as the banker to the Popes Alexander VI (the famous Borgia Pope) and Julius II (the warrior Pope and patron to Michelangelo and Raphael). The walls and ceiling of the villa are painted with the stories of the gods and mythological heroes in the form of the zodiac constellations that covered the sky on the day of Agostino Chigi's birth in November 1466.

Three rooms are painted by the masters Baldassare Peruzzi, Sebastiano del Piombo, Raphael Santi, and Sodoma. The result is breathtaking. Each room delivers more than the last. The four rooms that are painted are named: Loggia di Psiche, Loggia di Galatea, Sala delle Prospettive, and Sala delle Nozze di Alessandro e Rossane. The masters painted works named Council of the Gods, Wedding Banquet of Cupid and Psyche, Cupid and the Three Graces, Venus on the Chariot Pulled by Doves, Polyphemus, and Galatea.

The frescoes Polyphemus and Galatea are not only beautiful but the means of competition between two Renaissance masters. The frescoes are created by Sebastiano del Piombo and Raphael in the Loggia di Galatea. The work created by Piombo is the Cyclops Polyphemus and the work by Raphael the Nereid Galatea. The works are excellent examples of two distinct styles. Piombo comes from the Venetian school known for "colorito." His painting is rich in color and atmosphere. Raphael comes from the Florentine school known for disegno and delivers a balanced painting with complex movement.

Galatea was a Nereid (a nymph of the sea and daughter of Nereus and Doris). Galatea was the beloved of Acis, a Sicilian Shepherd. She was also desperately loved by the Cyclops Polyphemus. In a jealous rage Polyphemus killed Acis with a boulder to remove the competition for his beloved Galatea. Heartbroken over the death of her lover she created the river Acis from his blood. The river still exists today in Sicily.

The Renaissance competition was between Michelangelo and Raphael.

Michelangelo disliked Raphael of Urbino. The great Michelangelo was convinced that he conspired against him. (Michelangelo was high maintenance.) Pietro Soderini in a letter to the Cardinal of Volterra writes of Michelangelo, "we certify that your Lordship will find him to be a fine young man, and in his craft alone in Italy. Likewise, perhaps in the universe. We cannot recommend him more strongly. He is of the sort who with good words and stroking, if one gives them to him, will do anything; it is necessary to show him love and do him kindnesses, and he will do things that will amaze whoever sees them."

Raphael was masterful at court. He was graceful. He earned great commissions not only because of his artistic ability, but because of his pleasing nature and his powerful relationships with Pope Julius. He also had Bramante, the Papal Architect (also from Urbino) working for him behind the scenes.

Michelangelo felt that Bramante and Raphael wished to disparage him. He thought they talked of him to the Pope and other rich patrons in order that he not earn prominent commissions. His untrusting nature tied to rumors of the day and forced the great Michelangelo to utilize del Piombo in order to compete with Raphael. He would design the art of del Piombo in the Florentine style and allow del Piombo to utilize his skill of color to deliver a powerful combination at Chigi's Roman villa.

Piombo was also known as Sebastiano Veneziano or Sebastiano Luciani. His name del Piombo was given to him due to his well mannered courtly style. A piombo is the name of the Papal seal for letters and documents. He ingratiated himself with the Medici Popes (Popes Leo X and Clement VII) after the great patron of art Pope Julius II died.

Sebastiano del Piombo worked on eight lunettes for the garden loggia of the Chigi chapel. The name of the chapel is a giveaway to the victor of the indirect competition. The name of the chapel is Sala di Galatea. On the previous page you can see how Polyphemus yearns for his love Galatea. He turns his head to gaze at her beauty. His movement is Michelangeloesque. He is ready to explode and agony seeps from his soul. The body of Polyphemus is all Michelangelo. The psychology of the scene and its color are Venetian. His face is hidden, his lips parted as he softly sings about his unrequited love. The details are left to the viewer allowing pity for this brutish monster. The lunette adjacent to the cyclops is done by Raphael. It is of Galatea. She is coveted by Polyphemus. She is coveted by Polyphemus much the way del Piombo coveted the skill and ability of Raphael, much the way Michelangelo coveted the grace of Raphael.

Michelangelo wrote, "All of the discord that was born between Pope Julius and me was from the envy of Bramante and of Rapheal of Urbino."

In 1511 the Sistine Chapel ceiling was partially unveiled. The ceiling commission came from Pope Julius. Raphael was present at the unveiling. One of Michelangelo's biographers, Ascanio Condivi, writes,

"Raphael, having seen the new and marvelous style, as one who was remarkable in imitation, sought through Bramante to paint the rest [of the

- Michelangelo worked with Piombo in some of Piombo's greatest work. In fact, Piombo was hired by patrons hoping that Michelangelo would have a hand in the work.
- One of the greatest examples of competition by proxy for Michelangelo was Piombo's Raising of Lazarus. This image competed with the great final work of Raphael called the Transfiguration. Raphael easily won this competition. The Transfiguration hangs in the Vatican Pinacoteca.

ceiling] himself." Throughout his life Michelangelo was honored by Raphael. In two of Raphael's greatest works Michelangelo was honored with places of distinction. First, in the School of Athens as the front and center pensive Philosopher Heraclitus. Raphael added this image after the partial unveiling of the ceiling next door. Second, as the bearded poet under the Laurel tree on the right in Parnassas adjacent to the School of Athens. In this image Michelangelo is graced as one of two people in the scene to directly address the viewer. Not only does Raphael honor Michelangelo directly by placing him in his composite scenes right next door to the Sistine Chapel, but Raphael directly quotes the hand of Michelangelo in other works. In the Stanze d'Eliodoro Raphael copies the image of God above the Expulsion of Heliodorus exactly as he is represented by Michelangelo in the ceiling.

Why did Michelangelo take offense to the honor given him by Raphael? Was it because it too closely represented or copied the hand of Michelangelo?

The competition carried over into other works done by Piombo. It ended with Raphael's final work named the Transfiguration.

The Cyclops Polyphemus

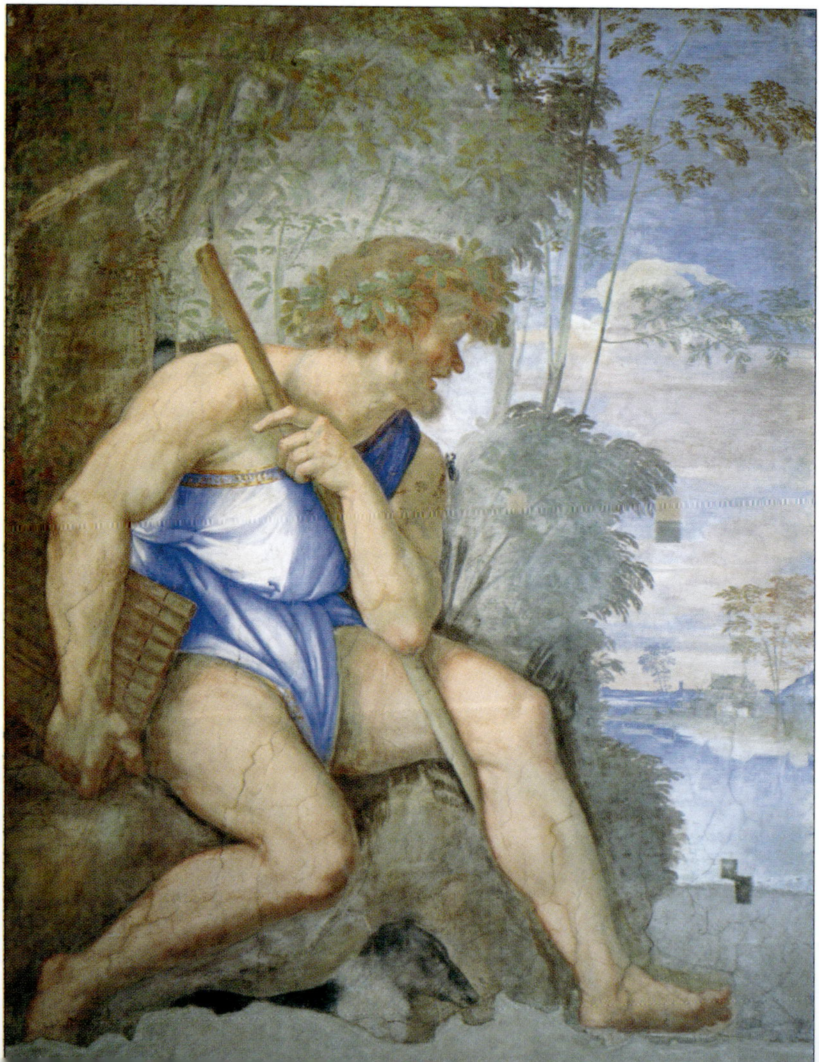

71 ▪ Sebastiano del Piombo & Raphael Santi

Galatea & Polyphemus Villa Farnesina

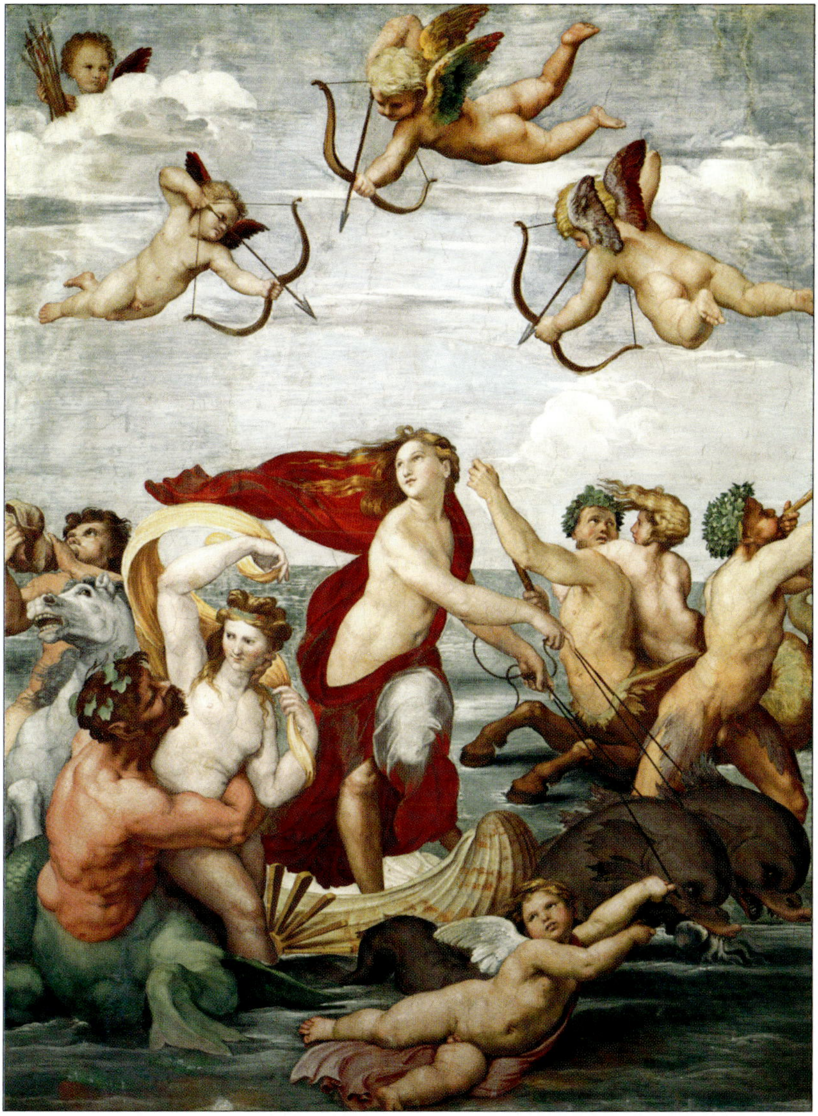

The Nereid Galatea (Gal-uh-tee-uh) – *She who is milk white*

Notes

Notes

Notes

Notes

Notes

Notes

Notes